TOKEN OF A COVENANT

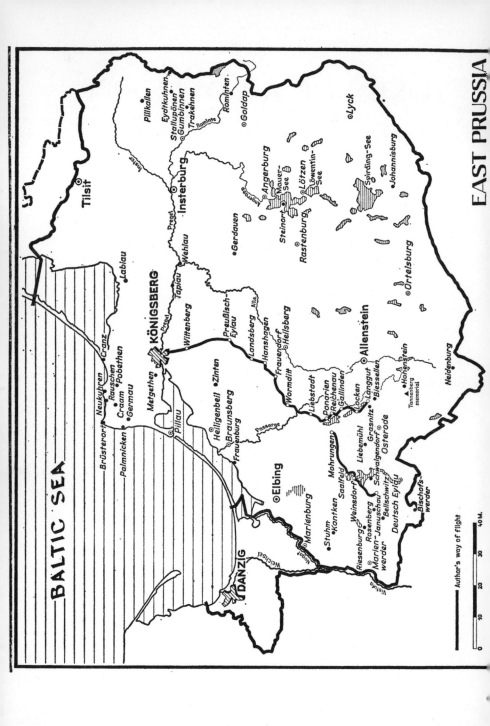

EAST PRUSSIA

BALTIC SEA

Tilsit

KÖNIGSBERG

Insterburg

DANZIG

Elbing

Allenstein

Pillkallen
Eydtkuhnen
Stallupöne-
Gumbinnen
Trakehnen
Raminten
Goldap
Lyck

Labiau
Cranz
Neukuhren
Rauschen
Craam Pobathen
Germau
Brüsterort
Palmnicken
Pillau
Metgethen

Wittenberg
Tapiau
Wehlau
Pregel
Tilsit
Memel

Gerdauen
Angerburg
Mauer-See
Lötzen
Löwentin-See
Spirding-See
Johannisburg
Steinort
Rastenburg

Preußisch-Eylau
Landsberg
Frauendorf
Hanshagen
Heilsberg
Ortelsburg

Zinten
Heiligenbeil
Braunsberg
Frauenburg
Passarge
Wormditt
Liebstadt
Donarien
Reichenau
Gallinden
Locken
Langgut
Biesselien
Hohenstein
Tannenberg memorial

Neidenburg

Marienburg
Mohrungen
Liebemühl
Saalfeld
Kontken
Weinsdorf
Rosenberg
Grasnitz
Schwalgendorf
Bellschwitz
Osterode
Deutsch Eylau
Bischofs-werder
Stuhm
Riesenburg
Marien-Januschau-werder

Nogat
Weichsel
Vistula

Author's way of flight

0   10   20   30   40 M.

TOKEN OF A COVENANT

Diary of an East Prussian Surgeon
1945-47

by

HANS GRAF VON LEHNDORFF

Introduction by PAUL TILLICH

Translated by ELIZABETH MAYER

Henry Regnery Company
Chicago

First published in Germany by Biederstein Verlag Muenchen
© 1963 English rights by Oswald Wolff Ltd., London
Copyright © 1964, Henry Regnery Company
Manufactured in the United States of America
Library of Congress Catalog Card No. 64-24065

PREFACE

"We beheld His Glory."

This account was written twelve years ago, partly from notes in a rescued diary, and partly from memories which were still very vivid. I have withheld it from publication until now, because I had not yet gained sufficient distance from the events of that time. But meanwhile they have become history, and the personal element has transcended the bounds of individual experience. I will, therefore, attempt to communicate this experience, even at the risk of stirring up past suffering again.

May these pages help to make comprehensible a fragment of the past and be of service to this life of ours which makes its demands on us day by day.

H. L.

1961

CONTENTS

INTRODUCTION

The events of the second "great retreat" of a Western army from Russian soil are, in their consequences, world history—felt by everybody, directly and indirectly. One of the best ways to get an idea of what these events have meant is through reports which, although limited to an individual's experience, make concrete and inescapably immediate what in history books tends to remain abstract and, despite its accuracy, pale and unexistential.

Of course, the diary of Count von Lehndorff covers only a small part of what was happening all over Europe and in the world at large during these years of retreat. But it covers it so sensitively that one has the feeling that these experiences truly epitomize the experience of a people in an invaded country, wherever it might be: the anxious anticipation of what will come, the attempted repression of half-knowledge, the breakdown of the power to repress, the revival of hope, often superstitious, the final resignation—and then the frightful realization that a world has gone to pieces. All this we live through with the author of this diary; this alone would justify its translation for American readers.

But there are other important elements in this diary, beyond dramatic history: the immensity of human suffering, the heroism of men and women, the devastation of cities and villages, of fields and woods, the vengeful savagery of the invading armies; and, in the midst of all this, the moments of human warmth, of life reaffirming itself against the overwhelming power of death, the timeless significance of Biblical verse, and, peculiarly German, the intimate human relationship to nature, the memories associated with special places and seasons.

The author does not politicize, although he was a part of the largely aristocratic group which tried to assassinate Hitler on July 20, 1944, and he is aware of the catastrophe which Hitler has brought on the German nation and most of Europe.

Later in the book, Lehndorff describes his work as a physician in the Polish-occupied territories. While this part lacks the dramatic character of the first, it shows the incipient transformation of the conquered provinces, first into deserts—without people, without production—and then into places for new inhabitants. With the last of the former inhabitants, the author leaves his homeland for the West, having escaped the threats of the new authorities. The surface of the earth in eastern Europe has changed, and much more has changed with it.

This book causes us, especially those of us who still have emotional ties with Germany, to participate in a rare historical event. Beyond this, it is of universal interest, drawing us back to a period of history which defies all imagination—particularly in a period of comparative security such as this.

PAUL TILLICH

University of Chicago

April 1964

· 1 ·

INSTERBURG
Summer 1944 to January 20, 1945

Once again, before the bulldozer of war went over it, my East Prussian homeland unfolded all its mysterious splendor. Whoever had lived through those last months with open senses must have felt that never before had the light been so strong, the sky so high, the horizon so far away. And that intangible element of the landscape, giving wings to the spirit, took shape with an intensity which only the hour of leave-taking can give.

At the end of June, the first harbingers of the catastrophe were felt—faint, hardly perceptible shocks which set the sunburned earth shuddering as if from a faraway earthquake. And then all at once the roads were overcrowded with fugitives from Lithuania, and ownerless cattle went straggling across the harvest fields, following the same irresistible urge toward the west.

It was still difficult to grasp what had really happened, and no one dared to give open expression to his fears. But by the time summer had passed, and the storks were getting ready to migrate, a clearer idea of what lay before us could no longer be brushed aside. Everywhere in the villages you could see people standing and staring up into the sky where the big familiar birds were circling, as though this time it would be the last goodbye. And all those watching them must have had the same feeling: "Yes, *you* are flying away. But what of us? What will become of us, and of our country?"

Soon afterwards, enormous herds of cattle came down along the stream beds and gathered in the flat valley through which the Pregel winds its way. They had been driven out of the eastern part of the province and now stood, an overwhelming sight, by the thousands in the wide meadows. For a short time there was food enough for them there; but if you went nearer and looked at the animals one by one, your heart was wrung with pity. With no relation between them, regarding human beings as enemies, they stumbled through the countryside, trampling down the hedges, forcing their way into paddocks and gardens, and stripping trees and bushes bare. They seemed to have come from a country where no order reigned. You could see that many of them were of an outstanding breed, but they had lost the instinct for mutual protection that made them into a herd.

At night we could see the eastern frontier towns lined up before us as if on a map. Memel, Tilsit, Schirwindt, and Eydtkuhnen were the brightest points, flaring up again and again under the air raids, and forming a line of fire which ran in a curve from north to south. And one day we heard that the frontier had been surrendered. The enemy had entered twelve to eighteen miles; then the front came to a standstill again. What things looked like behind it, none of us knew. You could only hope that nobody had survived; for what was reported of a few advanced points which the enemy had abandoned after a brief occupation froze your blood.

Another few days of fugitives' immeasurable misery on all the roads—then a sudden quiet, an almost inconceivable quiet. The rumbling at the front died down, the fires went out, even the nightly harassing planes had stopped coming. The deserted countryside with its farms and villages lay as if under a spell in the splendor of an incomparable fall, offering an indefinable experience to the few people who returned from districts farther west to get some more things from their houses or to look after the livestock they had left behind.

It was uncannily quiet even after the November gales had swept the land bare and the frost had withered the last blades of grass in the meadows. Scattered for miles over the fields, along the roads and the railroad lines, we saw the neglected cows standing, singly or in small groups, hardly able to move, with dried-up udders and prominent backbones, threatening and complaining. And when the first snow fell, they collapsed silently, one after another.

Christmas came and could be celebrated almost as in peacetime by those who had remained in their homes. Even hunting parties were organized, and people came together to see the old year out once more in traditional fashion.

Two weeks later all was over. The Russians had allowed themselves three months to prepare the final assault—now they came upon us with a vengeance.

January 13

About seven in the morning I was awakened by a monotonous roaring and rumbling. The windowpanes were rattling. It sounded as if many heavy trucks were standing around the building with their motors running uninterruptedly. In the dim light I could not distinguish anything. I stood at the window and collected my thoughts. This could only mean the end.

Toward noon the roaring became as loud as a falling avalanche. Violent gusts of wind made you gasp for breath. People looked meaningfully at one another, trying to take some comfort in the belief that all this was only the effect of our new Wonder Weapon.

Later on there was a sudden complete silence. At dusk airplanes made their appearance. Three, four fighters dived down out of the gray winter clouds and began firing on the railroad station and the airport. Others followed. Dogfights developed, and, in a few moments, the whole weird spectacle was over.

January 17

The Russians have broken through in several places and are advancing. Gumbinnen is on fire. At night the whole east is a sea of flames. Single planes come over and drop flares. We have brought all the patients left in the hospital down to the ground floor.

January 18

We can still use the telephone. I have talked to my mother and my elder brother, who has just come home on leave from the southern sector of the east front. They are in the midst of preparations for a trek. It has to be done secretly, because no official permission has been given up to now. My father is toying with the idea of giving one more hunting party. There are more red deer in the forest than ever before, but he doesn't see how he can get the hunters together.

January 19

Our hospital is being evacuated. All the patients and most of the nurses are going to Pomerania, where they will be given shelter in a private house in the country. We are left with nothing to do. I packed a few things I value in one of the thousands of crates they have been turning out for months for transporting the whole inventory of the town to the west, and took it on the toboggan to the freight station where it vanished among hundreds of other crates.

On my way back I noticed a lady standing by the roadside, surrounded by packages. As I passed her, hesitating, she said to me: "Oh, could you please tell me of a furniture mover? I want to send away the antique furniture from my apartment. I've just got it out of Gumbinnen with the greatest difficulty, but the soldiers who helped me with it couldn't take it with them any farther. They are all valuable pieces which I took from Wuppertal to some friends in Gumbinnen two years ago because of the bombs. These here are only the small things; the large ones are over there in a courtyard." We went across the road to look at them. There were eight enormous pieces, including an oak buffet weighing at least half a ton. I cannot imagine how she managed to get all that out of the burning town, surrounded on three sides by the enemy. We went back to the road again and stood there trying to stop one of the military vehicles which were rushing past at breakneck speed, for it would be almost impossible to find a moving firm still working. Meanwhile, I made a timid attempt to persuade the lady to leave without her furniture; but she would not hear of it. Her husband had been killed in the war, she had no children, her house had been destroyed. These were the only things left and she was very attached to them.

While we were talking, heavy aircraft appeared over the town at low altitude. I could not believe my eyes when I saw all the soldiers leave the road and dive with lightning speed into the houses around. Only the civilians were left. But then a flashing and rattling started overhead. So that was the explanation! It was the Russians! And so near! Never had we seen them so near in daytime. They circled and began firing on the railroad station. Then our flak went into action at last. Like ships in a rough sea the heavy bombers rose and fell, followed by our fighters, and turned off to the east. As though he had burned his fingers, the giant withdrew them again; but he had pushed open the gate. On my way back to the hospital I felt an icy chill.

All was quiet in the afternoon. High up in the sky invisible planes kept tracing their bold condensation trails. In sunshine and deep snow I walked once more across the Tilting Square and along the Angerapp. The waxwings were pecking red berries off the bushes. Not a soul was around; everybody has already cleared out.

And in the evening I went once again into our church. Ever since the air raid of last summer we have gathered there daily for evensong. The doors were all smashed in, and through the main entrance the snow had drifted between the pews. I sat down under the pulpit and sang the hymn *"Mein schönste Zier"* by way of farewell.

January 20

On my way to the station to inquire about trains, I found all the furniture belonging to the lady from the west where she had left it. She herself was busy making a few moderate sized parcels out of the smaller things, which she intended to ship by express. I went with her to the station which was swarming with people wanting to send off more and more crates and trunks. While we were standing in a long line at the ticket office, there was a sudden bang, and broken glass flew about our ears. Everybody rushed to the exit, glanced up, ducked their heads, and took to their heels. I seized my companion's hand and ran off with her. Ten or twelve bombers were hovering like dragons above us in the air. We raced across the station yard and dived into the already overcrowded shelter. At the same moment the load of bombs came crashing down. A short, earsplitting shattering and detonating, then the human stream welled up out of the ground again and scattered at lightning speed in all directions. Close to us two dead horses, steaming, were lying on the pavement. The hotel in back was riddled like a piece of theatrical scenery. The fire was crackling all around. Memories flashed through my mind of happy childhood days which had so often led me past this spot when we came to Insterburg from Trakehnen to see the Tilting Show. Now Judgment has come over the world.

So far the station has not been hit. There are hospital trains standing with a great many wounded. This time our flak was silent. They say the airport has also been evacuated.

Walking along Danzig Street, I saw more bombers coming, rushed into the cellar of an empty house and waited until they had released their bombs—this time apparently more in the center of the town. And then, all at once, I saw them shuttling back and forth north-east of the town. It looks as if the front must be there. Another formation was approaching when suddenly three fighters appeared from the west and hurled themselves straight at the enemy. Like a skein of wild geese attacked by falcons, the unwieldy machines staggered about, and dogfights started up close above the housetops. With only a few yards between them, two fighters raced over our heads, the pursuer pouring continuous fire into the other which disintegrated before our eyes. Just as he reached the power plant we saw the pilot bail out and fall on the ground with a thud before his parachute had opened. His burning plane was flying on while the pursuer turned away in a steep climb.

When I turned around I saw Doktora, our young assistant doctor, standing beside me. She had just returned from Königsberg, where we had sent her to recover from a severe attack of diphtheria. But she could not stand it there any longer; worried and restless, she had traveled all night in one military vehicle after another, in a roundabout way, as far as the outskirts of the town, where she met the stream of fugitives pouring out. She nearly turned back because they informed her that the Russians were already in the town. We were both delighted that she had got through, though there is really nothing left for her to do here.

Around three in the afternoon bugles were sounded—the sirens are no longer working—to call the last inhabitants to leave the town for good. We took the nurses who had remained behind to the railroad station, where the last train was standing with steam up, and waved to them with a feeling of relief when, in the gathering darkness, it drew slowly out of the threatened place toward the west. Left behind with us on the platform was the lady from the west, who had looked us up earlier at the hospital and had helped to push to the station the wheeled stretchers loaded with the nurses' trunks. Meanwhile, she had freed herself, inwardly and outwardly, of her furniture and promised us, laughing, to clear out as soon as she could get a lift in a car.

Back at the hospital we sat down for the last time to a really good meal. All the cupboards were standing open, and something of everything was left in them. As we had been taking leave of the place in imagination for months, it was now impossible to feel sad. The last hours of an epoch should be lived with clear and happy minds. God is demanding the return of the talent He had entrusted to us, asking what we have made of it.

Late in the evening the head of our hospital arrived in his car to pick us up. He was followed by a Red Cross truck which we loaded with the most valuable objects from our operating room. While we were loading, a few isolated planes came back again to drop flares and incendiary bombs. Men of the Volkssturm, armed with hunting rifles, stood around on the street watching us. At the last minute I threw my bicycle on the truck, and then we drove slowly out of the burning, firelit town, avoiding the debris of walls and the dangling wires overhead. We reached Gerdauen around midnight. We had wanted to avoid both the stream of fugitives and the military vehicles coming the other way, but we had not expected the roads on this detour to be so completely empty. Not one vehicle, nowhere even the slightest sign of any intention to defend East Prussia on this side. It was like driving through no man's land already.

Around four in the morning we drove into Königsberg in bitter cold. The snow-covered ruins of Sackheim glided past us like ghosts. Then our ways parted. For the time being I am going to room with Doktora's parents in Juditten, a suburb of Königsberg.

· 2 ·

FORTRESS KÖNIGSBERG
January 21 to April 8, 1945

Sunday, January 21

A radiant winter day! Gardens snowed under, tall snow caps
on the fence posts, all the children out with toboggans. I went
to the Central Office of the Red Cross in the Kastanienallee where
I met my chief. Somebody gave a lecture on the military situation with the aid of a large map. Judging from this, there is no
reason for any apprehension. The Führer has ordered East Prussia to be held; and in the event of Russians advancing to the
Weichsel and cutting off the province—an idea that had not yet
occurred to me—the sea route would still be open. We listened
attentively, and refrained from asking what this route might be
like for several million people and in the middle of winter.

From the medical board, where I went to ask for work, I
was sent to the main railroad station, where a transport with
wounded civilians had just come in. Somewhere near Tapiau a
train had been hit by bombs or had run over a land mine. It had
happened so suddenly that nobody could say what it really was.
A doctor and several nurses' aids were already on the spot, bandaging the wounded and arranging for their transportation to
the various hospitals. One of the nurses with whom I had a
chance to talk told me in a whisper that Russian tanks had advanced from the south as far as Elbing, and that trains to the

west could no longer get through. I caught my breath because that meant the end of all the places that mattered most to me. My parents, brother, sister, and brother-in-law—my anxiety would not reach them any more. "There go all the big shots with their baggage," said the nurse, when some transport planes roared over our heads. Thank God, we are rid of *them!* At last we can breathe freely!

Doktora turned up to lend me a hand. More and more fugitives from the eastern part of the province were gathering inside and outside the station, often in the oddest combinations. I was suddenly surrounded by fifteen Polish women, all of them in the last stage of pregnancy. Three of them were actually in labor. We first put them up in the newsstand, and later on found tolerable quarters for them in the barracks for foreign workmen behind the station.

It was getting dark when we bicycled back to Juditten. On our way we passed the mental hospital and called on the director who, as a senior medical officer, was more or less advised about the military situation. According to his information the Russians are advancing toward the Deime Line. The Deime Line! How grand it sounds! I wonder if the enemy colossus, when he has reached this lovely little river valley, will even notice that it was meant to be a line of defense. In the last fall, the men building the East Wall were felling the trees in the parks on the west bank, cutting away the slopes to make a vertical wall and surrounding each village with a circular trench to make so-called "hedgehogs" of them. By now the whole place is probably manned by Volkssturm men with hunting rifles and artificial legs.

January 22

This morning I went to the suburb of Ponarth. In the Südpark restaurant, a great glass box next to the brewery, emergency quarters are to be prepared for patients who may be coming in from the country. The restaurateur, whom I told of this intended alteration, was very glad, because the three thousand workmen there at present, who have to get their meals, had obviously given him a lot of trouble. No patients had as yet arrived, only a few men who were told to bring over the emergency beds stacked up in the nearby school.

As I had the afternoon free, I took advantage of it to visit my relatives in Preyl. The road there was completely deserted; I rode my bicycle all alone through the crunching, untrodden snow. Even the new airport which I passed looked as if it was no longer used. In the fields, to the right and left, a few communication trenches had been dug. My relatives were still there; after a long search I found my aunt in a corner of their house which is occupied by the military. My uncle came back later from a ride on his white horse Jaromir. They still have no fixed plans and do not know what their daughter has decided to do; she lives some sixty miles away and can no longer be reached by telephone.

We spent the evening sitting quietly together, not worrying about the near future. It no longer matters what will become of us, for one after another has fallen—the sons of this house, the brothers, the hope of the country we love. I stayed overnight and dreamed of all the lovely days we had spent together in this house.

January 23

Next morning I found the large square in front of the Königsberg main railroad station packed with refugees. Farm wagons, piled high with baggage, were drawn up in close lines, and more and more, mostly driven by women, were coming out of the side streets. You dare not think how this is going to end. Already the trains are coming back from the west because the line is blocked, and only one road to Pillau is left. But this does not seem to be worrying people for the moment. They drive slowly along the streets, only watching the wagon in front, and trying to stay in line. Pastor Müller, whom I visited on my way back, took me into a large room in which a number of these refugees had spent the night. Among them were a few sick people he wanted me to look at. Everything was quiet and orderly here too. I got the impression that nobody had a clear idea about the actual situation. One woman stretched out her leg toward me, on which was a big varicose abscess. It was a couple of years old already, she said, but up to now she had never had time to have it treated. Now I should do it. I tried to explain to her that in my opinion it was more important to get out of Königsberg first. She could then have it treated somewhere else, where she would have a better chance to rest. "Where are you supposed to be going?" I asked her. She did not know; only that they were all getting into the Reich. And then she added surprisingly: "Our Führer will never permit the Russians to get us; he'd rather gas us first." I looked furtively around, but nobody seemed to think that there was anything unusual about this statement. Good God! I thought, if only people had as much faith in You!

Sick people have arrived in Ponarth, hospital patients from various towns in the east, and with them several dishevelled nurses who had to evacuate, at a moment's notice, a hospital thirty miles away. The doctor and the head nurse had cleared out earlier, taking with them, so the excited nurses assured me, two hundredweight of butter. A young woman doctor had stayed behind with the seriously ill.

My new patients are already in their beds. Hardly one of them has the slightest idea why they have been brought here. They have been provided with food, and I was given a festive meal such as I had not enjoyed for a long time. I have taken a room close to the Südpark and left my rucksack there.

In the afternoon I went to Maraunenhof to say goodbye to my chief. He is going to try and get through to the west in his car, via Elbing and Marienburg. The Russians are said to have advanced to Elbing so far with only a few tanks. Later I went to the Red Cross again to try and recover some of the operating material we had brought with us from Insterburg. It is lying among a great pile of similar material from other hospitals which have been evacuated. The ambulance drivers, sitting idle in front of the barracks, had evidently been left to their own devices and seemed inclined to take up a threatening attitude toward me; but with the help of my elbows I managed to haul out as much as I could carry away on my bicycle.

In the evening I met Doktora at the mental hospital as we had arranged. There they had heard that the Russians had crossed the Deime Line and that their spearhead was outside Königsberg. So far the town has not taken any notice of the fact. The streetcars are running as usual, and people are having their hair cut and going to the movies.

January 24

Today the main mass of the refugees who had come from the country began slowly to get under way again. One wagon after another drove out of the line and headed for the old Pillau highway, along which an endless chain of vehicles is rolling westward. We hear that a number of overcrowded ships are lying in the harbor of Pillau, unable to leave because of mine danger. The patients from several evacuated hospitals in Königsberg are among the passengers aboard.

I met Doktora at her parents' house in Juditten. She has turned down several opportunities of leaving the town as a physician in charge of refugee transports, and has taken over the practice of a doctor here who has been called elsewhere for official duties. We were discussing with her parents whether and how they should get away, when we were called by telephone to the children's hospital. A large transport of children was expected there, but we found the hospital empty; only a few members of the personnel were still about. The house was heated. We seized brooms and mops and tidied up some of the wards, but waited in vain for the children we had been told to expect.

Around midnight a rumor spread that one of the ships had left Pillau and had been sunk. On the ground floor the head physician walked past us, unseeing. He had just come back from Pillau where he had put his wife and their seven children aboard that ship.

January 25

In the morning everything was still quiet. I stayed in the Ponarth Südpark, where a lot of old, frail people had meanwhile gathered. They are in need of care, but not of any special treatment. In the evening Doktora came to have a look at my new field of activity. When she was getting on her bicycle late at night to return to Juditten, we heard aircraft approaching. I tried to keep her back, for—aside from the danger of the long ride—it had grown very cold and she had lost her gloves. But after debating with me for a while, she rode off. Hardly had she turned the first corner when the whole region was lit up by a sulphur-yellow blaze. Close overhead the flares hovered like hanging lamps in the workshop of a giant. I ran after Doktora and stopped her; we stood and stared. Beyond a wide yellow expanse of snow, Königsberg with its roofs and towers stood in full view, clearer than by day. While we were walking slowly toward the town, single bombs fell here and there.

January 26

Russian artillery has started firing into the town. Not having much to do in Ponarth, I went to the military hospital in Maraunenhof to offer my services as a surgeon in case of need. But the hospital had just suffered two direct hits, and while I was talking to an acquaintance, working there as a surgical nurse, the order came to evacuate. Some of the wounded will be taken to Pillau, although the news from there is not very hopeful. The dunes are jammed with people. Russian planes appear from time to time, circling over the harbor. The ships, lying there crammed with people, are in constant danger of being sunk by bombs.

I called on the chief general officer of the army medical services and asked him if he could make use of me in one of the other military hospitals as my time was not fully occupied. I am no stranger to him, for he has been trying for years to lure me into the army service. But even today we were both unlucky. A telephone call to the medical board disclosed that they cannot yet release me.

I found Pastor Müller alone this evening. He had taken his wife and daughter to the harbor where there was still room for them on a small motorboat which belonged to someone they knew. Quite a number of his parishioners are still in town, because most of the houses on the Haberberg escaped the air raids of last summer. He is planning a church service at his house for next Sunday and has invited me to it.

Later on I met Doktora again at the mental hospital. Several professors of the medical faculty were assembled there; as holders of high military ranks they have received orders to leave the town. There is evidently no intention on the part of the Supreme Command to treat Königsberg differently from any other town which had to be surrendered to the enemy. It is something one has to get used to at first, but it rather annoys me to see these gentlemen obeying the order so readily. I cannot help thinking of the seven new professorial chairs which were founded with such arrogance only six months ago, on the occasion of the four hundredth anniversary of the university, among them several for the medical faculty. Now it seems that for a thousand wounded only one physician will be left behind to hand them over to the enemy. Nothing definite is known, but one big hospital, now a military hospital, has already been left without any medical supervision, and when it was suggested to me that I should take it over, I accepted the job gladly as a gift of God. Doktora got one of the professors to give her the key to his office, which is said to be still very comfortable. A certain cupboard with food in it was especially recommended to us.

It was dark by the time we left. Along the Old Pillau highway wagon wheels went creaking past in endless succession. Between them people of all ages and stations were dragging their toboggans or pushing baby carriages piled high with their belongings. Not one of them looked back. Who would not think of the words in the Bible: "Pray ye that your flight be not in winter"? It is a blessing to have the "Brotherhood" watchwords at hand,*—the only chart by which you can now find your bearings.

The surgical clinic is more or less intact, although it is almost on the edge of the town center which has been destroyed by bombs. The upper floors have been evacuated; all the wounded, some one hundred eighty in number, are lying on mattresses in the basement, and on double-decker army cots in the wing of the building. If you go down a few steps from the yard, you are right in the middle of them. Exactly opposite the entrance is the room

---

* The Moravian Brethren, a Protestant sect, founded 250 years ago, publishes every year a selection of biblical texts—one from the Old Testament and one from the New—regarded by many Protestants as "watchwords" for their daily conduct.

in which operations are performed. There we found, to our surprise, a gynecologist from Insterburg whom we knew. He had dropped in by chance, and the nurses had persuaded him to carry out the operations which were due. We worked together for a few hours, and then he left the field to us.

January 27

At daybreak work began again after a few hours' interruption. Gunfire had become somewhat heavier, and as there is no indication that the town will be defended, we take it for granted that the Russians are going to appear here in the course of the day.

Today, the watchwords had a special surprise for me: "Give me thine heart, My son, and let My ways be pleasant in thy sight." It is my baptismal text and can only mean the final alert: Stay here, keep your eyes open! Stop thinking: how can I get out of here? See how all those who think like that are losing their heads. Stay here, very close to Me, and you shall behold My glory!

In the afternoon the shelling suddenly stopped. Combat planes arrived and began firing on the street from a low altitude. The harsh ack-ack of the machine guns alternated with the rough toff-toff-toff of the aircraft guns. Now people realized for the first time what they were up against. Not far from us they were all crowding into the large air-raid shelter under the square by the church. It is surprising that the foreigners, who far outnumber the other men, had not taken the situation in hand long ago. As soon as airplanes appeared, people came pouring from the street into our cellars for shelter. When the raid was over, casualties were brought in to us; they were accompanied by their relatives who refused to be parted from them. Like a lifeboat our place got more and more crowded. I did not object. Nurses and orderlies remained magnificently calm, and we carried on as though we had been working together as a team for years.

In the evening we got a call from the chief of the army nurse corps (it is a wonder that the telephone still works), ordering all female helpers to be discharged at once and to leave the town during the night on their own responsibility. Our nurses talked it over for a moment; then the head nurse came to me and asked if I would agree to their not obeying the order. It was more important to them to stay with the wounded, she said. I told her how happy I was that they had come to this decision. The female domestic helpers were officially discharged with a warning against the dangers threatening them at the hands of the Russians. But as they refused to be parted from the nurses, everything remains as it was, and the work can go on without loss of help.

Meanwhile, the former attending physician of our hospital, Dr. Hetzar, has turned up again, after having been detained for several days at some military post, but then released when the post was disbanded. The seat in a car, which had been promised him, was taken by someone else, and as he did not feel like walking on his lame leg, he had come back to our hospital. He seems to be a heartbroken man, and is the only one who keeps talking of his imminent death.

January 28

We have had a quiet night. Early in the morning snow began to fall in big flakes. It was so quiet that we could only assume that the town was already in the hands of the enemy. But toward ten o'clock shelling started again. It suddenly occurred to me that Pastor Müller was probably just about to hold his service; and as there was nothing very important to do at the moment, we thought we might allow ourselves this short

outing. It did not take us long to get there on our bicycles.
To our great joy, the first person we met at the parsonage was
Brother Martin. He had come from Insterburg with his military
unit, had landed in Königsberg and was quartered in the Trommelplatz barracks. About forty people attended the service and
heard a sermon on the epistle for the day, the First Epistle to the
Corinthians: "Know ye not, that they which run in a race run all,
but one receiveth the prize? So run that ye may obtain." During
the following Communion Service, combat planes were roaring
over the town again.

Back in the hospital we found more wounded. The Trommelplatz barracks had been hit by heavy artillery fire, and several
women helpers in the intelligence service had been so badly injured that nothing could be done for them. They were left lying
on stretchers in the entrance hall because there was no room for
them anywhere else. Other wounded had come on foot and were
patiently waiting their turn. Some of these, too, were badly injured, although they had not yet realized it. One woman, for instance, held out her left arm to me, with a splinter of wood as
thick as a broomstick right through the elbow joint, sticking out
on both sides like a cross. She begged me to pull it out. She and
other people had tried, but had been unable to do it.

Late in the afternoon we went to Juditten to look after Doktora's parents. They have not been able to decide if they should
leave and are thinking of putting an end to their lives. The idea
of perhaps being forcibly separated after thirty years of happy
married life is more than they can bear. We could do nothing
to dissuade them; we only pointed to the eternal truth that it is
not *we* who determine our lives.

They are not the only persons facing this decision. Whenever you listen, you hear people talking of cyanide which seems
to be available in any amount you wish. The question whether
or not you should resort to it is not at all debated; only the

necessary amount is discussed, and this in a casual, nonchalant way as people might talk about food.

At night we went to Juditten again and found the couple dead in their beds, carefully laid out by their elder daughter who had already left the house. The window was open and the room was icy cold. We stood for a moment in silence. On the stairs outside we said the Lord's Prayer. When we came out of the front door, a woman rushed up from the other side of the street, screaming: "Frau Doktor, is that you? Come quickly, my husband has poisoned himself with gas!" Doktora went into the house with her and I followed after a while, finding the man lying on the floor. Doktora, who had been kneeling beside him, got up and told the agitated woman to leave him in peace. Then she gave me a short straight look and said we could go.

Doktora's sister was waiting for us at the hospital. She had come by a detour, and wants to work with us as Nurse Ina.

January 29

Nothing happened last night either to change our situation. In the morning a sudden revolt flared up among the patients when a Czech medical orderly, whose slick manners I had noticed before, had started to take away their guns. When I took him to task, he explained to me that it was absolutely necessary to prevent the people shooting at the Russians when they came. I gave him to understand that this was not his business, and asked a wounded major, who had been in the hospital for quite some time and could walk about, to take the necessary precautions. He suggested discussing the matter with the attending physician, and that we should meet around one o'clock in the latter's room.

When the time arrived, I was busy in the operating room, and Dr. Hetzar went up alone to the first floor, not wanting to keep the major waiting, when suddenly there was a roar overhead followed by several deafening bangs. The walls rocked and we were smothered in a cloud of plaster. The orderly standing opposite me was bleeding from his forehead; in the background a woman was yelling at the top of her voice. Then through the smoke cloud came the soothing voice of the old surgical nurse Ida: "Be quiet, no harm has been done." When the cloud settled, we saw that she was right. The people around us had been only slightly injured by fragments of brick. The orderly in front of me was the first to recover his senses; he beckoned to me and ran out of the room, and I followed him upstairs to the first floor. Everything was in an awful mess. All the doors and most of the partitions had been blown out; in the attending physician's room the entire outer wall was missing. On the floor lay a heap of splintered wood, covered with a reddish layer of brick and mortar dust. Under this we found Dr. Hetzar, dead, a big gaping wound in his head; then, after a moment's search, the major who was still alive. We dragged him out. His face was pierced by a thousand tiny fragments of brick and looked like sandpaper. Both his eyes were destroyed, otherwise he was unhurt. We carried him downstairs and sent for his wife, who is working at a Red Cross post nearby, to stay with him.

I ran through the building to ascertain the damage. In the cellar only the store rooms had been blown open, nothing had happened to the wounded. On the yard side an enormous bomb crater filled the whole space between the operation wing and the side wings. The housewall, behind which the wounded were lying row upon row, was still standing. Outside, the gray winter air smelled of gunpowder, iron and snow. Trees had been uprooted, fire was raging in the nearby houses. One dead, one blinded, and I, myself, completely unhurt. Doktora came quietly up to me. We stared for a while into the gray haze.

Meanwhile, the operating room had been cleared. The raid had brought us more wounded. We spent the next hours with a wonderful sense of cooperation among all the helpers. Even the kitchen personnel, although much overworked, was in great form, and had posted guards to make sure that the food would be served at the right moment.

To our surprise, three officers of the active forces turned up late in the evening to inspect the condition of the hospital. I had to explain the reason for my being on the job here. Then they assessed the damages, and promised that several ambulances would, if possible, arrive during the night to take the wounded to the railroad station. A train was standing under steam and would try to leave the town before daybreak. They took the blinded major with them to be examined by an eye doctor at his request.

Meanwhile, a change had come over the place for which I could at first find no explanation. The medical orderlies, who had functioned up to now in exemplary fashion, were in a state of increasing restlessness. They were running in all directions, and suddenly I met one of them with several bottles under his arm. I blocked his way; he fell and rolled in a pool of red wine. Alcohol had started to appear on the scene. Strangers from the street had found their way through the holes in the walls and were plundering our stores. Some of our own people had become engaged in a scuffle with the intruders and then started to grab bottles themselves. There was no longer any consideration for the wounded, the chase went on over their heads; it was a desperate situation. Fortunately, the ambulances arrived at this moment. Our people came to their senses, the strangers ran away, and the wounded could be transferred in peace. Only the dying were left behind.

Toward eleven at night the long train of ambulances started moving, each carrying nine patients, and there followed a ghostly ride through the snow-covered old town, now reduced to a field of ruins in one night of bombing. Not a soul could be seen on the streets. The moon stood cold and clear above the rows of roofless houses. Isolated shells whistled through the air, to strike somewhere with a crash.

The ambulance drivers were very nervous; they made a wide detour to get to the freight station. On the very last track stood a long train, in which many wounded from other hospitals had already been accommodated. Most of them had their arms and legs in splints and were lying two to a berth. The loading platforms slanted so steeply that the ambulances threatened to overturn. It took an endless time to get the wounded aboard. The medical orderlies were cursing; the man in charge of the transport was hardly approachable. Doktora spent the whole night going back and forth between these overwrought men, trying to pacify them. Judging from the fiery glow, the town was by now completely surrounded, and there seemed small hope that the train would be able to leave. From beyond the heights of Ponarth, on which a few houses were burning, isolated shells came plunging between the tracks. The night was bitterly cold.

Around four in the morning Doktora succeeded in persuading one of the drivers to return to the town where we wanted to pick up the nurses who, on my advice, were holding themselves in readiness in case of emergency. A second ambulance followed us. As soon as we stopped at our hospital, a horde of strangers flung themselves with their baggage upon the ambulances before the nurses could get in. I told the drivers to proceed slowly in the wrong direction, until one passenger after another had dropped off again; then they drove back by a detour to where the nurses were waiting. They got in quickly and were whisked off; there was still room for them in the hospital train, where they were needed.

It was very quiet in our hospital. The Czech had stayed and now received us more or less as our host. Two ladies, one fair and one dark, had joined him. They had made themselves at

home in the operating room and offered coffee to warm us. Then
we visited the dying, the care of whom had been taken over
by the Czech. Between two of them, on their mattress, a newborn
child was lying. A Polish woman had come in to give it birth and
had disappeared again, promising, however, to come back and
take it with her. It was almost day when we went to bed.

January 30

During the afternoon two young men came to say goodbye
to us. For the last few days they had been very helpful assistants.
I now discovered that they were medical students who, for want
of a better opportunity, had spent their three days' army leave
with us. Luckily there was still a bottle of champagne—red,
moreover—in the cupboard, and we finished it between us. I
wrote out a chit for each of them, saying where they had been
in the interval. Then they left us to look for their unit, though
they had no idea if it still existed.

A change had now come over the streets. Officers were going
around singly, with pistols drawn, searching bunkers and cellars
for hidden soldiers. At my request, one of them came with me
to the cellar where the looters were at work again. He fired a
few shots, whereupon they all vanished through the exits like
rats.

We said goodbye to the Czechs and took our baggage to the
children's hospital. Fifty civilian patients are lying there in a
bunker built into the slope of a hill. Most of them are in plaster
casts and, therefore, almost immovable. An iron door leads into
the hill, and behind it runs a narrow passage between double-
decker bunks around several corners to a second door leading
into the open again. The five nurses working there, still have
room for us and received us very kindly. In the empty children's
hospital next door there is still hot water for baths—an oppor-

tunity we welcome with enthusiasm. When my turn came, the bombers were on their way again, and I was twice forced to get out of the bathtub for a time, as it is on the second floor.

By afternoon deep snow was on the ground and the sun was shining. Not a soul on the street which only a few days ago was filled with a stream of fugitives. Single enemy fighter planes swept like hawks over the town. I set out for Ponarth, this time on foot, for the snow was too deep for bicycling. Doktora and her sister were going to explore the center of town to see if there is new work for us anywhere.

I tramped through the powdery snow in a curiously exalted mood, as if the whole town and its fate belonged to me alone. While walking I sang a hymn in praise of God, and my voice moved me to tears of joy. The crowning moments in a man's life arrive when the Last Judgment is quite near. He feels the earth revolve under his feet like a ball.

When I was passing the railroad station I saw to my horror that the train with my wounded was still standing there. It had started at daybreak and could not get through. Now it was back again, waiting for tonight. One dares not think what will become of those thousand young creatures in their helpless state if they are unable to get away. Now they are still hopeful that they will be lucky the next time.

Ponarth has already suffered from shell fire; the houses on the south side have big holes. The house where I have taken a room was also hit, and an old couple on the second floor was killed on that occasion. On my way I met some women who were in a great hurry; they were going to try and escape to Pillau.

German tanks drove past, and the crews were tossing bars of chocolate to the children playing on the street. Perhaps it was done to boost morale. The children grabbed them with delight.

The Südpark has lost the greater part of its roof, and the premises are littered with glass. The patients have retreated into the cellar. A young woman was standing by the kitchen range, surrounded with nothing but debris, and was cooking dinner for the personnel. Beside her stood a young N.C.O., peeling potatoes with his pocketknife. I sat down at the kitchen table and had the situation explained to me while an ear-splitting roar was going on outside. A tank battle was going on at that moment. The Russians were aiming at the crossroads, where the Südpark is standing; they were firing too high and, therefore, kept hitting only the roof. Our tanks, which were returning their fire, were stationed about a hundred yards away. I asked him if you could see the Russian tanks from here. No, he said, they were standing on a lower level, some fifteen hundred yards away, in the direction of Wundlacken. While we were both eating his potatoes I heard more about his tanks. They had come from Tilsit a short time ago and had driven twice through the Russian lines on their way; they would do it again when the Russians arrived here, perhaps within an hour. I looked at the girl, calmly going on with her cooking as though the whole business had nothing to do with her, and I listened to the rest of the story with only half an ear. When the N.C.O. had finished, he suggested that I should accompany him; his captain was a splendid fellow and would be delighted. I hesitated for a moment. The idea of a drive, almost at the eleventh hour, with people who could defend themselves, was a great temptation. But just at that moment the detonations suddenly stopped. I changed my mind, and we parted with mutual good wishes. He had come from somewhere near Berlin, and Königsberg was for him only one of the many stages of his adventurous expedition.

On the way back to town I noticed that the tracks at the station were empty, so it looks as if the train has left again

after all. Across the fields I saw soldiers coming towards me at
top speed, throwing themselves flat on the ground in the snow,
getting up again and running on. I asked one of them who
had thrown himself down next to me what all this meant. "In-
fantry fire!" he shouted and ran off again. My ears were still
drumming, so I had not noticed the small dull thuds on the
field. When I passed the houses I saw women sweeping in front
of their doors, and children building snowmen in the gardens.

Near the Haberberg parsonage soldiers were hastily putting
up a barrier of branches and logs across the road, which was
meant to be a barricade against tanks, but looked more like a
hurdle on a racecourse.

The pastor was at home and invited me to a cup of coffee.
We sat at the window and looked out in the direction from
which the Russians should be coming. While we were waiting,
he told me about the heavy task now laid on him. Every morning unknown corpses were lying in front of the church door,
some of them completely naked. They had to be buried, which
was almost impossible in the hard frozen ground.

When I was walking a little later toward the town along
the Altstädtische Langgasse, people came running toward me
again, soldiers and civilians, scattering right and left down the
side streets. The cause of their headlong flight seemed to be a
tank which blocked the Pregel bridge. Was this a Russian one
already? If so, it was too late to run away. I walked calmly up
to it, but when I came nearer I recognized it as a German tank,
and that the man standing on it was delivering a fiery speech.
Apparently, every passer-by was being held up. When something about "our beloved Führer Adolf Hitler" reached my
ears, I, too, chose to vanish quickly down a side street.

It was nearly dark when I returned to our bunker. Doktora,
who had been in the Samaritan Hospital with her sister, had
already returned, bringing with her a poster they had found

stuck on several trees and street corners. It was headed "Hate and Revenge," and this was followed by a long-winded defamation of the Russians full of obscene expressions, and ended with a summons to use all possible means to dispatch the invading enemy. This appeal aroused our indignation; and not being inclined to sail under these colors, we decided to go and see the commandant of the fortress and call him to account in regard to these posters. It was just possible that he knew nothing about them; his name was at the bottom, it is true, but only in second place, below the name of the Kreisleiter, who had obviously grabbed the last shreds of power for himself.

After a useless walk to general headquarters, which took me once more through the town, I found at last the man I wanted to see at the General Post Office, where he had taken up his quarters. To give myself a more military appearance I had buckled on my Russian Kommissar's pistol, given to me by a friend. The guard let me pass without difficulty, but at the General's door I was stopped by a major who simply barred my way. The General would not see anybody—under any circumstances. If it had anything to do with defense, he himself was the man I should speak to: authority for this rested with him. I asked him for what other matters people had assumed authority in this place, and we got into a rather heated altercation, in the course of which I discovered that nobody here had as yet thought of acting on their own responsibility but that everything was still subject to Hitler's orders. Even the Hate-and-Revenge appeal seems to have met with general approval. "Can you think of any other way?" asked the major in a quite friendly and rather helpless tone. I said I could and urged him again to let me see the commandant, because I could only say this to him directly. But it was useless; he refused to let me enter. I asked him his name, and finally he promised to deliver a letter to the General. On the back of a temperature chart I wrote to this effect: "Herr General, what do you hope to gain from the appeal we have found put up everywhere with your signature appended? Königsberg is not just any sort of town; it has a great history. Would it not be better to honor the truth which probably we all must soon acknowledge before the throne of God? You can no longer catch anyone with 'Heil Hitler,' least of all the poor soldiers who are now hiding in their foxholes. 'Kyrie Eleison' seems to me the only war cry left us. Many desperate situations have been saved by it before. I am at your disposal."

It greatly relieved my mind to get all this down on paper, although I very much doubted that it would reach the addressee. I came back to the bunker late at night, completely exhausted. Clattering and crackling was going on all around the town, and colored flares soared up on all sides out of the ring of fire. Mortars rattled like the wheel of fortune at the country fair. But it is still very difficult to grasp the harsh reality as a whole.

January 31

After many hours of dreamless sleep we came out of our bunker into broad daylight again, astonished to find everything still unchanged. Airplanes were buzzing about; artillery fire from somewhere near the old railroad station came at intervals flat over our heads. Now and then a shot was fired in return.

In the children's hospital I met the director of the hospital, who had been aboard a ship, but was hauled off again by force; as he is not in uniform, he has to stay here. He made unfavorable comments on Hitler and Gauleiter Koch—criticism which seemed to us rather belated.

Doktora went to Juditten with her sister to look after their house and dead parents; but the front being very near, soldiers had stopped them, and they had to turn back without achieving their purpose. On their way back they discovered that a field hospital was just moving into the mental hospital; and as we foresaw the possibility of being wanted there, we were on our way at once. At first we hung around the entrance to see what was going on. One ambulance after another drove hurriedly through the narrow gateway and was unloaded at the main entrance. Everything had to be done very quickly because a second field hospital was known to be on its way from Ballieth at the edge of the town where it had been under fire, and had to be evacuated at a moment's notice. Many wounded were lying naked or only scantily covered in the ambulances.

We pushed our way into the hospital and saw that it was already crammed with people up to the roof. In the corridors they were lying on the floor and the tables in utter confusion, almost on top of one another, and in the lecture hall they were clinging to the tip-up seats. Many were obviously no longer alive. Faced with the excess of suffering suddenly closing in upon us, I felt everything in me resisting any contact.

Stepping over arms and legs, we reached a door at the end of a corridor on the ground floor behind which much seemed to be going on. Wounded were being carried in and out; we were jammed through the door into a small room swarming with medical personnel. In an adjoining room we saw a tall, stout man with bare arms, wearing a rubber apron. On the operating table before him lay a stark naked casualty on whom he was working. He looked like one of the Caesars. Above his enormous, bulging forehead a strip of gauze held back his sweaty hair. In a voice hoarse with shouting, he was hurling outrageous swearwords at the orderlies to speed them up. "What a butcher!" I thought to myself and gave Doktora a meaningful look. "Who knows if there is not more to it than that," her expression seemed to reply.

Suddenly he looked up, noticed us and asked gruffly what

we wanted. "Adam," I thought, "a man all of a piece." I explained to him that I was a surgeon, and asked if he could make use of me and the two women. To our surprise he put down his knife, and almost embracing me, pushed me out before him into the corridor, where he croaked: "Look at this beastly mess! I've been coping with it all alone for days. It can't go on like this. Do try and clear things up somewhat. Start wherever you like. And if any of those internists get in your way. . . ." Here followed some more than drastic instructions how I should treat them on his behalf.

We went to work. On the first floor, which had the best light, some of the wounded had already been laid in rows. Two assistant surgeons and a number of orderlies helped us to change the bandages which were hanging in rags from the shattered arms and legs. We knelt on the floor, trying to immobilize the limbs to some extent with the help of splints. The wounds were running with pus, and we would have needed at least an hour to fix one of them properly; but it had to be done in five minutes because hundreds were waiting. Many of the men were still in uniform just as they had come out of the trenches, and nobody had yet looked after their wounds. While the work was going on, our helpers provided us very kindly with coffee and the best canned food. Doktora and her sister were the first women, we three the first civilians, who were allowed to work in this military hospital.

Some time during the night I was called down by Captain Bode, the stout surgeon, to assist him in an operation. I was much relieved, for after kneeling for six hours, the task of dressing wounds had become an ordeal. The women, on the other hand, were still as fit as a fiddle. Downstairs they tied a rubber apron around me and we set to work. Our schedule of operations was indescribable, and the next hours passed like a grotesque dream.

Toward morning I was operating alone. Captain Bode was sitting in a corner grunting to himself, dozing, sleeping for a while, getting up again, settling the order of the surgical work, and alternately holding a cutlet, a cigar, a glass of champagne or a sandwich under my nose. Later on Doktora was called down to assist and was fed in the same personal way by Captain Bode. All the while heavy firing was going on outside, and the not very stable building shook ominously. Suddenly the rumor spread that six Russian tanks had driven past on the Old Pillau Road and had penetrated into the center of town.

At one time or other work was temporarily stopped. I lay down on the floor among the orderlies and slept for an hour. Then we went on again for at least the whole day, for when we finally stopped and walked, half dazed, out of the front door, it was getting dark again. The wintry air and bluish snow were a relief to our eyes. The soft glimmer in the trees of the cemetery beyond the pond was a sign of thaw. With a sense of deep satisfaction we groped our way silently, in single file, back to our bunker.

At midnight we set out again, four of us this time, because I took Nurse Minna from the bunker along with us. She has done four years' work as surgical nurse. It was thawing. Only a faint glow came from the front, and it was so dark and slippery between the cemeteries that it took us half an hour to get to the hospital. As soon as we arrived there, we were again engulfed in our work. On the left beside the main entrance, where the lab used to be, the new arrivals were lying on the floor around the big lab table. They all had head or abdominal injuries, or both. All other injuries were sent straight from the front to the five main first-aid posts inside the fortress.

There could still be no question of working systematically. The man lying next to one's feet was put on the operating table, though we tried to sort out among the newly admitted those whose pulses could still be felt to a certain extent. We cannot do anything for the others as there is no possibility of treating them for shock. After-treatment is out of the question, too; we can hardly even keep account of those who survive the operation or know where to find them again. We can only take thought for the present.

Meanwhile, on the upper floors more sorting out is going on. The patients are laid in rows, and the dead carried out and stacked against the back wall of the building like cordwood. This gives us more room indoors, so that mattresses can be laid down and double-decker bunks set up. Another surgeon has joined us; he belongs to the second field hospital which, with its personnel, has taken over one-half of the house.

The internists of both field hospitals dislike coming into the operating room, because Bode always showers the most obscene swearwords upon them. Nurse Minna was fully employed at once. The orderly who had been taking care of the instruments up to now yielded his place to her with relief. And should it ever have occurred to me that she might feel rather shy among all these men, I was soon to see that I had been mistaken. Hissing and rolling her eyes, she chased the tired warriors in all directions, seeing to it that no one should stand around doing nothing. Even Bode contemplated her at times with a certain respect, and toned down his peculiar way of expressing himself to a minimum of forcefulness, visibly glad to save for once his totally exhausted voice.

An eye ward has been opened too. There I found the blind major again, lying on a stretcher. His wife, who also takes care of the other wounded, is still with him. Still other women have been roped in as nurses; a few deaconesses are already at work. Order is appearing here and there in the chaos, making it possible for us to get into personal contact with some of the wounded. And out of the gray mass of humanity for which mere compassion did not seem any longer enough, because the suffering had been too overwhelming, one single human being would now and then stand out in need of a kind word.

As we occupied ourselves with the wounded, days and nights melted one into another, and we were always surprised to see that it had grown light or dark again. The Russians were evidently allowing themselves and us some time. Defenses were now built on the streets, barricades of brick, brushwood, planks, and old wagons left lying on the roads by the fugitives. The dead, stacked up against the wall of the building, were buried in one enormous grave in the cemetery on the other side of the pond with the two hospital chaplains officiating—one Protestant, the other Catholic.

One day we had a visitor. The chief general officer had flown back to the town and resumed his office. Bode and I, both of the same height but of very different girth, received him in the operating room, standing side by side. The General, formerly famous for his corpulence and still very portly, noticed Captain Bode first, looked him up and down with disapproval and started rebuking him for the disorder in the hospital. As I was afraid that Bode would become aggressive, I seized his right wrist and held it with a firm grip. Fortunately, however, the General had now recognized me and turned to me in a more amiable manner, wanting to know the date of my enlistment. I told him that I was still a civilian and hoped to remain one.

A few hours later the first of the two field hospitals, to which Captain Bode belongs, received orders to move into the East Prussian power plant near the Northern Railroad Station, which will be cleared for this purpose. The move took place as follows: before we realized what was up, everything in one-half of the hospital that was not actually a fixture was taken apart, dragged out, and loaded on the ambulances. Only the wounded were left behind to be taken over by the second field hospital. As a result, three hundred patients were left without any medical personnel, tableware, bed pans, or wash basins, all of which had so far been available, if only in meager supply. We parted regretfully from our friend Bode who had endeared himself to us with his fierce humanity. By way of farewell he gave me some more drastic pieces of advice about how to treat soldiers and, in particular, internists.

My team now consists of Doktora, her sister, one assistant, four medical orderlies, and Nurse Minna as surgical nurse. The wounded will be brought in by *hiwis,* Russian prison volunteers. I have supplemented our supply of instruments from unused stockpiles in the town; and I have even hauled out a plastering table from among the ruins of the surgical clinic. Our new admissions consist exclusively of people with abdominal wounds, though they have usually been hit by shell splinters in other parts of the body too. All those with head injuries are henceforth to be taken to the power plant.

We have given up our quarters in the bunker near the children's hospital and have moved into the house of the director of the mental hospital, together with all the other doctors—internists, eye, and ear doctors. We know the rooms well from more peaceful times. I have been given the children's bedroom on the first floor, overlooking the pond. I reach it through a room in which the Protestant hospital chaplain lives. We have come to know him better through his frequent visits to the operating room.

The two operating groups have now arranged their working time so that each of them is on duty for twelve hours. My group works at night, and we get to sleep around eight in the morning. At that precise moment the Volkssturm starts anti-tank practice on the other side of the pond, and the resulting double detonation causes the rooftiles above me to flap up and down like chicken feathers in the wind, and the holes in the roof are getting bigger and bigger.

In the wooded cemeteries on either side of the Pillau Road mountains of ammunition are piled up. Two guns posted there fire at random behind the rampart encircling the fortress. Now and then there is a shot in return. But in general it has become much quieter. Fights are going on only near the outskirts. We can tell it by the rattle of the "Stalin organs," the shuttling back and forth of the airplanes, and that new wounded keep coming in all the time.

Once, during her time off, Nurse Ina succeeded in getting as far as Juditten and persuading two old men to help her bury her parents. The front is only a few hundred yards away from there, and the houses are occupied by the military. The following day, February 7, Doktora and I went to the Juditten cemetery. In the middle of an open field, in the deep, melting snow, a grave had been dug. Nurse Ida had gone on ahead to help the men. We met her at the graveside, and when the men had left we recited the 139th Psalm together.

For days the town was completely surrounded; then the road to Pillau was temporarily free again by force of arms. Fresh troops came in, the wounded could be evacuated. Transportation is only possible at night, however, and is not always successful even then because of the shelling of the road; and the ambulances are frequently forced to turn back.

Still more problematic perhaps is further transport to Pillau, where numerous homeless people are huddled together in the dunes. Wounded are arriving there even from Heiligenbeil across the Haff. The Haff itself is at present the scene of immeasurable suffering. Thousands of refugees are trying to cross the ice in their wagons to the Nehrung sandhills, with the Russian bombers circling overhead. At night the whole region is lit up by flares.

Meanwhile, the Russians are advancing through Pomerania

toward the sea. Some of their detachments have already reached
the Oder, so the radio informs us. Very few people realize what
this means; they hardly give it a thought. The Führer has planned
everything up to now and must have some definite reason for
letting the Russians push so deep into the country. They also
put their faith in the new weapons, although nobody knows
how they can be used without annihilating friend and foe alike.

The suburb of Metgehten has been in Russian hands for a
few days, but is now retaken. What happened there, in what
condition the inhabitants, especially the women, were found, is
reported with all the gruesome details by leaflets. It is probably
done to rouse us to desperate resistance. But there is little appearance of any deeper reaction to news of this kind. People are
still incapable of realizing that such things exist and are happening in their immediate neighborhood.

With the return of the active medical officers to the fortress,
paper warfare has broken out again and demands its victims,
of whom I am one. I have been sent for by the General to
explain my relation with the military, for it is apparently considered inadmissible for me to be working as a civilian among
the soldiers. With my pistol buckled on, I went to the proper
office next to the theater, where I was received by an officer who
tried, tactfully, to convince me that I should now become a
soldier. I asked him if that was worthwhile for such a short
time, and if I could not do without a uniform. As far as I was
concerned, I would not feel myself more committed than before,
and it would only cause inconvenient complications in the hospital. They always addressed me there as Captain, and so far
nobody seemed to have noticed that I was wearing civilian
clothes. But to take me away from my work in the operating
room would be very inexpedient, because we had never yet been
able to get through our assigned daily task in any case. I was
then told that was not at all the intention. In recognition of the

voluntary work I had done up to now, I was to be appointed second lieutenant with three weeks' reimbursement, and my basic training would be deferred to a later date. Aside from this I would be better off in the army, from the point of view of maintenance. I assured him that I was satisfied to remain in the hospital without pay and that I had enough to eat too; and I also reminded him that we would probably be unable to put forward claims for maintenance to the Russians. But this seemed to fall on deaf ears. We were obviously talking at cross-purposes. Therefore, I submitted to my fate and asked him about the necessary formalities after my return to the hospital. The first step, he told me, would be to report to the sergeant major; all the rest would have to wait.

When I was taking leave of him, someone came in with news about the hospital train with my wounded from the surgical clinic. In spite of repeated attempts it had not been able to leave the town and was still standing at the freight station. Those of the occupants who have survived will now be distributed among the military hospitals and first-aid posts in the town. Several of the accompanying nurses will have to be admitted as patients as well. My imagination fails me when I try to picture to myself what they must have been going through in the last two weeks.

After my return to the hospital, I duly reported to the company sergeant major, who had no other choice than to arrange further details with embarrassed condescension. Of what they consisted remained a mystery to me for the time being, because I was once again engulfed in my work as a surgeon. I learned only incidentally that objections had been raised in regard to my taking my noon meal at the doctors' table. This was good news, for I had never cared much for the arrangement and would have preferred to sleep at the usual dinner hour instead of having to join in polite conversation. To my general relief, however, the situation was cleared up sooner than expected, due to a sudden

change at headquarters. The General's successor came in person
to inform me that everything could go on as before. To conform
to the demands of the paper warfare I would be officially listed
as "consulting surgeon."

In the middle of February two new surgeons were sent to us
via Pillau, and this lightened our burden considerably. Only two
groups out of four are now on duty at the same time, and this
gives us a chance to visit the patients, which up to now had
been hardly possible. Each group has a trained surgical nurse,
and trained nurses are working on the wards. The ground floor
is reserved, as far as possible, for new admissions. This means
a continual coming and going, for many of them are carried
out again as corpses in a few hours' time. Unforgettable people
are at work there; first of all, frail old Nurse Ursula from Ko-
blenz, who almost glides over the ground from sleeplessness, and
Galla the medical orderly, a man of unparalleled loyalty. The
hospital chaplain has succeeded in getting Brother Martin, whom
he has known from his student days, out of the Trommelplatz
barracks, and has found a post for him in our hospital as a
medical orderly. He was assigned to my group and had to go
immediately into the operating room, of which he had never
had any practical experience. He was also given no time to get
used to the work there, but at once had to take hold of several
arms and legs which had been amputated and carry them away.
We are grateful to have him with us, and not a day passes without our meeting at some time to read the watchwords together
and discuss the Bible text for the day. This gives a meaning to
our work—often so desperate in appearance—and a special tone
to each day.

Our very cramped operating room has now been enlarged.
The larger adjoining room has been cleared out and added to
it, and now we are operating there, while the wounded are
sorted out, undressed, examined, and X-rayed in the anteroom.

Moreover, the bandaging and plastering for transports are done there too. We have made a valuable acquisition in the person of the old male nurse Didszus, who worked for thirty years in the surgical clinic. I engaged him off the street at his urgent request, and, as he has a knack of doing everything in the right way, he saves the work of two men and a lot of talking.

At midnight we usually have a "luncheon" break, squatting in a circle on anything available in the way of seats, both operating groups together, and have coffee and sandwiches, which Brother Martin gets from the kitchen. We all look forward to this because it is an opportunity for good talks; and also many secret worries can be given attention. But the extra meal has become important to us too, for our official rations are becoming daily shorter. The only meat is horsemeat—plentiful it is true, owing to the number of horses constantly killed by bombs.

Among the wounded sent to us, an increasing number can no longer be termed regular soldiers. Many of them are over service age, but have been put in Volkssturm uniforms and let loose against the enemy at once. Some of these have performed astonishing feats. One of them was sent to us accompanied by six men with a chit from the Kreisleiter demanding special treatment for him. In spite of his serious injuries he was almost crazy with self-admiration, because he had succeeded in destroying four Russian tanks with his anti-tank gun.

In addition to these men we get boys of fifteen and sixteen, who have often been taken from the street only a few hours before they were sent to the front. As they are local youths their mothers, of course, soon make their appearance. We let them stay with their children, for, as we only get those with abdominal injuries, most of them haven't long to live.

I have had several surprise visits from my relatives. B. Finckenstein, who is in command of a battalion in Metgethen, has come twice. The second time he brought me brandy and cigarettes—

things we have been kept short of in the hospital since our stout friend Bode left, though there is reason to suspect that our stocks are not as depleted as the authorities maintain.

Another day my cousin Knyphausen, who is quartered in Vierbrüderkrug, came to see me. He is on the staff of the fifth Panzer Division, which is divided between Königsberg and Pillau. Nobody in his division any longer believes in the possibility of effective defense, once the enemy starts the final assault. I am glad to have heard such an honest opinion.

Over against this we have been indignant at a so-called NSFO, or national socialist public relations officer, who visited the hospital toward the end of February, and delivered a brazen lecture to the wounded on the military situation. Hundreds of tanks, he declared, had just arrived in Pillau. They were soon about to advance with the help of the new weapons and join a second lot of tanks, now on their way from Breslau, to the rear of the Russians, somewhere near Warsaw. This was the Führer's longcherished plan—to let the Russians in, in order to destroy them more surely. If the population of East Prussia would now retreat to the west, every man could be sure of returning in peace in a few months' time. They would all be back in time for the spring sowing. Those who chose to stay at home were defeatists and would suffer the fate they deserved.

It was useless to talk back; he knew himself what outrageous lies he was telling. But it gave me some pleasure to stare him in the face, from two yards' distance, all the time he talked. I gladly declined an invitation to the "informal gathering" arranged for the evening with the lecturer; but next morning, my apprehensive colleagues reprimanded me on my provoking behavior toward such an important personage.

We were treated to all sorts of other things. A prancing cafe violinist in uniform with ten other non-military musicians played the latest sentimental hit tunes for a whole afternoon to the wounded men. We were also urged to see the movie *Kolberg,* which was being shown at the theater. As it was bound to consist of the most vulgar mass propaganda, we gladly excused ourselves with our heavy duties.

At the beginning of March it began to thaw and the sun came out. Now and then we felt a quite unseasonable breath of spring. Swans were flying in orderly formation over the town, keeping us constantly on tenterhooks for fear that they might be shot down by the flak.

Our work at the hospital had become such a routine that we began to wonder again how the outside world might look. The first time I took a walk I came upon a red deer between the cemeteries; it scented me, crossed the Pillau Road, and disappeared into the park. I was on my way to post office five at the main railroad station, the site of a main first-aid post. Now and then we got wounded from there, who had already been given proper treatment. But the most remarkable thing were the carefully written medical records they brought with them, for that sort of thing went out of fashion long ago in the general confusion. I was curious to meet the man who signed these reports: First Lieutenant Bothmer, M.C.

The walk to that place was more hazardous than I had bargained for. As I was about to turn right from the Pillau Road, I saw some people suddenly throw themselves on the ground at the crossroads. Automatically, I did the same and heard planes roaring above us. Lying on my back, I saw them appearing between the clouds at a moderate height, and then down crashed the bombs with a noise as deafening as the roar of a powerful waterfall. The hits followed, and then everybody jumped up, and all went on their way again.

A few minutes later I passed the spot where the bombs had fallen, near the Holländerbaum Station. The houses on both sides of the street were riddled through and through; they had obviously been empty before. But the bridge, probably the target for the attack, was undamaged. I crossed it running as fast as I could, because more planes were coming. One bomb hit the water, the others fell farther away among the ruins. A third formation came streaking along the railroad line just as I reached my destination. I slid down the nearest cellar entrance and found myself in a large, dimly-lit room, leading to other large rooms in which the wounded were lying. People in white coats were moving about in the background. I looked at them closely, one by one, trying to determine the man I was looking for. Not one of them struck me as being exceptional. Then I saw him coming in my direction, almost like an old acquaintance. I let him pass and followed him, unnoticed, to the X-ray screen, where he asked to be shown some radiographs. While he was holding one of them against the light, I asked him a question with reference to the subject. He answered first, and then turned slowly round to the questioner. He looked me up and down with a touch of curiosity. "Are you a soldier?" he asked. "No, I am not, anyway not a proper one. I am merely working at a military hospital, and wanted to see the man who is sending us such excellent medical reports." He put down the radiograph and took me into the next room. There we sat on a table and were soon far away from this dark cellar hole. He comes from Kiel, where his wife and two small children are living. We managed to say much in a few words, and mean to keep in touch as long as it is possible, even if only by telephone, which is working again between the hospitals.

On my way back I called on the Haberberg pastor. Once again he and his house have escaped damage, but the houses behind the church, which had survived the air raid last summer, have been hit this time. The dead were carried out from under the heaps of splintered boards lying on the road. More and more I feel it is a miracle that I am alive.

After walking through the ruined town, which never ceases to fascinate me by its powerful grandeur, I ended up at the power plant. Our portly friend Bode received me in a silk coat reaching almost to the floor; he had found it in an abandoned medical depot of the SS. He looked like a maharajah in it. He still has some very good brandy and showed me a beautiful spaniel which he intends to train for hunting as soon as he gets a chance. He really seemed to think this was possible.

When I left him it was almost dark. The prosecuting attorney's office which I passed looked exactly as it did last fall; the front building torn open by an air mine, the prison behind it undamaged. My mother had been inside it at that time as a prisoner of the Gestapo, having been arrested in June.

Without saying a word about the object of her journey, she had gone to Königsberg to inquire about the whereabouts of a pastor who was a friend of ours. He had been taken to this prison a short time before. For four days my mother could not be found; then information seeped through where we could look for her. But it was four weeks before we could get permission to speak to her under supervision. I shall never forget the moment when, after waiting for an hour in the anteroom while all the close-cropped famished men and distressed women in their prison clothes were driven past me, I heard her at last coming along a long flagstone corridor, and the attendant unlocking the iron door that separated us from each other. In what condition would I find her? I was immediately reassured. She was still wearing her own clothes, and was obviously treated with respect by the matron who supervised our conversation. Full of energy and indignation at being deprived of her liberty, she placed a long list of commissions for me on the table, which we went through one by one. They consisted mainly of instructions concerning my brother's household, which she had been running during his absence. The actual danger threatening her had not yet entered her mind.

My subsequent interview with the prosecuting attorney in charge of her case was far more disturbing. He wanted to persuade me that she had committed high treason by not denouncing the pastor. He said she must have known that he listened to foreign broadcasts. Two years' penal servitude was the least she deserved. Undoubtedly he would have liked me to plead with him on the grounds that my brothers had fallen in the war, and that their death had caused us grief; but I could not give him this satisfaction, and when we parted the gulf between us was wider than before.

At precisely that time Königsberg was celebrating the four hundred years' existence of its university. The rectors of all the German universities turned up in full regalia; for days on end there were addresses, torchlight processions, and concerts, and seats of honor were fought for as in times of complete peace, while you could already hear the dull thudding of the Russian guns in the east. I had just returned, full of painful impressions, from Berlin, where I had been trying to visit a friend in the prison of Moabit, seriously damaged by bombs. He had been condemned to death by The People's Court. No wonder the racket in Königsberg seemed still more weird to me.

Three weeks later the whole situation was changed. The attempt on Hitler's life had taken place on July 20, and many of my friends and relatives were in custody, confronting an entirely uncertain fate. It now seemed almost a piece of luck that my mother should have been arrested earlier, and that she could not be implicated in this new affair.

When I was allowed to see her for the second time, I realized at once from her behavior that she knew everything about the events of that day. She had already picked up some of the prisoners' means of communicating by tapping on the walls, and was this time prepared for anything, because she had evidently realized into whose hands she had fallen. Knowing her passionate temperament, I admired seeing her as alert as an animal in danger, every word, every movement under control, so that I felt ashamed of being still at large.

Her trial came up soon afterwards, and I was allowed to attend it. The pastor who had been singled out for a show trial, was no longer alive, and this had considerably reduced the interest in my mother and the other persons arrested on the same charges. She was sentenced to nine months' imprisonment, and I calculated that the Russians would have arrived long before.

In that very same month Königsberg was destroyed by bombs. From the roof of our hospital in Insterburg we could see at night, fifty miles away, the fiery glow rising into the sky. The prisoners there were meanwhile raving in their cells, until at last a few courageous guards came running along the corridors, drawing back the bolts on their own responsibility.

Three days later it was possible for me to travel to the town. Everything was still smoking and smoldering under a radiant September sky. A road had been cleared for traffic through the unimaginable wilderness of ruins, and on either side of it lay the iron girders which had come down as whirling firebrands. The prison was still standing; destruction had stopped right in front of it. Only the roof had caught fire; but it had been extinguished by the prisoners. The front building had been torn open by an air mine, and you could go in without being stopped and rummage among the prosecuting attorney's files, which were lying knee-deep on the floor.

Referring to the destruction and the obvious challenge to the Russians to make further attacks on the outskirts of the town, I asked one of the attorneys if he would not let me take my mother away. He was sufficiently upset by the events to give me at least a hearing. But he demanded to see the files, because, he said, he could not decide anything without them. I asked him where they might be, and was directed to a large room on the first floor.

After having searched at random through an enormous pile of papers for at least an hour, an old office clerk sitting at a table in the adjoining room approached me. I explained my situation to him, and found him a most sympathetic ally. He knew about my mother's case, and told me in a whisper what he thought of our present rulers. It was incredible, he said, how they treated people. Then he advised me to give up my hopeless efforts, and went himself to the attorney to whom I had spoken before. Half an hour later he came back to take me to him, and worked on the already half-softened attorney in my presence, until the latter promised to release my mother on a month's parole if I could set up a well-substantiated appeal. This was quickly done. The helpful clerk called in a secretary and told her to type out on the spot the appeal we had drawn up together. Then I was sent around to the prison, and after barely five minutes' waiting my mother came downstairs, escorted by several matrons who took leave of her very affectionately and expressed their hope that she would now be free for good. She had received official instructions to report to the women's prison in Stuhm in West Prussia in a month's time. Fortunately, even this could be prevented when the time came.

At the entrance to our hospital I met Doktora, who had been in Vierbrüderkrug on her bicycle. She gave me an enthusiastic report of this daring enterprise.

One evening soon after this my new friend at the first-aid station rang up to tell me that he was coming to see us. As he did not know the way, I went there to meet him. When I left our hospital around eight o'clock it was raining hard; you could not see your hand in front of your face. I had walked only a few steps when I was stopped by a sentry who asked me for the password. "Theater?" he said. "Curtain," I replied and was allowed to proceed.

Immediately afterwards I heard airplanes approaching again. A few bombs fell, and the nearby harbor district flared up a dull red. The clattering machines of the enemy circled slowly at a low altitude over the town. Now and then one of them was caught in the beam of a searchlight, only to disappear again in a thick bank of clouds, pursued by the tracers of the anti-aircraft guns. The bombers returned heavy firing. The whole region was growing lighter because of the fires. I hesitated for a moment, then summoned my courage and ran along the deserted streets until I reached the main railroad station, where we had arranged to meet. We waited until the attack was over, and then walked back the way I had come, which was lit up by a fiery red glow.

In the course of the evening Bothmer told us about his experiences in Africa where he had spent two years, substituting for a very busy doctor. When the war broke out, his fiancée was on her way to join him, while he, unaware of this, was trying to get back to Germany by an overland route. Her ship was torpedoed off the coast of Capetown, and she had to swim ashore and remain there for a year until she too managed to return to Germany.

When I accompanied our guest home, the night was nearly over. We talked of the only things that were still of any importance; he is one of the rare people who have no illusions about what is to come. When we parted at the Holländerbaum Bridge a flock of large birds rushed over our heads through the early spring night.

Most people are still convinced that the Führer's present strategy is in accordance with a definite plan. And the fact that the Russians have already reached the Oder, and that we are now living, so to speak, on a small remote island, is hardly felt as a reality. This is confirmed to us every day in a partly ghastly, partly humorous, way. The reopening of the banks, for instance, has spread a wave of reassurance; the possibility of paying money in again and drawing it out is evidently proof for the people that things cannot be so bad after all.

I came across much the same attitude when I talked to one of our nurses. She had been a parish nurse for years in L., and I said to her that I wondered what it looked like over there now under the Russians. She stared at me, speechless. The Russians in L.? It simply wasn't possible! And I have the impression that this nurse has been considerably more reserved towards me ever since.

The following is significant too. On my way to the children's hospital, where many patients are still lying in plaster casts in the bunker, I met a number of horse-drawn wagons, loaded with people driving westward—a sight I had not encountered for weeks. I asked one of the deaconesses in the bunker what might have induced people to leave their homes and attempt the dangerous journey to Pillau just now, when things had quieted down a bit. She explained it in this way: "At first they didn't want to leave, as you know, but they have probably been told that the English bombers may come and raze everything to the ground—so now they are going."

General von Thadden, who, as C.O. of the so-called First Division—which may no longer exist—has come to Königsberg via Berlin, told me a similar story when I called on him in his bunker in the general post office. A Königsberg artist had come to see him, raving about the stimulating material he, as a painter, had now found in this town. The general had complimented him on his work and had asked him, among other things, where he had sent his family. "Oh, they were still at home and doing very well." "But isn't there too much shelling going on? The Russians are, after all, less than a thousand yards away from you." "That's true, and the upper floors of our house have been hit twice. But we live on the ground floor." And when the general asked discreetly if it would not be better perhaps if he took his wife and children out of the town while it was still possible, he received the naive answer: "Do you really think that it is necessary, Herr General?" "Necessary? That depends on . . . your feelings about your family." How was he to convey the truth to him unobtrusively without being cried down as a defeatist? In the end his guest thanked him for the suggestion and promised to talk the matter over with his wife.

The radio is imperturbable. We were told about the frightful air raids on Dresden, and heard Goebbel's brazen speech in which he admits that we could now say like the Romans: *Hannibal ante portas!* But that we should remember there was not only one, but three Punic Wars, and in the end it was the Romans who were the victors.

Among the internists in our hospital who feel rather out of place, because of the almost exclusively surgical character of the work, I have the reputation of attracting enemy aircraft. And it is true that almost every time I go out, whether by day or by night, hardly ten minutes pass before they arrive. I have been asked quite seriously to let everybody know before I go out, so that they can take shelter in time.

These airplanes can really wear you down. One by one they drone over the town for hours, dropping a bomb from time to time. Our hospital is, moreover, the only large building within a wide radius, and can be considered a worthwhile target. Those who have nothing to do go down to the cellar if they can; only Doktora and her sister show an almost offensive indifference to the bombs. During the raids they can always be found on the top floor, cheering up the patients.

Only once did we witness a counterattack, equally surprising to both sides. I saw an approaching formation suddenly scatter, as though a hawk had butted into it. A single fighter, three times as fast as the Russians, swept repeatedly across our range of vision. One of the bombers caught fire, eight men bailed out and were hanging with their parachutes over the harbor docks, while the rest of the bombers beat a retreat. We were told later that the fighter had shot them all down, one after another. Even if that is much to be doubted, this effective act of defense at least provided us with an element of tense excitement in our fortress existence.

What a lot of different people pass through our hands here! And what horrible injuries! The "right to health" has become a special grace. A few isolated cases in which we have become interested by chance have been accommodated next to the operating room, so that we can take a quick look at them from time to time. Foremost among them is nineteen-year-old Seppl, a husky lad from Innsbruck. He has lost an eye, and one of his legs has been amputated high up in the thigh. We often hear him screaming with pain. But when I visit him, he stops at once, and his expression seems to say, "Dear doctor, I know you have no time, and I am only one of many, but stay with me for a moment; I'll be a good boy." Then he tells me about all the plans he is making in case he should not be able to ski again. When I leave him I feel comforted.

A stud groom from Trakehnen is here too, whom we, as children, used to admire for his daring horsemanship. While serving in the Volkssturm he stumbled on a mine, and I had to amputate his right hand and foot. He has reminded me that years ago I had sat by his bed for a whole night after he had had a bad fall, and told me how happy he is to be again in my care.

As far as the whole question of surgery is concerned, I am daily and hourly staggered by the measure of responsibility imposed upon you, and even more by the necessity to make up your mind quickly for the gravest decisions. What is it in you that decides? Is it merely practical considerations, or does your momentary frame of mind play a part? I have sometimes amputated ten legs in succession, which I had until then hoped to be able to save.

In decisions of this sort the question always arises, too, as to what will become of these people if the Russians suddenly arrive. Will not the amputated be the worst off? I try to ignore this consideration as much as possible, because it is beyond what is demanded of me. But it keeps haunting me, and if I did not believe in forgiveness, I would not know how to bear up under all this. The people are dying like flies in one way or another, from exhaustion and also because we cannot give them the necessary post-operative care. Used bandages are piling up yards deep in front of the house, and begin to slide down into the pond, while in the cemetery the rows of new graves are steadily extending. Lately, we even have wounded coming to us via Pillau, where all accommodations are filled to overflowing, and ships can sail only rarely because of mine and aircraft danger. We hear about desperate fighting around Heiligenbeil, where a whole army is encircled by the Russians and driven towards the Haff. Thousands of wounded are being transported across the ice under impossible circumstances. A few pockets of resistance are still holding out in the cliffs on the shore of the Haff, with the Russians only a few yards above them. Airplanes are shuttling back and forth over the beach, firing into the cliffs. When that is over it will be our turn.

Pastor Müller has been transferred to Pillau, and Brother Martin has taken his place as hospital chaplain. We are glad that his gifts are no longer exploited in the operating room, and he is able to devote himself entirely to the wounded.

On March 20 I was asked by the chairman of the medical board to take charge of the surgical department of the municipal hospital, which has not been properly staffed for some time.

I am now free for this new duty, because another surgeon has come to our hospital and can take over my team. In this way I shall become a civilian once again. Doktora and her sister will stay for the time being; they are indispensable.

This evening I succeeded in bringing Bothmer and Captain Bode together. We met in Bode's room at the power plant, and the two of them were soon deep in a professional discussion on head surgery, assisted by a neurologist from the former mental hospital, who is also working at the power plant. Our host treated us to the last drop of his Martell, which we drank out of little red-rimmed glasses.

It was at first difficult for me to find my bearings in the organization of the municipal hospital. The separate blocks have been badly damaged in parts, and the wards which can still be used lie far apart on different floors. You feel like you are in a labyrinth and never know where you are. The operating room in the basement of the second block, which belonged originally to the gynecological department, is really splendid and I feel at home there. It is as well equipped as in peacetime with instruments, linen, and lighting, and also with two perfect surgical nurses, Martha and Ruth, who are both longing to set to work, and glad that operating is to start again.

The outpatients' department, which is in the front building on the street, is also run by two very capable young nurses. They live in an adjoining room behind a curtain. Left for weeks without any medical support, they have been extracting shell splinters themselves and have done all the necessary plaster bandages. Anything that is beyond their capacity they send to the Samaritan Hospital across the street. The basement in which they work is not quite below street level, but it is well protected on that side by a bricked-up screen. Here, as on the other side, a lot of patients have been accommodated near the operating room, although in a very narrow space, still fairly safely. There are about one hundred and fifty all told, half of them foreigners, French, Polish, and one single Russian, including a certain number of women. Fifteen Frenchmen and one Russian medical student are working as stretcher-bearers, in addition to Stantus, a male nurse with years of experience in surgical work. Among the domestic personnel are a few Russian women. The nursing staff is very mixed; some belong to the Brown Sisterhood. They say that many nurses have already left the hospital. The director, Professor Boettner, stayed on with one internist and two women assistants. I myself have been given a young Ukrainian doctor as an assistant, and am living in the former attending physician's room on the second floor.

On March 22 I bicycled to my old hospital to take my leave. When I passed the Treasury Building, a huge black airplane flew over the town like a demon in the twilight. Followed by a thousand pairs of eyes, points of light shot up in long chains from innumerable guns on the ground, up and up, only to ricochet ineffectually from the armored fuselage. The demon pursued its course imperturbably. And then a thick black column of smoke rose out of the immediate neighborhood of the main railroad station, followed by the heavy boom of the impact. A single bomb on a whole town—but how deeply disturbing! It must have fallen quite near Bothmer's place. I did not have time to go there and find out what had happened, and my anxiety was not relieved until I returned to the hospital and found a letter from him. He has sent me a wounded Frenchman, but kept four German soldiers who were hit by the dreadful bomb just outside his door.

Next day I visited my colleagues in the Samaritan Hospital. On a table in their dining room stood a photograph of Churchill, and everybody was busy learning Russian words of welcome. I was advised to do the same, and they thought I was very much behind the times because I considered these efforts pointless.

Their cellars are overflowing with patients, and they intend to send fresh arrivals over to us in the future. They have lost some of their staff already, including their X-ray nurse, who was killed by a shell while at work. The X-ray department at the municipal hospital is run by a tall blonde woman who makes excellent radiographs and is glad to have something to do again.

I have been given a pass allowing me to circulate freely inside the fortifications. In recent weeks a number of barricades and barriers have been built from the wreckage. In times past the whole place might have almost been called a fortress. The area between Castle Pond and the university has become completely unrecognizable. The debris has been mostly removed, and you have to wind your way up and down along narrow paths between high piles of brick. Every now and then the region comes under heavy gunfire; you have the definite feeling of approaching the end. At night the Russian radio stations are blaring from the outskirts of the town; between intervals of music they appeal to the population to surrender unconditionally.

I am using the opportunity of operating on peacetime lines as long as time allows. With the consent of the medical commission I have even brought over a soldier from the field hospital to operate on him for cancer of the stomach. Having been released from the field hospital, Doktora is coming to assist me and will stay on afterward.

March 23, Palm Sunday

Brother Martin held a community service in the Ratshöfer Church and we attended it. What a springlike March! There has been no snow on the ground for quite some time. Swans and geese fly over the town; the cemeteries are dripping wet. There are still mountains of ammunition between the black tree trunks, and the guns for which it was intended are still standing there in more open places. The service was well attended. In the absence of wine, strawberry juice was administered at Holy Communion. At the end a small child was baptized.

Maundy Thursday

I was ordered to report to the mayor to have my new appointment at the municipal hospital confirmed, and to settle the question of my salary. The mayor was supposed to be at the Town Hall next to the northern railroad station, but my search for him in the badly damaged building was unsuccessful; and as my salary does not interest me particularly at the present time, I gave up the attempt to find him and instead paid a visit to the medical institute behind the police headquarters. There I found the chairman of the medical board with a few younger colleagues and also the senior medical officer of public health, Dembowski, a man entirely equal to the situation as one can see immediately. With him you can risk an outspoken word.

While I was there two general practitioners from the Insterburg district, with whom I was acquainted, came along. Together with an older colleague they have taken over the abandoned Red Cross Headquarters. One of the young doctors is about to get out of the fortifications, and I could give him a letter to take with him. A short time ago I received a field postcard with the immensely comforting news that my sister and her husband had got through, and that my father was in the west too. The fate of my mother and brother, on the other hand, is still uncertain. They have not yet turned up with the members of their trek on the other side of the Oder.

I paid a short visit to the nearby Girls' Industrial School, which now houses a main first-aid post. It had suffered that morning several direct hits in the top floor. I was pleased to find there the two students who had given us such loyal assistance in the

surgical clinic at the end of January. They are in charge of the
X-ray department and are in thoroughly good spirits.

Then I went with my two Insterburg colleagues to their place,
which is now in a bunker of the general hospital. They still have
astonishingly good food and invited me to dinner. Afterwards
they brought me back to my hospital in their official car, having
filled my pockets with provisions. When I got out I asked where
they were going. On duty to Juditten, they said, to a Nazi
Women's League coffee party. One of them had to make a speech
there. "Good God!" I burst out, "is the Nazi ghost still not laid?"
They shrugged their shoulders.

March 30, Good Friday

Brother Martin had promised to come and hold a prayer meeting here, but we waited for him in vain. In the evening I went
through the house and invited all the nurses, and everyone of the
personnel I met, to a meeting I would hold myself. I read the
Gospel of the two crucified thieves: "Verily I say unto thee, this
day shalt thou be with me in paradise." It was not difficult to say
a few words on this text. At least we know now only too well
what we will have to face. The Russians have dropped leaflets,
telling us that we may celebrate Easter, but that all would be up
with us after that. We have heard that Danzig was destroyed
two weeks ago, but that Breslau is still holding out. The towns in
the west are plagued by air raids as before; Dresden has been
burned down with ten thousands of refugees aside from its own
inhabitants. Where are people to go?

Late in the evening Bothmer came to see me, having found
his way on his bicycle, although you can hardly see three steps
ahead in the fog and drizzle. Over a bottle of bad wine, which we
had obtained with difficulty, we spent the night in our wonderful yellow-tiled underground delivery room, talking about the

redemptive event of Good Friday, and what meaning it has for us. Toward morning I accompanied him through the rows of ruins in the Rossgarten, which were now and then lit up by the moon, as far as the Rossgärter Market Square. When we said goodbye, I asked him his first name. "Unfortunately I am called Adolf," he replied, "but my friends call me Alf." I remained silent and did not tell him that the person on whose account he said "unfortunately" was also called Alf by his friends, as long as he had any left.

April 1, Easter Sunday

The story of Christ's resurrection according to St. John formed the central point of a private service we held in the operating room. We even managed some singing, although very few of those present seemed to be familiar with church hymns. Doktora went to the field hospital and saw her sister and Brother Martin, and found both of them well. A corner of Brother Martin's room was blown out in his absence. An artillery shell crashed through the window and was found lying, a dud, on the bed of one of the internists.

April 3, Tuesday

Very early in the morning I began to feel uncomfortable in my room on the second floor, because heavier shelling was going on. Although I had figured out that nothing could actually hit the room directly, I took almost all my belongings downstairs and stored them in the room next to the operating room. An hour later, just as we were operating, a load of small bombs rattled down on top of us. Parts of the house wall became detached from the upper floors of the old, high, box-like brick building and crashed to the ground. We were well protected in the operating room and hardly felt the impact. Soon after somebody came in and advised me to have a look some time at the opposite house wall. I ran out into the yard and saw a big hole in the second floor. The only bomb which hit the house from the side had gone into my window and torn a round hole out of the wall. I found nothing but debris up there, the inner walls had been torn out and my bed, with the rest of my belongings, was in fragments.

April 4, Wednesday

The night was quiet again, but in the morning drumfire started up. All day long the ground shook and the sky reverberated. We could only distinguish details when stones came rattling down close to us. We were like a ship tossing on the ocean. All the patients were taken down to the cellars. New arrivals were left lying on the floor of the operating room and in the adjoining rooms. Doktora and I operated on two tables; one was not enough for the number of wounded arriving. Not only women and children with serious shell wounds were brought in, but soldiers as well. We, too, have now become a kind of field hospital.

April 5, Thursday

Today it was the turn of the airplanes. From early morning until late in the afternoon on this lovely sunny day they circled, first at fifteen hundred feet then much lower, over every quarter of the town. More than a hundred were always in the air at the same time, dropping heavy bombs and firing on the streets with all their guns. There was no sign of any defense. The bombers pursued their course calmly and steadily. A powerful spectacle met our eyes every time we passed the exits of our building facing the Castle Pond. In the steel blue sky a violent storm,

blowing toward the center of the town, sent the rising smoke
clouds whirling about. Over the center of town lay a black cloud
bank like a mountain range out of which flames were shooting,
and above it circled the planes, pressing in from all sides, plunging into the witches' cauldron and climbing up again unharmed
on the other side. The stone stairs in front of our door were littered with shell splinters; but only when the planes were directly
overhead, did we run back a few steps into the cellar. Otherwise
we stood outdoors, staring spellbound at the infernal racket. We
could not hear what the other said, but it was not necessary, because we knew that we were both thinking of the same thing—
our Savior's advice and promise for days of terror and destruction
like these: "Then look up, and lift up your heads, for your re-
demption draweth nigh."

I noticed that Doktora was singing, and then we sang together
into the tumult:

> Praise the Almighty, my soul, adore Him!
> Yea, I will laud Him until death.
> With songs and anthems I'll come before Him
> as long as He doth give me breath.

We are living an ardent life these days; all our thoughts revolve
around the one everlasting center, and believing has almost become seeing.

As for our fellow workers—no better functioning of the body
of helpers can be imagined. The Frenchmen as stretcher-bearers
performed miracles, walking unafraid across the yards from one
block to another. I assembled them for a moment, thanking
them for their magnanimous services which nobody could force
them to render any longer. One answered for all of them, saying
that they were here as conscious representatives of their country,
and would render us the services demanded of them to the end.

When the engine house between us and the Castle Pond started burning, we organized a fire-fighting squad with the help of the Frenchmen to prevent the fire from spreading to the hospital. In single file we ran down to the pond with buckets and succeeded in extinguishing the flames without anybody suffering an injury.

The nurses too were beyond praise in their fearlessness and readiness to risk their lives. One of them, our touching, absolutely devoted Nurse Maria I remember particularly because of the unexpected answer she gave me when I asked her how she had come to join the Brown Sisterhood. "Well, Herr Doktor," she said, "at first we belonged to the Christian Community; but then the Englishman came with his bombs and destroyed our trombones, and so we had nothing left to attract people. That's why we joined the Brown Sisters."

When towards evening it had become quieter, we found to our joy that we were all still there.

April 6, Friday

After a rather quiet night, the day began again with drumfire. Our nerves are already so overstrung that we live in a strange state of split consciousness. While I am doing my work with more or less outward calm, trying to accept with composure the hits on the thick walls of our building and the crumbling down of the brickwork as a matter of course, I am increasingly invaded by a dream world. I see us sitting in a thatched cottage at the foot of a wooded slope under deep snow. It is night, and swarms of Russians with torches in their hands are gliding down upon us through the trees. They have not yet quite reached us, but we are staring into their strange wild faces.

In between I catch remarks which because of their unique naivety bring me completely back to reality. I shall never forget the following, uttered by one of the wounded soldiers lying in rows on the floor of the operating room. Just as a fresh hail of shells came rattling down close to us, I heard a loud clear voice declare in the purest East Prussian, "Well, now they'll conquer us all right, but never in *spirit!*"

During the night we too stretched out on the floor for an hour at a time. The town was a sea of flames.

April 7, Saturday

I was awakened by the sudden fall of the four ceiling lamps in the operating room, one of them on my body, accompanied by the reverberation of a terific shock throughout the whole building. A moment later heavy hits were heard a little farther away. It was day. Stantus, the male nurse, came staggering up to me in the hall. He had been going to the upper floor to get something from the evacuated ward when the bomb fell, and was hurled with tremendous force against the wall. So was Wally, the Russian girl who had accompanied him, and she was now lying there unconscious. We quickly brought her down because the bombers were coming close over the houses again. On the upper floor the last of the remaining doors and partitions had been ripped out. The east entrance was blocked by a crater forty-five feet wide. A rack wagon carrying beds, which should have been standing there, had vanished into space. Another crater of almost the same size was separated from the operating room only by the outer wall. The third bomb was an enormous dud, which had come to rest on the first floor just overhead.

In the course of the afternoon we found ourselves between the two fronts. Armed units retreated across the houses of our block, fired their guns at a high angle over the roofs, and ran around the Castle Pond toward the town. On the other side of the pond a new defense line had apparently been formed. Shots from that direction came flying uninterruptedly flat over our heads, splitting off parts of our roof. There was hardly a hundred yards distance between us and this line, but their defense sounded like small caliber shooting compared to the vicious "toff toff" of the aircraft guns when the bombers were approaching.

The other side of the pond looks like a cabbage field destroyed by hail. Involuntarily, I am reminded of pictures of Douaumont and other battered fortresses of the First World War, except that those had been built in case of war, whereas the shore of the Castle Pond had always seemed to have taken a perpetual lease on its civilian peace and quiet. Now it is being completely ravaged.

Nerves are beginning to break down here and there. I sometimes notice people lying in a deep sleep, obviously the result of taking an over dose of sleeping pills. Afraid that the idea of suicide might become infectious, I gave a short address in the operating room on the text "Fear not those which kill only the body, but cannot kill the soul. But rather fear the one who can destroy both body and soul."

In the course of Sunday, April 8, firing became gradually less frequent, like machinery slowly running down. The continuous roaring and booming dwindled to a rattling at several isolated points. Rumors circulated that the town had been summoned to surrender by parley. The Commandant had wanted to consent and had been shot by the SS who had now entrenched themselves in the Castle, determined to fight to the last man.

Peculiar individuals, storm-driven and no longer quite in their right mind, keep turning up, looking for a place to stay. They talk like wandering Fates, and you wonder what they used to say and do when they were still normal. You listen to them, nodding agreement, and realizing the meaning of war from the fact that it makes human beings become that way.

Late at night the firing stopped altogether. After the pounding and shaking of the last days you no longer feel the ground under your feet. You imagine yourself falling, sinking into an eternity. We look at each other with a melancholy smile, almost disappointed that we were still alive, and that everything has to go on some way or other. We had not expected to come up once more out of the fiery sea. Now we are again floating on the surface, and the only thing we know is that we will no longer be equal to any new demands. Having read once more in the Bible and prayed, we lay down on the floor to sleep.

· 3 ·

KÖNIGSBERG UNDER THE RUSSIANS
April 9 to April 24, 1945

Once I saw a cat playing with a mouse. The mouse was very lively and seemed to amuse the cat. It kept trying to escape, and more than once I thought it had really got away. But when I went closer to the bored-looking cat, I discovered that it had seized the mouse in its teeth again. Many hours later the mouse was still alive. The tiny mangled creature no longer wanted to run away; it rolled aimlessly about, at the cat's pleasure. The cat still tried to find some amusement in this unequal game; its eagerness seemed greatly overdone, considering the condition of the mouse.

I could have rushed and killed the little animal for my own peace of mind. But what use would that be, I thought, to all the thousands of mice threatened with the same fate with nobody there to help them? Should we not harden ourselves to a problem which is always recurring in the same form? And can I find the solution anywhere else but in a situation in which I recognize myself as being the mouse?

April 9, 1945

Towards five in the morning I was roused out of my sleep by a babel of voices and hurrying footsteps outside my door. I woke

Doktora and told her to get dressed. "What's the matter?" she asked, still half asleep. "I think the Russians are here," I said, "I'm just going to look." "The Russians? Oh, have they really come? I had quite forgotten them." "What is to be done!" I said. "You wanted it like this!" She nodded. I put on my white coat and went out into the corridor.

Czernecki, my Ukrainian assistant, came running, calling me to receive the Russians. The patients I went past craned their necks. "Two of them have been through here already and taken our watches, and Wally has been knocked out." Wally, our plucky Russian girl, was lying among the patients, blood streaming over her face, not stirring. The Russian she had tried to stop had seized her by her hair and hurled her, face down, to the floor. Her upper jaw was broken, and several teeth had been knocked out. She was conscious but made no sound.

Outside the main building two Russians were rummaging in a trunk. There was something frightening about the sight. I felt like someone who had gone bear hunting and forgotten his gun. When we approached them, they left the trunk alone and transferred their interest to us. Automatics pressed to our bodies, we were honored by a thoroughgoing search. An attempt by my companion to talk to them had no effect. They reacted with short, growling noises and carried on with their work methodically. Meanwhile other Russians came out of the main block, hung around like sleigh horses with the most fantastic objects. They too frisked us quickly; my fountain pen vanished, money and papers flew all over the place. My shoes were too worn for them. They hurried away with a short-legged gait over ruins and through bomb craters to the other blocks and disappeared in the doorways. Their way of moving with a set purpose was bewildering: if the situation demanded it, they used their hands and ran on all fours.

In the main building they were already hard at work. As I was forever having to stop and let myself be frisked, I advanced along our basement corridors as if through a jungle. Stifled sounds of protest came from all the wards. Patients were rolled out of their beds and their bandages removed; here and there masses of paper were burned to improve the lighting, and our people tried desperately to extinguish the fires. We kept looking in vain for an officer; for if this sort of thing went on, there would soon be not much of us left.

In the out-patient clinic the young nurses were fending off some particularly impudent fellows. I dare not imagine what it would be like when they had become more assured. For the moment they seemed determinedly keen on hasty looting, as we discovered when we came to the storehouse. I was dumbfounded by the sight of the amount of foodstuff there, which we had been denied during the months of the siege; it infuriated me to think that I had let myself be hoodwinked into allowing both ourselves and our patients to go hungry all that time. Now a wild, howling mob was fighting over the finest canned goods; provisions on which hundreds could have lived for a whole year were destroyed in a few hours.

In the middle of the main storeroom lay a pile of broken glass jars and opened cans. Sack after sack of flour, sugar, and coffee were emptied out over it. Alongside, half covered, lay a dead man. On top of it all the Russians, soldiers, and civilians, were rampaging, raking down more and more piles of valuable provisions from the shelves. I tried to fish out a couple of unbroken jars, but a Russian knocked them out of my arm.

In the operating room Doktora was busy dressing patients' wounds. A crowd of nurses had taken refuge there and were pretending to be very busy. In the background the Russians were prowling around the patients, searching for watches and wearable boots. One of them, a mere boy, suddenly burst into tears because he had not yet found a watch. He held up three fingers: he would shoot three men if he did not get a watch at once. His despair brought about the first personal contact. Czernecki entered into a long palaver with him, and finally, somewhere or other, a watch was found, with which he ran off, beaming with joy.

The arrival of the first officers destroyed my last hopes of coming to tolerable terms. Any attempt to talk to them failed. Even for them I am only a coat rack with pockets; they see me only from the shoulders downward. A few nurses who got in their way were seized and dragged off and then released again thoroughly disheveled before they realized what was happening. The older nurses were the first victims. They wandered aimlessly along the corridors, but there was no place to hide, and new tormentors kept pouncing upon them.

I crept through our basement as if in a dream, trying to understand what God was demanding from me here. Czernecki had found out from a Russian who proved to be approachable that we could not count on any kind of order for the next six or eight days. The town had been handed over to the soldiery. I then realized that this was the first time during their campaign that women had fallen into their hands in any number, a fact I had completely forgotten and which was now brought home to me in its naked truth.

Had we not already laid the responsibility we had been allowed to shoulder during the siege back into God's hands, commending ourselves and those entrusted to us to His mercy? Now it was thrown back at our feet in an unbearable form. I had expected that a savage horde, determined to take a justified revenge, would descend upon us and destroy so much at the very first moment that a single person would have no time for reflection. For anyone coming through alive, the situation would be so novel that his behavior in it would result automatically. He would then be able to start, as it were, a new life. The former one we had written off already, though all too rashly.

What, actually, is our situation now? Nothing has really changed except that the process of attrition which began with the houses is now spreading to the people. The final decision concerning us has not yet been made. I am so exhausted that I can't even pray.

At the same time, to my horror, a quite new sense awoke in me, a sort of cold curiosity. What is it really, I ask myself, that we are witnessing here? Is it simply an expression of natural savagery, or of revenge? Of revenge perhaps, but in a different sense. Is it not the animal revenging itself on the human, in one and the same person—the flesh on the spirit that has been forced on it? Where do these types come from, human beings like ourselves, in the thrall of impulses, in horrible disproportion to their outward appearance? What effort to display the chaos! Moreover, this dull, growling speech, from which the word seemed to have withdrawn itself long ago; and these maddened youngsters, fifteen-, sixteen-years-old, flinging themselves like wolves on the women without really knowing what it is all about. All this has nothing to do with Russia, nothing to do with any particular nation or race—it is mankind without God, the caricature of man. Otherwise all this could not affect me so painfully—like personal guilt.

If it were only the Mongols. In any case I can get along better with them. They are individuals, more disciplined and, therefore, perhaps not so vulnerable to western influence. Their wildness is not offensive. Among them are wiry figures with remarkably slender limbs and a natural poise.

With Czernecki's help I succeeded in establishing the first human contact with a non-commissioned officer of this type. He is going to try and find a command post and arouse some interest in our patients, many of whom are foreigners. I'm placing my last hope on him; if he gets through and comes back we may be able to save something. Meanwhile we must try and hold out as long as it is possible.

Towards evening our courtyard was transformed into an enormous gypsy camp. Hundreds of small carts harnessed to shaggy little Russian horses drove up at intervals. Nondescript figures, civilians, and a few women among them, were crouching everywhere around little fires, over which, on two bricks, cooking was busily carried on. I felt as if I were in deepest Asia, and all this had been planned long ago. It was all so much beyond reality, like the confirmation of an always recurring dream. They were all busy sorting out their loot. Among them, unnoticed and dumbly resigned, stood our patients and their relatives, watching the distribution of the contents of their trunks. My brain reeled when I thought of the night. But to my temporary relief the crowd suddenly broke up and dispersed down the Rossgarten towards the town.

Night fell, and our Mongol had not returned. We did our best to go on looking after our patients. The Frenchmen were still there and helped as much as they could. They, too, have been robbed of everything. One or two had managed to rescue some foodstuff—a few cans of meat, a little bread—and we shared it among us.

During the night the operating room was a scene of ghostly activity. In a dim light, fifteen or twenty muffled figures, mostly younger nurses, busied themselves with a patient lying on the operating table. Now and then a large number of personnel was detailed to bring another one to be bandaged; so many were still lying around with two or three days old wounds. The Russians seemed to find the atmosphere slightly sinister. They stood around for a while in the next room, coming in now and again to snatch a pair of scissors from among the instruments, but the nurses were in less danger here than elsewhere.

Relief was provided unexpectedly by a major, who watched us some time and then asked me to remove a tiny wart from his face. He seated himself on the operating table, and large white sheets were thrown around him with theatrical gestures, which obviously impressed him; but he suddenly jumped down and told his orderly to stand by my side with his automatic ready. Feeling safer, he climbed on the table again and gave orders to begin with the operation, the need for which struck us as greatly exaggerated. However, it had the desired result: the major was delighted, and defended us for a long time afterwards against intruders. Having taken a liking for us, he showed himself a man of feeling.

We took turns lying on the floor to sleep, the nurses having been distributed among the patients. Towards morning there was hardly a Russian to be seen.

April 10

Trouble broke out again in the morning. For a time our corridors were teeming like the inside of a beehive. Women were heard screaming on every side, and a new tone had crept into the infernal racket, the origin of which was at first not quite clear to me. Up to now it had been possible to shake the intruders' self-assurance by an energetic attitude. Even Doktora had frequently been able to save a situation by her sudden intervention. But now? It looked as if the Russians had discovered some alcohol.

Then suddenly our Mongol appeared in the midst of the crowd at the entrance. I nearly embraced him. He had discovered some sort of responsible office and was going to take us there. Czernecki and I started off at once, taking another Russian with us who helped to hold off the snoopers who were forever trying to stop and search us. Walking down the Rossgarten, we got into a denser and denser crowd. On our left the Samaritan Hospital was on fire. I wondered what they would do with their patients who were all lying in the basement. All the way to the Rossgärter Market Square everything that had not yet been destroyed was on fire; the heat was so great in places as to be almost unbearable. Up the Königstrasse, over the Rossgärter Market Square and toward the Castle an immense coil of incoming troops was winding, in which we now became engulfed.

I pinched myself hard to convince myself that all this was reality and not a dream. "Königsberg 1945," I told myself again and again. To think that the good old venerable town, which we had hardly ever taken quite seriously, had only been waiting for this grandiose spectacle to expire. How cleverly it had guarded its secret from us, when, not so long ago, we had been strolling about unsuspectingly and with a feeling of superiority in its unchanging friendly folds. Only the storms of last summer—the two English air raids—had torn the mask from its face, making it outwardly ripe for this moment.

We were swimming in a stream of lava pouring down on the earth from some malevolent star. Now it curved to the right. Why? Of course, there used to be houses standing here: just about here our dentist used to live. He worked up there—in the air. In those days he may have sometimes looked out of his window at the peaceful street below, as if waiting for something. Now, between flaming ruins, a wild, yelling mob, without beginning or end, was pushing its way along the street. Was this really today, this very day? Wasn't it two thousand, ten thousand years ago, or as much later? At that moment time was twofold, threefold.

Impossible to describe all that was moving along—people, animals, and vehicles. All I knew was: this is victory, victory as it looks, is bound to look, in the year 1945. The ridiculous and horrible details of which the picture was composed seemed to me like compulsory acts, reactions within a consistent physical-dynamical process. The sloping plain seemed also to have something to do with it, and I wondered with a shock if Königsberg had always lain so much lower than Central Asia that the gray lava could slide down into it like this. Floating in it, emerging and submerging again were figures, figures! No, no! I am such a figure myself. I saw myself stopping, stumbling on, gaping with a dead, forgotten face. Who was I today? Who were the others? How strange to think that people had once been standing for hours to watch marching men pass. Here, perhaps, on this same spot. Therefore, there must have been something worthwhile seeing in it. And now this scene, surpassing all bounds of the imagination—for whom was it happening, who saw it anyway? Was it not completely purposeless? Or was God here putting on a show for Himself?

We were drifting toward the Castle. Out of the ruins rose the tower like an exclamation mark, split all the way down, riddled, shredded, and slashed by a thousand shells. You could look right into it—the bell was still hanging at the top. And all at once a voice in me answered and commanded: Open your eyes and look, for what is happening here would indeed be senseless, purposeless, mere diabolical laughter, if you didn't see it. This is not a glimpse of world history, momentary and passing again, it is world history in a glimpse. Therefore, look—and you will behold the glory of God. And the dirty, exhausted human worm that I was shivered with profound bliss.

The stream had seized me again. Riflewomen, standing in cars, came sailing past, both terrifying and ridiculous. Their gestures showed that they felt themselves to be the representatives of Victory. I laughed to myself, although I knew that my outward appearance matched exactly what they expected of the conquered.

Right and left among the ruins the remainder of the population was creeping around like half-drowned chickens. You had to look hard to discover them. Now and then a weak fluttering of wings betrayed their presence, when they were startled and run down by one of the tireless sleuthhounds. They are probably already searching for bread.

Our small party was increased by a cilivian who was suddenly pushed over to the Mongol from another group. In some mysterious way there seemed to be a certain method in this bedlam. The man spoke Russian, had apparently been seized as a spy, and looked like a fox in a trap. After a few more steps, an idea occurred to the Mongol. He pushed the man down on a heap of stones and ordered him to take off his boots. Then he held out his feet to him, one after the other, and ordered him to pull off his boots and put on the pair belonging to the man. As the Mongol's boots did not fit the latter, he was obliged, like so many others, to walk in his socks. I doubt that he will ever have a chance in his life to wear boots again.

After a while the Mongol asked us to stay on the left side of the street while he disappeared down a hole. It was probably the cellar entrance to a former house, perhaps a big store; it was impossible to guess what had once stood there. We did not see him for quite a while; but in the meantime other figures emerged from the hole, and still others were creeping in. It really seemed to be the command post we had been looking for. The ludicrous entrance was used with an inimitable seriousness. Like ground wasps people were flitting in and out. After a time our Mongol came out too, and escorted us back without saying a word. Gradually we got out of him that, for the moment, nobody was in the least interested in us—later on perhaps, in a few days. He was obviously sorry to tell us this, and probably guessed what was in store for us.

April 11

Dawn is just breaking; our operating room is packed with people. A small candle-end serves us as illumination. We have got through the night somehow or other. Only a few Russians still haunt our basement. A dead woman is lying on the operating table and is always attended to as soon as a Russian appears. Lying on the floor and dozing, I can hear Doktora's voice in the next room, comforting some one. It is a miracle that she has come through this hellish night unharmed.

Just as we had feared, the Russians had found some alcohol. Right next to us in the Menthal liqueur factory some thousands of gallons, carefully hidden, were still lying, saved up by the irony of fate for just this moment. Now something like a tide of rats flowed over us, worse than all the plagues of Egypt together. Not a moment went by but the barrel of an automatic was rammed against my back or my belly, and a grimacing mask yelled at me for sulfa. Apparently most of these devils have got venereal disease. Our dispensaries were burned out long ago, and the huge supply of drugs was lying trampled to bits in the corridors. With a certain malicious glee I could point again and again to the devastation caused by their buddies. They burst in here from the factory in crowds—officers, soldiers, riflewomen, all drunk. And not a chance of hiding anybody from them, because the whole neighborhood was lit up as bright as day by the burning buildings.

We kept close together waiting for the end to come in some form or other. The fear of death which had hardly figured in our thoughts since the days of the last air raids was now completely dispelled by something infinitely worse. On all sides we heard the desperate screams of women: "Shoot me then! Shoot me!" But the tormentors preferred a wrestling match to any actual use of their guns.

Soon none of the women had any strength left to resist. In a few hours a change came over them; their spirit died, you heard hysterical laughter which made the Russians even more excited. Is it really possible to write about these things, the most appalling things human beings can do to one another? Isn't every word of this an accusation of myself? Hadn't I many opportunities of flinging myself between them and finding a decent death? Yes, I felt guilty that I was still alive, and that is why none of all this should be passed over in silence.

After my return from the town, a major who seemed to be still relatively reasonable, sent for me to come to the isolation barrack. Thirty to forty Russians were rampaging among the patients. I was to tell him who these people were. Sick people, of course, what else? But what sort of sick people, he wanted to know. Well, all sorts: scarlet fever, typhus, diphtheria. . . . He gave a yell and hurled himself like a tank among his men. But he was too late; when the tumult had subsided, four women were already dead.

Later in the evening I was standing with Doktora among the milling crowd which always blocked the exit of our basement, watching the battle hyenas busily hurrying past, intent on their purposes. We were just figuring out how we might get my pistol which, with fifty cartridges, I had hidden nearby under a rubbish pile when all at once we heard a terrific rumble overhead and saw several Russians trying very hard to roll the dud bomb which had been lying for the last three days above the operating room toward the iron stairway. It was much too late to take cover. We looked at each other, laughing and no doubt both thinking: "It'll be worthwhile, anyhow, here in the midst of the densest crowd!" But then the heavy thing rolled back again and remained peacefully lying on the landing.

When it was dark we succeeded in retrieving the pistol and fastened it in a handy position under the top of the operating table, in case of an emergency. Apart from this we merely carried on with whatever needed to be done at the moment. We found, for instance, several German officers lying among the patients, although they had not been wounded; they implored us to give them civilian clothes, thinking they would be safer in them. Of course we couldn't think for a moment where to find them, but then remembered the dead who were lying on the first floor among the debris. We stole up there and undressed them, as soon as the terrain was more or less safe from rummaging Russians.

About midnight a Russian physician turned up in the operating room, accompanied by a woman in uniform. A small spark of hope glimmered again. Perhaps he would have some fellow feeling for us. But he, too, was drunk and only out to impress his companion. He took his stand beside the operating table and kept pinching the knee of the wounded man lying there, until the victim exploded with a choice Bavarian curse—"You son of a gun, take your dirty paws off my pins!"—and released us from the spell of this atmosphere of listless resignation to fate.

It was obvious that the riflewoman saw through our maneuver of keeping so many nurses in the operating room. I was afraid of some dangerous move on her part concerning these poor helpless women, and was greatly relieved when she marched off, only wrinkling her nose in contempt.

The Frenchmen were particularly decent. "Adieu, docteur!" one of them called out to me, just as I was knocking over a Russian who was about to use his automatic in earnest from the middle of the crowd, because I had succeeded in chasing him away. He rolled on the ground, and I retreated into the background to take off my white coat for a time, so that he should not find me again immediately. Shortly after, the Frenchmen must have left, for I never saw any of them again.

It is moving to see how sorry the Russian patients are for us. Four men who had been successfully operated on for abdominal injuries feel especially obliged to us. When other Russians are present, they have to be rather highhanded with us and order us around because they are afraid. But afterwards they always apologize to us in private and assure us how dreadful they think all this is.

Towards morning I found a Russian all by himself in our burned-out dispensary. For a few seconds I felt a mad thirst for revenge when he blundered along in front of me in the darkness. What thoughts flashed through my brain! Moses and the Egyptian! But where should I take the body? It would be found here at once. Never mind, things cannot get worse than they are! No, leave him alone, he, too, is only a poor, miserable tool.

I had a long struggle with the surgical nurse who wanted to take her own life. I begged her to stay with us, for Jesus Christ's sake. At present no other argument has any effect. Finally she yielded.

Oh, what envious glances the dead have to bear! The little woman on the operating table is the symbol of peace to all those around me. What more is there to tell of the night? Now, at daybreak, I have nothing left in me but the feeling that I am standing in an empty station and have missed the last train which might have carried me to a decent "other side." Indifference, the worst enemy of all, creeps slowly into my bones.

In the morning only a few Russians came and bothered us, but one of them is horror incarnate. Not an Asiatic, but a type you may meet everywhere in the world. Judging from his uniform he belongs to the navy. His behavior is so outrageous that I noticed him at once and decided to keep an eye on him. His ghastly grimacing face keeps cropping up everywhere. Once, when I was crossing the yard, he was cutting the clothes off two old women with a pair of scissors. They remained standing as if asleep, bleeding from a number of gashes. I took out my pistol and hid it in the big bomb crater by the main entrance which every intruder must pass. This would be the only chance of finding him alone. I hung about there for a long time, feeling cold and numb. Then I had to give up because there was something wrong again in the main building.

When I went into the operating room later, I realized at once that something had happened. The nurses looked at me with terrified faces. Doktora was standing by the table, bandaging wounds as usual. But those eyes! My God! A knife ran through what was left of my soul. I crept away and dropped down somewhere on an iron cot. Now sleep, sleep, and see nothing more. It is enough.

After a while she was standing beside me in her torn training suit, trying to comfort me with her hand. "Will you please find my Bible for me?" she said. "It must be lying somewhere on the landing. It was pulled out of my pocket." I went in a daze to look for the Bible and found it. Then we sat side by side for a while on the cot without making a move. She wants me to try and get away; alone, I would certainly get through to the west somehow. "There is nothing more you can do here. I have my pills, and anyway I know that God does not demand the impossible." I was much too tired to answer and was so deeply disturbed that I would not have dared to say anything. I saw clearly what had happened in my absence. It could have only been that devil who defeated her—the Power of Darkness against which there is no defense. (I read the confirmation of all this some months later in the notes she left me: "For the first time in all those months I was afraid," she wrote; "I knew at once there was no escape.")

The Russian was nowhere to be seen. We walked down a few steps to the shore of the Castle Pond where a number of up-turned boats were lying on the grass. Nobody was watching us. I wrapped Doktora in a blanket and pushed her under one of the boats.

In the afternoon the whole building was full of Russians again. They started fires everywhere. A house next door burned so rapidly from bottom to top that our roof caught fire. Although the experts declared that it could not reach our basement, I gave the order to evacuate it to be on the safe side. To make a beginning I carried a fat man, with a recently fractured thigh in an extension on my back down to the Castle ditch. With astonishing speed the house was emptied behind me, and after frequent pauses all those unable to walk were dragged across the small footbridge to the opposite slope.

The Russians had again become very active and were on the rampage in our midst. Doktora, who had taken part in the transport in spite of my pleading, was suddenly attacked by three quite young boys and carried away. I made a half-hearted attempt to run after them; a few shots from an automatic passing close to my head stunned me for a moment. Czernecki was just going past with a Russian major and tried to intervene, but in vain; the major just laughted at him. Doktora had soon freed herself—they had only been rude, silly boys—and hid among the patients on the slope, where she could rest at last.

Meanwhile I noticed that another caravan of nurses and patients, being carried, led, and more or less crawling along, was also heading for our slope. They belonged to the Samaritan Hospital which, because of constant outbreaks of fire, had had to be evacuated too. Soon the whole hillside was occupied by patients, and the Russians were rushing wildly among them like a horde of baboons, carrying off indiscriminately nurses or patients, harassing them and demanding watches for the hundredth time. (Mine was still safe around my ankle between two pairs of stockings.) With my pockets turned inside out I went back and forth among the patients. It was bitterly cold. Snow showers fell on us. The patients were moaning; some were getting abusive, others had already started talking with the Russians in a none too trustworthy manner. The last shreds of internal order were disintegrating.

I sat for a while by Doktora who was lying very quietly under a blanket, crying. A Russian had helped her carry a sick girl, and this had released her tears. I was glad that she had let herself go at last.

I left her alone again so as not to betray her whereabouts, for the Russian major was after her. When I could not see him any longer, I began exploring the immediate surroundings. Although our buildings had stopped burning, fire might break out again any moment, and as it would soon be night I had to look around for some emergency shelter for the patients. On the road along the upper pond, which looks like a newly plowed field, many small Russian carts were shuttling back and forth, getting stuck in the mud, pulling out of it again, and hurrying on. I had to keep reminding myself with an effort that this had once been Königsberg.

In my once white doctor's coat I reached the Dohna Tower without being stopped; it was swarming with Russians. There are supposed to be the remains of a German military hospital around there. With determination I walked up to the entrance and the sentry let me pass. In the back rooms I found several German medical officers, one chief surgeon, and some assistant doctors. They are taking care of a few wounded, but have not the slightest idea about their own future. The Russians were busy outside at the walls; perhaps the Tower is to be blown up. Anything is possible. We cracked a few poor jokes, and they fed me with peppermint patties from a big glass jar they had rescued. On the operating table a Russian was lying, groaning terribly; he had an abscess in the hollow of his knee which had to be lanced. They were just debating with what kind of narcotic they should make him happy, when I quickly seized the knife and cut into the abscess with great gusto. The Russian, though much taken aback, was suddenly quiet and let himself be carried away completely satisfied. As nothing else was happening at the moment I took my leave, inviting my colleagues to pay us a return visit if they were not blown up meanwhile.

When it got dark, the personnel of the Samaritan Hospital started moving their patients to Maraunenhof, where some empty houses are said to be assigned to them. I can't imagine how they will manage to get that far. We were left alone with our patients and began to move them back into our basement. I shouldered again a rather heavy man, and had just crossed the footbridge when I was stopped by a Russian accompanied by Tamara, one of our Russian nurses of the Fortress days, who was already dressed as a riflewoman and behaved like one. I begged her to help me, because the Russian was bothering my patient. She hissed under her breath, "Today I'm scared too," and went on acting her part. I had to drop the man. The Russian ransacked him, then shot him in the belly as if by mistake, and went on. The man sat there, looking at me, an inquiry in his eyes. If only I could have given him the finishing shot! I gave him a dose of morphine and left him lying by the side of the road. Before going on I looked back once more at the slope, taking in the whole before it would be cleared—a picture forever engraved in my memory. Up there, against the sky, the Cross should have been standing.

The next moment I collapsed. I had cracked my breastbone, which in normal times would probably have handicapped me considerably, but was now a quite welcome excuse. The others went on lugging their burdens with their last bit of strength. A new colleague who had lately joined us helped with great devotion. Czernecki is no longer here, and the foreign patients have left as well. At midnight only eight persons were left lying on the slope, all dead, our surgical nurse among them.

The whole town is now burning. Airplanes circling over it were constantly dropping incendiary bombs into the ruins. Our tormentors, in the meanwhile, have suddenly vanished from sight. A Russian told us that our district would be cordoned off to be blown up. We don't mind. I have taken out my pistol and have deposited it with all the sleeping pills and drugs I could find, together with the last hypodermic syringe, in our latest cache.

Why hadn't we hit upon it before? Behind the windows of the operating room, bricked-up on the outside, is an empty space about two feet deep, which cannot be seen from the inside in the bad light, not even when you are standing directly before it. Behind each of the three windows is room for two persons. Now the nurses are sitting there by turns, and we have quartered Doktora there for part of the night. I was sitting by her side for a while, reading to her from the Epistle to the Hebrews, of which she is so fond. "We have an High Priest, which hath pity." A great quiet has settled on us. I have promised to shoot them all if we should be trapped in the rubble and could not get out. This has comforted them for the time being.

Below us, Dr. Hasten is lying on the floor with severed arteries. He was brought to us in the morning from the Samaritan Hospital, where he had been found lying when it was evacuated. One of the nurses who brought him gave me Bothmer's last greeting. She was present when he was wounded on April 8; he died on April 10.

April 12

The night passed without any special incident. Around five o'clock the front building started burning again. Most of the rooms in the basement could still be evacuated; only two very sick people were left in one of them, because it was impossible to get to them. The fire was so fierce that we had little hope of putting it out with our inadequate equipment. Nevertheless we made the attempt, more to dull our senses than in actual self-defense. Starting from the well, we formed a long chain, along which all available buckets and containers drawn up by rope from the depth were passed from hand to hand. The Russians kept tossing incendiary bombs and firing anti-tank rockets from the street; but in spite of that we managed to get the fire under control, advancing in turns with protected faces. When all was over Gudat, our administrator who had turned up again from somewhere, came to take me with him for a walk around the town. He had heard of a command post supposed to be near the university hospitals.

Blackened with smoke we started out. The streets were almost empty today. The main body of the Russians seems to have left. Large formations of bombers are still flying westward. I did not dare to imagine what our people there will have to face; they have already receded for us in a distance beyond our reach.

Like ghosts we wandered through the deserted streets. The Russians whom we asked now and then for the "Kommandatur" pointed toward the chemical institute beyond the Castle. There we fell in with a crowd of miserable people who had evidently been straying around for the last three days with nothing to eat and no roof over their heads. Their houses had burned down, and nobody had paid any attention to them. Among them were many mothers with small children.

Suddenly three Russians appeared on the scene, separated about fifty of us from the crowd, and marched us to the former Red Cross shelter in the courtyard of the general hospital. (It surprised me how open the view of the whole area was since I last saw it.) Assuming that this was the command post we were looking for, we waited impatiently to be admitted. After we had been standing around for quite a while, a Russian came up to me, hung his loot bag and a military overcoat round my shoulders, and ordered each of us to take two cans with vegetables from a pile. Then we were surrounded by several armed Russians and marched out of the entrance. I tried to protest and looked around quickly for a chance to escape, but Gudat held me back—it would be useless. At the same moment a heavy weight was lifted from my mind. I was a prisoner—free. Free from this appalling responsibility. I felt like Jonah in the whale's belly, waiting with a grateful heart to see where it would spew me ashore again. My second life had begun.

Loudly whistling I walked along at the rear of the procession. Those in front looked round at me with disapproval. But with the best will in the world I could not be sad now. Life was so extraordinary. It would be a pity to miss the joy of it. And the only thing I prayed for was a spark of humor and an open eye for all that might still happen.

We walked past the smoking ruins of the Town Hall and the northern railroad station. The surface of the street had been churned up by bombs. The Gestapo prison was, of course, still more or less intact. Down the General Litzmann Street—one huge gutter. Keep your eyes open! Yes, but they simply cannot take in more; there are even limits to seeing.

Where could they be taking us? To the sea, perhaps, and from there by boat to Russia? It was all the same to me. My Bible, torn from my pocket a hundred times, was still there—for the moment I needed nothing more.

At the boundary of the town we stopped. We all sat down by the roadside and dozed. The sun was shining but it was cold. I suddenly remembered that twenty-three years ago to the day we had come as children to Trakehnen where the most wonderful time of our life began. It had been a day just like this: the starlings were whistling in the leafless trees; then they swept away before the wind into the clear East Prussian countryside and my heart flew with them.

I did not join in the attempts to argue with our guards. It would have been useless. They never gave information and you only risked a heavy blow with the butt of a rifle. Hardly two of my companions belonged together; their relatives were waiting somewhere in the vast field of ruins for their return; but they would probably never get a chance of seeing one another again. And all this was accepted with the utmost impassivity, as a matter of course. Our present experiences were, moreover, in no way different from what millions of human beings had been going through for years. It was simply the new way of treating one another, less out of hatred than—well, indifference, lack of imagination. I today, you tomorrow.

We walked through the completely devastated Fuchsberg district. The villages looked like half-decayed fish standing up in the air with their bare bones. It looked as if they would take us to the front. We could watch the bombers roaring over our heads circle not far away, calmly select a target, and come back again, while over there one smoke mushroom after another rose up in the air. Probably our poor soldiers were still sitting there in their foxholes. What must it be like to see death simply falling upon you, I wondered.

Because of the lively traffic on the road we had to walk alongside in the slippery fields. Vehicles with "Stalin organs" and other heavy guns were driving back and forth, all of them regular V.I.P.'s with their staff of servicing personnel. *"Gitlair kaput!"* the men yelled in triumph as they overtook us. Bravo! I thought, if it needs all *this* to make *that* happen.

By evening Königsberg was some fifteen miles behind us. Two old people had collapsed on the road; the others were still together. To the right of the road was a small farm towards which we were led. A few Poles were living there, probably the volunteer workers who had stayed behind. We were first crammed into the village smithy, but there was not room for all of us. They then decided to put us up in the cowshed where we had at least a roof over our heads. It was cold and we huddled close together on the floor, Gudat and I lying next to the steps which led to the hay loft.

When it was dark, our guards came with bull's-eye lanterns and searched the whole place. The women, whimpering or cursing, were dragged out with the help of the Poles. This devilry would probably never end. *"Davai ciuda!"* "Woman come!" It sounds more horrible than all the curses in the world. When something that means life bears the signature of death, Satan's triumph has reached its peak. It did not matter to them at all that they were handling semi-corpses. Eighty-year-old women were no safer from them than unconscious ones. (A patient of mine with head injuries, as I heard later, had been raped innumerable times without being aware of it.)

April 13

Last night, too, passed. To be alive is a constant reproach. Stiff and dazed, we were routed out at dawn. The ground was frozen hard. We ate the remains of the canned food cold, and then had to stumble on in a north-westerly direction behind the front. My military coat weighted me down almost to the ground. Other people were lugging all kinds of objects along, with the idea that they might be useful some time later.

The surface of the ground was thawing again in the morning sun. We slithered up a long hill of clay and were suddenly directly behind the front. We suspected that we would be thrown into the battle. I would not have minded, and Gudat was not against it, either. I told him that today was my birthday. Thirty-five years, a round number.

But even without us, they seemed to be getting on quite well. The artillery was firing from the rear over our heads; we saw the heavy shells flying. When we reached the top of the hill the sea was lying before us: so that at least is still here! You are by now prepared for anything. The nearest place, Neukuhren, was under heavy fire. We were taken across the field a little closer to a small wooded valley, the slopes of which were dotted with dugouts. Our guards immediately appropriated some of them and met other soldiers who had to guard a group similar to ours. At first we stayed in the open, sitting at the edge of the woods, evidently as a target for any German flyers who might turn up. But they were nowhere to be seen. However, a whole swarm of Russian planes was circling over the unfortunate little village in front of us.

After a while I was singled out with two other men and three women and taken into the woods. We were ordered to stay there and boil potatoes for the whole group. And this out of the blue again, as if it were the most natural thing in the world! Potatoes were lying around plentifully, a large tin tub was also at hand, and water in a brook running through the valley.

We slipped a stick through the handles of the tub and hung it on two forked branches we had driven into the ground. Then we built a fire under it. Going in search of kindling wood I clambered up the opposite slope and surveyed the terrain. Directly before me stood a quick-firing gun, from the barrel of which some hundred shells issued in a few seconds. I could hear the hits resounding from Neukuhren like the slow collapsing of a wooden shed. I began turning over in my mind thoughts of escape, but I could see that it would be impossible to get through on this side in daytime.

The sight of the boiled potatoes warmed our hearts. One of the three women shared her piece of bacon with us. The women were already going almost barefoot, their shoes not being made for such marches. After our meal we sat for a while on the slope and dozed. Then a Russian appeared with a hatchet and explained to us how we should build a shelter for ourselves out of branches. With united efforts we put up a hut like those we used to build as children, on a smaller scale, for the Easter Bunny. In the evening we moved into it. Although the rain came through, we felt in a way protected.

When it was dark, they suddenly began to take an interest in us individually. Close in front of us in a dugout on the slope, a small, square-built Russian had established himself and now sent for us, one after another. Toward midnight it was my turn. Stooping, I crept into the bunker where a stove was spreading an extremely pleasant warmth, and I immediately decided to make my interrogation last as long as possible. Aside from the stove there was room only for a short bunk and a small table. The Russian and I sat on the bunk, a Polish interpreter before us on the floor. The few papers I still had with me were thoroughly studied. Then came the questions. Listening to my statements of family circumstances, landed property and buildings, the number of horses, cows, pigs, sheep, geese, ducks, and chickens which my family had possessed, the Pole opened his eyes wide and asked me if I was completely crazy; it was stupid to tell the fellow all that stuff. It was touching how sorry he was for me. He knew the rural conditions in these parts quite well, having worked on an estate for quite some time. When the Russian left us alone for a moment, he told me that he had lived for the last two years very comfortably in Königsberg and had earned no less than forty thousand marks.

The Russian did not quite know what to make of me and brought in another expert to help him. This one was slightly more cultivated, spoke German well, and questioned me about medical matters. I asked him what they intended to do with me, and he began telling me about big modern hospitals in Moscow and Odessa, and that I would work there in my field as a surgeon. My over-excited imagination transported me at once into an entirely different world. I saw cube-shaped rooms with walls of dark glass where a few silent men were working. Everything was dark, only their hands were in a strong light. All that had belonged to me until now was extinguished. Nirvana—Russia!

When the interrogation was ended—the Pole had long before been allowed to squeeze himself under the bunk—I signed five closely-written sheets of a questionnaire. I had no idea what was said in them, as I did not know what lies the Pole had told the Russian to help me. Then I was marched off and shut up with those of our group who had made the most dangerous impression—twelve men, among them a prosecuting attorney, Gudat, and a railroad man because of his blue uniform. We were lying in a small dugout in two layers, one above the other. Outside was a barbed wire fence and two sentries were posted before it. The second part of the night was chiefly taken up again with the raping of the women.

April 14

At dawn we were taken out of our hole again, rising like Lazarus from the grave—once again, after all. We had expected they would blow us up or else subject us to some sort of ceremony. We were gradually getting ripe for some ritual sacrifice.

Cold is much worse than hunger. In your wet clothes you are anxious to move as little as possible. Your facial expression freezes, so to speak. You can laugh only deep inside.

Slowly our procession got going, we twelve dangerous men first, and then the other forty including the women in the rear. Most of them were already moving with difficulty. We went up the hill again and then west behind the front which had meanwhile been advanced considerably. The villages were smoking, the inhabitants nowhere to be seen. The farms, riddled by bombs, were covered with bedfeathers. Not a chicken, no livestock of any kind except for a few half-wild dogs. And the smell of burning! Never will I get rid of that smell.

After a few stops in the wet fields beside the road we reached the highway to Rauschen towards evening and turned north on it. Where it forks—to the right toward Kranz via Pobethen, to the left toward Rauschen—there lay two long potato pits in which a large number of Russians were digging. We were drawing nearer the advanced lines again. The stretch between the roadfork and the next village, Watsum, was a terrible sight. Obviously there had been strong resistance quite recently. The houses, scattered on the slope to the right, had not been burned down but riddled by shell fire. The trees were splintered, the fields churned up by bombs. Many dead were lying in the ditches or rolled flat on the road. But none of this particularly impressed us for the present; our longing for warmth was so overwhelming that the prospect of the burning village ahead of us silenced every other feeling. Shortly before crossing the Samland railroad line we met the first detachment of captured soldiers. Unbelievable that human beings had actually come out of the inferno alive! With gray, expressionless faces they stumbled past us—to the east. I made an effort to nod to them, but then looked the other way. It was impossible to face them.

To make the most of the warmth, we dragged our feet as slowly as possible between the burning houses. When we left the village the icy wind met us again, driving wet snow into our faces. Because of a blown-up bridge, we turned left and saw a column of vehicles and tanks crossing by torchlight the small marshy valley in front of us. The heavy machines staggered like elephants through the swamp. On the opposite side the troops were gathering around several fires. Among them were some powerful, sharply outlined figures, and the sight of them had something reconciling about it.

Soon after we stopped for a while, and squatted on the ground or stood with our backs against the wind. When it was completely dark, we walked a little way to an almost undamaged solitary farmhouse. A trap door in the floor was opened, and we twelve dangerous ones went down into the cellar, a hole about six feet long, wide, and deep. Because of the potatoes kept there, we could stand only in a stooping position. A young Russian, who was evidently serving a sentence, was pushed in with us; then the trap door was closed. One of our fellow prisoners still had matches, another a candle, so that we could at least inspect our new abode. First we had to portion out the space. Six men could lie down on their sides at the same time, the others had to squat at their feet, leaning against the wall or against each other until their turn came. The poor attorney had a tough time; he had a high temperature and horrible diarrhea, and was very upset at being such a nuisance to us. The Russian horde was rioting over our heads with the feminine part of our main group who had been put up in the upper rooms.

April 15

The night and the whole next day passed without any change in our situation. Once, around noon, we were let out and taken to a ditch running behind the farmyard. I ventured another attempt at escape, wandering some distance along the ditch, but was forced back by the sentry. The next minute we were squatting in our cellar hole again. We had long given up speculating what they intended to do with us.

The Russian was the only one who was given some food; but in the evening the Polish interpreter secretly brought us a few boiled potatoes. A second night passed for us in this cramped space. At least we were not cold. On the other hand we were sitting in our wet clothes like in a wet pack. We noticed the first bugs but could no nothing about them. I was glad that it was dark and we could not see each other's faces.

April 16

At four in the morning we were driven out of the cellar. The sky was starlit and it was freezing cold. We walked on in a westerly direction. For a short while the attorney was hanging like a weight on my arm until he was flung on the wagon which followed us, because he kept falling on his knees at every step and held up our march.

The renewed cold paralyzed my capacity for making a decision for the time being. I let myself be driven on, but hobbled and dragged my feet on purpose in order to avert any suspicion that I might plan to run away. I had slowly come to the conclusion I need not put up with this absurdity which meant a slow but sure death as long as I still felt the faintest spark of self-assertion.

At daybreak we reached the highway to Palmnicken. I had by now become thoroughly acquainted with a great part of Samland, because a man who is thinking of escape looks at the terrain with quite different eyes from those of a man who drives through it in a car with no special purpose. For the first man every rise in the ground, every clump of trees becomes important and burns itself into his memory. After reaching the highway we turned north again, in the direction of the sea. The farms on our left looked pitiful; here and there in the wide fields cattle with severe shell wounds were standing motionless. A stork, probably just coming back from the south, was fired at with automatics by the Russians leading our group. Astonished, the bird rose into the air and winged its way towards Gross Germau which lay before us on a small hill. Over the village a volley of a hundred shots brought it down like a stone.

In Gross Germau we turned left and walked on to the next village, which the Russians had apparently invaded only a short while ago. A few old people were running around helplessly, while their possessions were dragged out of their houses and either destroyed or loaded on trucks. I took a sharp look at the surrounding terrain. A few hundred yards to the north I could see a narrow strip of wood running along the sea. I would have to try and reach it.

We were pushed into a small woodshed where the wind whistled through the cracks. Every now and then we got a gratuitous cold shower from the pond which the Russians were splashing up with hand grenades. Through the open door we could watch the looting going on. The most useless objects, sofas, life-size photos, and other pictures in good taste were hurriedly thrown into the yard and carted off on trucks, whereas old cupboards and tables were chopped up for firewood. Here, too, no animals were left alive.

Our attorney was very sick; he was lying on the floor and hardly moved. One of our guards came along with a tall, black-bearded man, the local country doctor of this district. He was ordered to examine the sick man, who was then carried away to be housed somewhere else. We got a couple of new people in his place, among them a well-fed and still vigorous farmer of my own age. I looked him over closely, in case he should be willing to escape with me as soon as there was a chance.

The Russians were still busy screening out the remaining villagers. When they had finished, they took us out and shut us up in a partition in the loft, which might have given us a chance of communicating with the less dangerous ones, had we not become too lethargic to take advantage of it.

We were brought down again at dusk and drawn up in two lines in the yard. It was rumored that some trucks would be coming to take us to our final destination. The farmer I mentioned before was standing next to me. I told him in a whisper that I would probably take to my heels—did he feel like coming with me? He did not even give me an answer. Of course, it could not be done straight away. Something would have to happen to make it possible to break through the sentry lines. For that special something I was waiting, gathering all my strength like a race horse at the start.

And then came the signal for the start. The Russians must have thought that the war had come to an end, for light rockets suddenly shot up into the evening sky from several points at once. *"Gitlair kaput!"* shouted our guards who were delirious with joy. At the same moment I broke out of the ranks, heard an excited hubbub behind me, got around the pond, thirty, forty steps, and still no shot. I vanished behind a wall and ran toward the forest. Far behind me things were stirring; a few shots fell. Fortunately it was very foggy. The Russians I passed took no notice of me. I kept running inside one of the many defense trenches, clambered out again, was out of sight against the dark forest, and dived into it unharmed.

Freedom! Freedom! Like a moon-calf I was for some minutes in a frenzy of joy, not caring what my next step should be. The mouse had escaped—look out how you catch it again!

Sitting by a small pool in the dense underbrush, I took stock of the countryside I had left behind. It was snipe flighting time. A thousand peaceful memories crowded in upon me. What a miracle life is!

My thoughts turned to people who were no more. I saw cousin Heinrich Lehndorff standing before me. Only a year ago, in wintertime, we were hunting together in his forest by the Mauer Lake, picturing to ourselves what living there together after the catastrophe as partisans would be like. Might not our homeland then reveal to us for the first time its deepest meaning?

Half a year later he came to see me one night in Insterburg and told me about the attempt on the Führer's life which had been planned for a few days hence. He wanted to know whether I was willing to be at their disposal if they should need another man to help. As I already knew that this question would come up, I had asked a young pastor whom I trusted to go with me to the railroad station. Sitting there on a bench for several hours and waiting for the train, we looked for advice in the Scriptures. The thirteenth chapter of the Epistle to the Romans gave us particular qualms—how could it have been otherwise. "Let every soul be subject unto the higher powers . . . the powers that be are ordained of God." Should we, as Christians responsible for our country, really put up with everything? Should we go on idly watching a madman bringing disaster on the whole nation? One thing at least became clear to us: the Apostle Paul gave no one the right of appeal to the Epistle to save our own souls. He only helped us to realize that we were confronted with an extremely grave decision. There was no other choice than a choice between guilt and guilt.

I lived the following days under intense emotional strain. Again and again I asked myself what would give me the strength to walk up to a man with an explosive in my pocket, and to kill him. Would I not suddenly feel closely bound to him and feel it my duty to do everything to warn him? Or—this was still more difficult to overlook—supposing there was a latent possibility not to destroy the man but to make known to him God's judgment and to do it in a way that his eyes would be opened? How terrible it would be not to take this incredible chance because of one's own spiritual incapacity!

July 20, with its horrid reality, brought this dilemma to an end. And while I myself remained safe from any suspicion, I knew that my cousin was first arrested for high treason and then was fleeing through the forests, not from the Russians but from Hitler's executioners, until he fell into their hands again through betrayal. Compared with that all I was going through now was merely child's play!

When it was completely dark I got up and started to walk in

an eastern direction. A camouflage jacket was hanging on a bush and I took it with me. Cautiously I crept along in a plantation of young trees. In several places I could see the light of fires and hear the Russians cutting down trees. I came to the older part of the forest again and took a path which led deeper into the main stand. Suddenly I felt that something was trying to hold me back. Pricking up my ears, I thought I heard movements, and then noticed a few steps ahead of me the remains of a smoldering fire. I heard shouts and ran, first straight ahead and then in a curve through the underbrush. Two lights were pursuing me. In the next fire lane I gained on them, turned sharply right, tried to take cover in one of the many dugouts, but jumped out again and hid close beside it under a small drooping spruce. My pursuers ran past me, a hand grenade flew into the dugout, the sand sputtered over me. I flattened myself against the ground, waiting for the next hours to pass.

April 17

The night passed unusually quickly; I must have slept without knowing it. Not far from my hideout trees were being cut, and heavy vehicles rolled on a road in both directions. The forest nearest me was too thin to hide there in daytime; I had to find a better place before it grew light. Like a wounded wild boar I searched for cover. Close to me ran a wood path and behind it, to the left, was a thick fir plantation which was very tempting, but I had to take into account that they would inevitably search the forest and start with the thickest parts. The large clearing on the right looked more suitable; only quite low fir trees stood there and would hardly be considered, from a distance, as a hiding place for a human being. One jump over the path, and I lay down under a clump of those trees, which were surrounded by hazel bushes. Two steps away was one of the many dugouts, connected with the next by a communication trench.

It was hardly light when the hunt started. An uninterrupted rat-tat-tat of small arms of every caliber gave me a rough idea of the measures taken to mop up the forest. The tree plantation next to me was combed for hours; some German soldier or other might be still hiding there. The rain came down in torrents, and this inconvenient fact was a godsend for me at the moment when I heard dogs baying. It was the only chance to throw them off the scent.

Airplanes were circling close above the treetops. They were surely going to some expense over this hunt. I was now quite calm and detached and watched everything as from a great distance. I thought of the occasions when hunting I had only wounded game. They had haunted me all my life and were now no longer a nightmare but only debts I was paying at this moment. There was not the slightest difference between myself and the whole suffering creation.

Around noon a series of shots at close range swept above me through the bushes. Immediately afterwards a Russian stood in front of the dugout, deliberating; that is to say, I could see only his feet which I could have touched had I stretched out my hand. I was not sure if I was sufficiently hidden from above but I did not dare move to find out. A few seconds passed during which I felt exactly like a rabbit, then the feet outside moved on again and disappeared from my range of vision. A short time later my situation became critical again when several Russians pushed through the bushes at the same time. I drew in my legs and waited, ready to run. I was not going to let myself be shot lying down. Then even that was over and I was left in peace and quiet at last.

Late in the evening the shooting ceased. I was lying on my back trying to sleep, but the cold and the rain kept me awake.

I sucked a little moisture out of my wet sleeve; I had not felt hungry for a long time. All around me the bushes were rustling and bluish flames flashed before my eyes. Gradually the shadows closed in on me; two great birds with outspread wings rocked on the thin branches. When I tried hard to see them more clearly, they dissolved into the indistinct grayness of the night. But soon they were back again, beginning to whisper to each other. I wished they would fly away and leave me alone, but they stayed, and I became more and more entangled in their dialogue—until I jumped up with a jerk.

It may have been around midnight. The birds had vanished, and without hesitating I started on my way. I crossed the big fir plantation in a south-east direction, left the forest, walked through pastures which were intersected by deep ditches, crossed the Palmnicken highway and landed on the other side in a small wood. I kept struggling to my feet without having been aware of falling down. Fires were smoldering at the edge of the wood. I kept away from them and walked past lighted windows along a slippery country road toward the east until I landed in another cluster of trees. There I lay down and gave up all further attempts to come to any fresh decision. The feeling of that place becoming gradually covered with wet snow was a last lingering memory.

I had been there for only a short while when I heard the two voices talking above me again. "He cannot stay here. We cannot leave him lying in the middle of the road." It went on like that without stopping until I could not stand it any longer and struggled to my feet again. I had been actually lying in the middle of a road, right across some rutted wheel tracks. I groped my way along a wire fence to the nearest house and dropped down on the doorsteps. My flight into freedom had come to an end.

A Russian in undershorts opened the door and called out to me; then he summoned two other Russians to pull me in. Sitting on the floor I was stared at by the three as if I were some curious animal.

One of them pushed his canteen with soup toward me—only then hunger overcame me for the first time. I said grace and began eating slowly, cautiously, like a child taking its first steps. Eating and being were one and the same at that moment.

Food and warmth put me on my feet again. The man in the undershorts took me across the yard to the barn, where I saw by the light of his lantern a lot of people lying in the straw. I threw myself down among them and slept until late in the day.

April 18

There was a light frost again in the morning. I found myself in the midst of a crowd of women with small children, elderly men and a few teen-age boys. We built a fire in the yard between two bricks, and boiled some potatoes. The guards made no objections. The women and children, among them one that is still pushed in a baby buggy, come from villages as far away as twelve miles. They have been hustled about on the roads for some days; the soles of their shoes are worn thin, their clothes are dirty and quite inadequate for the cold. They have brought a few things with them all the way on their pushcarts. Some of them are complete strangers to this part of the country, because they are evacuees from the west and had lived with their relatives until the Russians arrived. Several children have died during the last few days; but the mothers have no time to mourn for them, being much too busy looking after those left. They have been given nothing to eat. They could only boil the potatoes, lying around everywhere, when they rested on their march.

At noon my new company slowly got on the move. Marching eastward we crossed a highway. Beyond it, we walked along a deeply rutted and half-flooded, muddy road toward a village ly-

ing somewhat higher. Our group became widely scattered because the women often had trouble with their baby buggies,
which got stuck. When after endless trials we reached the place,
we were told that we could not stay there. We turned off north
and came, after a mile and a quarter, to the village of Craam.
On the way there some women at the end of the line were
dragged away from their children into a solitary house on the
left, and were released only after a long time. They are used to
it; it is the same everywhere.

Shortly before Craam we camped in a paddock beside the village pond. The place is evidently a rallying point for Russian
military vehicles. The farmyards are full of tanks and heavy
guns. New ones are arriving, others driving away. There was no
room for us here either. We had to walk on again towards the
east, this time along the highway. Cars were tearing past us. We
trudged for long stretches in deeply plowed-up fields, advancing
only at a snail's pace. Toward evening we reached the village of
St. Lorenz, lying higher and looking like a menacing skeleton.
We stopped beside a barn, and in a few minutes little fires were
burning and something was cooking over them. A sack of potatoes which I had dragged out of the road ditch was greeted with
cries of joy.

Soon we had to start on our way again, first straight ahead on
the road to Rauschen, and then in the opposite direction to the
village of Watsum, through which I had passed once before. On
this road too was continual two-way traffic. Next to me a woman
dressed like a nurse was pushing a blind and paralyzed man in
a wheelbarrow. I asked her where she was going. She was making
for Königsberg, she said, because the blind man had become
scared of all the Russians in his house in Rauschen. For a moment I felt I ought to dissuade her from her crazy undertaking,
and to tell her the truth about what she had to expect in Königsberg. But then it seemed to me more charitable not to deprive her

and the man of their illusions. To judge by human standards, it was out of the question that they would ever reach their destination. She had to stop every five minutes and set down her burden. It could not be long before one of the cars, rushing past at a reckless speed, would put an end to their plight and send at least her charge into a better kingdom.

The straggling village of Watsum was a scene of wild confusion. The houses had been shell-battered, and some ruins were occupied by Russians; others were still burning. After many futile attempts to find accommodation for our group, we ended up at the railroad station in total darkness. Meanwhile we had met other groups similar to ours who came from Königsberg looking wild and distraught already. No roof had been found to cover them either.

We finally occupied the station building, which happened to have just been abandoned. In the basement stood a few sofas, whose coverings had been ripped off as usual. There our guards moved in. Only a few days before German soldiers had been sitting there when Russian artillery fired through the first floor; since then many other things had taken place here.

The two rooms into which they put us were full of a mixture of straw and unspeakable filth. After clearing out the worst of the dirt, we lay down on the floor, as tightly packed as canned sardines. Mutual warmth outweighed the disgust we had slowly acquired for each other, less on account of the vermin or our disheveled, unwashed and squalid outer appearance than because of the lack of any good manners. My only consolation was a fifteen-year-old boy from Palmnicken, Helmut Z., who treated me with great politeness and respect in spite of my horrible condition, and even shared with me a piece of bacon which he had salvaged. He has only been dragged along with us for three days and still has a great deal more energy than I.

All through the night two of us men had to stand guard on the stairs. They did not tell us why and against whom; but we had long ago stopped asking for reasons. I too took my turn, utterly chilled in the horrible draft. We haven't taken off our clothes for two weeks; we've been wet and frozen for one week; we could hardly walk properly and yet nobody is actually sick; nobody feels the slightest symptom of a cold or of any kind of organic disturbance. Our bodies are behaving far better than we could have expected.

April 19

In daytime we were allowed to go out onto the one-time platform. The men stood around, still half-asleep, at some distance from a cauldron in which the Russians were boiling soup for themselves and those women who were in their special favor. As there would be none for us, we crept out of the wind and drizzling rain into the shelter on the platform and lit a fire there between some bricks. Beside the tracks water was spurting out of a drainpipe, and Helmut persuaded me at least to wash my hands and face with it. I myself would not have had the energy to do it of my own accord. We took advantage of a moment when nobody was looking, climbed up the embankment, and crawled on all fours as far as one of the many dugouts. There we found a sack of groats. We emptied out enough to allow us to drag the sack behind us and reached the platform again unnoticed. The men had put one of the cooking pots lying around on the fire, and we crumbled the lumpy groats into it, accompanied by good advice. I avoided looking around me. In their miserable greed the ragged figures reminded me of pictures by Hoegfeldt; and when you are such a figure yourself, you cannot have the sense of humor which would make all this bearable.

While the soup was cooking—and hot disputes were carried on

whether or not it should be stirred—it came to me in a flash that I had been here once before. Twenty years ago, when I was traveling to Rauschen with many light-hearted companions, the train had stopped at this station. I remembered everything quite clearly: it had been a hot summer day, the rye was almost ripe. And it seemed to me that even then I had a heavy heart because I had a premonition of what had now come true.

When the soup was ready, it was dished out in every kind of container. It far surpassed my expectations. How was it possible that in the old days people used to feed only pigs on it! While we were eating some Russians appeared, tied up a cow on the platform, and went into the station building. With a large can I ran quickly up to the cow, and while Helmut kept a sharp lookout, succeeded in drawing a few pints of milk before the soldiers came back. But the can must have been filled before with vitriol or some similar acid, because even we men could not drink the milk, and the children's mothers rejected it with tears in their eyes. For the rest of the day we continued cooking and distributing soup on the assembly line, so to speak.

In the afternoon one of the many Russians going past stopped and talked to us for a while. When it was dark, he returned with a pair of felt boots which fitted me. He could not have come by day, he explained shortly, and disappeared again. I looked after him with a grateful heart. But into the pleasant prospect of warmth crept the conflicting thought how much simpler everything would be if we had no human contacts at all with him and his kind.

April 20

The second night in the station building passed like the first. In the afternoon the men were taken to Rauschen, while the women had to stay behind. What is to become of them, we do not know.

My outfit at that time consisted of the following items: a short-sleeved tropical shirt, a pair of undershorts, a pair of cotton pants eighteen inches too wide in the waist, which I had found on the road, and on top of them my own long trousers, tied round my ankles, a jacket inherited from a relative, the military overcoat, the felt boots, and a hat, likewise picked up. In a bag over my shoulder I carried my old shoes and the camouflage jacket I had found.

The weather was a little better; the sun was shining now and then. Traffic on the road was still extremely lively, and the sky was full of airplanes heading for Pillau. I recognized a great number of East Prussian horses harnessed to wagons and with riders on their backs. The horses had become quite spiritless, used to the abominable paces forced upon them—a high-stepping trot changing into a furious gallop. It was torture to hear them tearing past on the paved road, heads jerked backwards, mouths torn and bleeding.

The big farm on the right before you get to Rauschen was completely intact. The new buildings with their bright red roofs looked provocative in this desert. In Rauschen we were quartered in back of a garage, which was also familiar to me because I had my car repaired there some weeks before the outbreak of war. For the sake of completeness you now experience the reverse side of everything.

Squatting close together on the floor, we were guarded by a good-natured, blond Russian who could speak a little German. At noon he cooked some thick porridge for us in a pail on a brick stove in the hall. Our hungry eyes seemed to please him.

In the afternoon we were called up, one by one, to be interrogated. My hearing was surprisingly short. Though the grim-looking major saw from the remnants of my papers that I was a doctor, he could not make anything of me otherwise. Apparently he could not understand how I came to be in this group of people. I was once again astonished that there should be any system in this chaos. Why do they still make any distinctions? Hardly anyone will come alive out of this sifting machine. Everything else I mentioned seemed exaggerated to the major. I was obviously in a condition which no longer aroused any special interest in my person. He would not believe that I had never been in the Party. The interpreter asked: "Why Party bad for you?" I could not explain that to him in a hurry, I said. After being repeatedly urged to give some explanation, I made the sign of the Cross. The interpreter tapped his forehead and nodded to the examining major, who pushed my papers back to me and dismissed me.

The interrogations of the other men lasted much longer. The boy was asked, among other things, how many Russian prisoners he had shot while he was being trained in the Hitler Youth maneuvers. An old man who had been with the police never returned.

April 21

To our great surprise we were simply turned out into the street in the morning. "Go home!" Our guard laughed good-naturedly. "Home where?" I asked. "To Insterburg?" "Yes, Insterburg!" "Give paper," I said. "Paper? Rubbish! Nix paper!" It was obvious that we would be arrested again on the next corner. Our company set out uncertainly. Actually, nobody paid any attention to us; it was almost unbelievable. Farther on at the crossroads Helmut Z. turned right to Palmnicken; he was going to see if any of his people were still there. As I had no plans of my own, I went with him, for I was no longer capable of a long march.

Again we walked through the villages of St. Lorenz and Craam; nobody took any notice of us. Where the road entered the forest, an old man came toward us pushing a wheelbarrow. We sat down with him at the roadside. He was a farmer from the neighborhood of Labiau and had fled with his wagon and horses as far as Palmnicken, where he was overtaken by the Russians. Since then he had been sneaking about on the roads with the rest of his possessions, and was now going to try and reach his hometown. He advised us urgently against going to Palmnicken, because of the Russians there. My companion, however, decided to go on, whereas I joined the old man, mainly because he still had a piece of meat in his wheelbarrow. We took turns in pushing the latter, now again in the opposite direction, advancing very slowly. In Craam we were overtaken by the Polish interpreter of my first interrogation, walking at a quick pace. I ducked my head involuntarily. He passed us without a sign of recognition.

The old man had to push his wheelbarrow all by himself, for I didn't have the strength to move it. Columns of military vehicles were racing past us; one of them brushed the side of the wheelbarrow and hurled it into the air; it was smashed to pieces and the contents flew far and wide over the fields. Fortunately, however, a tin tub with two handles was among them, and everything now had to be collected and packed into it, including a meat-chopper, an axe, a hammer, and a pair of tongs—very useful objects, of course, but not exactly suitable for being carried about the countryside as one's last remaining possessions. My attempts to persuade the old man to leave at least the meat-chopper behind were unsuccessful. I did not mind the other things: two white sheets, a few potatoes, a piece of meat, a rasher of bacon, and several shirts.

Carrying the tin tub between us, we trudged again through the field to a small wood on the right of the road. There we sat down and decided to cook a meal. As I was not quite sure if I would get any of it, I made myself useful by building a fire. For water I went to a ditch some distance away, which ran through a marshy meadow. As I was dipping it up, a couple of bullets whizzed past me. I looked around. A half-naked Russian was standing far away at the same ditch, firing at me. But he made no attempt to follow me when I retreated.

We boiled our potatoes in peace and quiet. When I went again to look for some dry kindling wood, a German soldier's head popped out of a communication trench. Two men of the 5th Panzer Division, a lieutenant and a N.C.O., had been in hiding there for three days. They belonged to a scouting patrol and had got behind the Russian lines. I asked after my cousin Knyphausen who was in the divisional staff. They thought it possible that the rest of the division might get away by sea. They had been without food for three days. My companion invited them to our potatoes and shared his bacon with them. They intended to leave from here in a southerly direction as soon as darkness had fallen.

We got on our way again, leaving behind the meat-chopper, the tools, and the tin tub. The rest we carried in my bag, from which I had discarded my useless shoes. Behind St. Lorenz we took a short cut across the fields to Watsum. There we hid in an empty house whose interior presented the usual sight: upholstered furniture with the coverings ripped off was lying in a knee-deep mass of bed-feathers, bottles, pictures, and smashed dishes. Window frames and doors had been torn out. On a window sill we found a piece of cheese which we finished on the spot. Two Russians came in, turned everything upside down again and departed without taking any notice of us.

The main body of the troops had left earlier, but planes were still busy flying around, from which we concluded that fighting was still going on in Pillau. Now and then the heavy thunder

of guns came over from the direction of the sea; and as the wish
is always father to the thought, we persuaded ourselves that the
Americans were already advancing against the Russians.

On the other side of the street was a house occupied by women
and children. They had all settled in one room on the now uni-
versally adopted principle: the old women in front, the children
behind them, in the background the younger women and girls,
camouflaged as old ones. They were all exhausted, with the exception of a talkative old woman who thought it highly interesting to be living in such apocalyptical times. We lay down to
sleep on a double-decker truss of straw left behind by German
troops. You could hardly believe that only a few days ago this
was still Germany.

During the night Russians came in and played their flashlights
on us. It did not bother us. We were at their mercy anyway, and
stretching out at full length was so marvelous that we did not
want to give up one second of it. Fortunately, they soon left
and we could sleep.

April 22

In spite of his seventy years, my companion was far more enter-
prising than I. He got hold of two lame horses left behind by the
soldiers, harnessed them with improvised reins to a rack wagon,
and loaded on it two more families, who came from the same district as himself and were going to try and get back there with
him. I hung on to the back of the wagon and passed for the
third time the Watsum railroad station which I will always remember. At the fork in the road we turned left and drove eastward via Pobethen. Craam, St. Lorenz, Watsum, Pobethen—the
sound of these names, so friendly and familiar to the people of
Samland, echo in me like an endless outcry rising up to heaven.

Slowly, slowly we drove along the road to Cranz, picking up

anything useful we saw lying in the ditches and taking it with us. In the cold strong wind of early spring soldiers passed us, singing while they marched. Everything went well for the next few miles. But then we were stopped by a sentry who searched the wagon, examined the horses, and ordered me to get off. The wagon was allowed to proceed. I waved to the old man. We had spent twenty-four hours together—a slice of life.

I lay down in the grass beside the Russians. First they searched me and then busied themselves with my papers, among which were some letters and photographs. I gazed at the sea and did not pay any attention to them. They held a photo of my sister under my nose. "Your wife?" I nodded. "Where your wife?" "At home." "Where home?" I mentioned some place or other. *"Gitlair kaput!"* The usual refrain like the amen in church. I did not respond to any further attempts at conversation.

A few hours later they were relieved and took me with them as the first occupant of their new prison, the large room of a laborer's house on an estate. The windows were boarded up; it was freezing cold. I sat or lay curled up on the floor. Now and then I put my feet up on a milking stool, the only piece of furniture in the room, to straighten my back. You gradually adopt some routine in these matters. I put my handkerchief over my nose and mouth, because it conserves a lot of warmth in your body.

The sentry posted before the door seemed to be slightly uneasy about me. He kept coming in, staring at me, and trying to teach me a different position. I lay quietly and watched him. He might have been eighteen years old, and was standing there like a young dog in front of a curled-up hedgehog. Then he disappeared again and returned to his post before the door. Once, when he came in again, I gave him to understand by signs that I was very cold. He did not know what to do about it. Instead, he began to teach me a few Russian words: "Give . . . me . . .

food." When I could say them, I repeated them as a request. He became suddenly scared and embarrassed and retreated slowly. From then on he only peeped through the door which was not quite closed. Toward morning he brought me a piece of bread; but when I wanted to shake his hand, he started back.

April 23

Around noon I acquired a companion, a young Lithuanian who had deserted from the Russian army and had been recaptured. He was given a bowl of soup which we ate in turns with his spoon. Later on we were joined by an elderly German with a wooden leg, a native of this village, who had just managed to get here from somewhere else.

Towards evening we three were taken in charge by two sentries and brought nearer to Königsburg. In a village swarming with Russians, we were locked up in a pigpen already occupied by ten other men. We heard that we would be interrogated again. You were thrown from one sifter into another. Meanwhile we boiled two buckets of potatoes in the mash copper and stuffed our bellies.

April 24

Without having been interrogated, we were again on our way via Fuchsberg to Königsberg. I was getting increasingly restless. I would not have had the courage to approach that town of my own free will; there was too much finality about it, and I had no resistance left.

In the suburb of Tannenwalde we turned left and were once again screened out on some mysterious principle. The Lithuanian was to stay where he was—to be shot, so he thought. When we were led away, he started playing furiously on a piano which had been left standing on the road.

We walked toward Königsberg. I just dragged myself along in my felt boots and thought I would drop any moment. Nonetheless I was intensely alive to the scene around me. The whole region looked like a lunar landscape, crater upon crater, and beyond them a sea of ruins. In the direction of the center of town you could see a few last fires dying down, smoldering. It was the end.

On the right side of the road a Russian's car had got stuck in the mud—one of those innumerable and hideous little American jeeps that look like public lavatories. We were ordered to pull it out. I simply flopped to the ground. The others struggled to no purpose; splashed with mud, they had to give up. We walked a little farther along narrow-gauged railroad tracks and found ourselves on the Cranzer road in Rothenstein in front of the Wrangel barracks. A sentry let us pass through the gates. We had reached the camp.

· 4 ·

CAMP ROTHENSTEIN
End of April to Mid-June, 1945

Nowadays everybody knows from hearsay what a camp is like. It is a place to which persons are sent whom people want to forget for a while, either because there are enough other matters to worry about, or because the problem of what to do with them is a headache.

Once in the camp, these persons are trapped in a process of attrition which, though not having any demonstrable connection with the intentions of those who have sent them there, meets their intentions insofar as it saves them any further thoughts or at least reduces them to a minimum. The ultimate effect of the camp is, in any case, a human condition which can evoke nothing more than a shrug. Nobody can really be expected to feel any further responsibility for such people.

The feeling that one has been consigned to oblivion in this way is hard to describe; and had I not known that God forsakes no one, I would have despaired.

The surrounding barracks were almost undamaged. We were led down the central driveway. The yards between the garages on our left were cordoned off by sentries; gray masses of humanity were creeping past them. We were pushed into Hall Eight where we could not see the floor for people. Followed by feeble curses we carefully picked our way over the many legs, looking for an empty spot; but there was really not an inch free. Two thousand people were said to be collected here—all of them men, some having been here for four weeks, the majority for two. Every one of them had made his home, so to speak, on his eighteen inches of cement floor. Only a few could lie down; most of them were squatting or standing.

I continued climbing, when a hand grasped mine, and an elderly man looked as kindly at me as his stubbly face allowed. He told me he might find room for me if I would sit back to back with him, and if his neighbor would spare a few inches. With a sigh of relief I bent my knees and took up the position he had suggested. Official introduction was unnecessary; we all were the same, and mutual introduction would have been only embarrassing. In the course of our talk, however, I did learn his name and that he was an engineer and town surveyor. He was sorry that he could not offer me anything to eat; with luck, they got once a day a cup of porridge and a slice of bread. Of the four coffee beans he had in his trouser pocket, he gave me two.

The mood of the seedy men around us was either petulant or plaintive. I gathered from their talks that they had not yet fully grasped their situation. They still believed they had fallen victim to some unforgivable error on the part of the administration. As soon as the news got around among the people nearest me that I was a doctor, I was besieged with questions as to what all this meant, and when they would be released. It was a crime, they said, to coop up human beings in this way. They would all get sick, and they never got the food which was due to them! I ought to go to the commandant and make energetic complaints about these abuses. There was no water at all and no latrines either. The whole thing was a scandal, and probably nobody "at the top" knew anything about it.

I behaved as impossibly as possible, for making public addresses was never in my line. An old man had the courage to recite in a loud voice the ninety-first Psalm: "He that dwelleth in the secret place of the most High. . . ." Nobody took any notice of him.

Toward evening a woman turned up who had evidently started a kind of medical service on her own. She was called over to us and told to take me with her to the other German doctors. I was to get full information from them and then set things in order.

She left, returned after a short while, and asked me to follow her. The guards, who already seemed to know her, let us pass until we came to Hall Two, where we pushed our way through another dense crowd to a room which had been partitioned off. The door opened and I saw several men in dirty white coats bustling about. My companion approached one of them, and I hesitatingly followed her. He gave me one look, came quickly up to me, and closed the door behind me. Without many words he directed me to a wide wooden bunk and covered me with a large overcoat. I felt ashamed and moaned under my breath. I could not have been better sheltered in Abraham's bosom.

From under the coat I had a good look at my benefactors. All three wore hats, more on the nape of their necks than on their heads, and civilian clothes under their coats. I could not recognize what they were doing. People kept coming in for treatment. When two Russians appeared, the overcoat was drawn over my head until they had left again.

Later they were joined by a fourth man who brought a saucepan of porridge which we shared among us. I came out of my corner and introduced myself to the others: a young medical officer whom I will call Schreiner, and two medical orderlies, Holter and Klein. They had all belonged to a unit which was last stationed on the outskirts of the town, and had been taken to the camp after the fall of Königsberg. With the help of a hypodermic syringe and a few medicaments they had brought in their pockets, they had set up a dispensary here. Even the Russians had begun to take an interest in it, and came occasionally for treatment, although clandestinely. In general the latter kept outside the cordons and left the restraint of the prisoners to the Poles who made exaggerated use of their rubber truncheons to get high marks—that is, better food—from the Russians.

As illness increased among the internees, Dr. Schreiner had enlisted the energies of some women and set up a voluntary medical service. These women, wearing Red Cross armbands, went through the halls, listened to complaints, made notes, and told the doctor where he was wanted. The guards usually let them pass and made no objections to their work.

Except for my feeling cold, I was in fairly good shape again but felt a coward at the thought of meeting some connection of mine in this place. In the absence of latrines, everybody, men and women, met in a grotesque fashion in a corridor about twelve feet wide between the halls. There was always a horrible crush, for some of the people already suffered badly from diarrhea. Added to that, it rained all day. It was not unusual to see someone collapse from weakness. That you should have lived only to end up in this place, literally "in the muck"! Involuntarily, a hymn flashed through my mind: "Thus far hath God brought me . . ." Or was that blasphemy? But who else had done it? Well, if He had stood by thus far, He must surely continue to help.

In the hall opposite men had been put up in one half, and women in the other. There was also a partitioned-off room like ours in which an ear doctor camped, together with two men I knew from the Fortress days—Giese and Röckert. At that time they had worked as medical orderlies with Bode in the field hospital. Giese had been pastor of a parish in Stockholm, and Röckert a medical student. They took me in for the night, as there was room for four in their compartment. I was lying on a

long table, and my comrades on the floor. They even had a small
stove in the room.

Next morning we went on a short expedition. Dr. Schreiner
had persuaded a Russian to let us out of the camp under escort to
look for medical stores. Quite nearby he and his aids had hidden
a larger quantity before they were taken prisoner. Holter directed
us to the place he knew; but even there everything had been
looted. In the little houses the rubbish was knee-deep. The only
useful object I could find was a large, slightly chipped coffeepot
which I took with me as a food container.

In the small garden lots the first rhubarb was venturing above
ground, still hardly visible, but I took as much as I could tear
up and ate it on my way. Vitamins! Unbelievable how life never
stops assuming importance.

In the camp, meanwhile, people had formed into wide lines in
the yards, waiting to get their food. At the end of our yard an
almost blind, toothless Polish woman stood behind a tin tub,
threatening with her ladle everyone who came too close. In the
tub was a thin, gray fluid with a few barley grains at the bottom.
It took hours to distribute the stuff. Everyone got a cupful. People who remained standing beside the tub begging for more had
to be pushed on by the Polish bullies. A great many did not get
anything, for the tub did not hold enough for all. Those assembled in our yard came from a distant barracks. They had brought
with them everything they still possessed because they did not
know if they would be allowed to go back to the same place or
would be put up somewhere else. Many were wearing three
suits, one on top of another; and since this condition had lasted
more than three weeks, vermin had increased on a large scale.
Even so, it was a miracle that relatively few persons were really
sick.

Nurse Hedwig, the woman who had taken me to my colleagues, called for me again to go with her through the halls

under her care. She had found some people who were running a temperature. I examined them superficially, so far as it was possible in the crush, and gave them pills of some kind, leaving the requisite instructions to Nurse Hedwig. She dragged me from one person to another, and I followed her directions as long as I could. Examining those who were lying on the floor was not an easy job, and it took the last shred of my strength to get on my feet again. Near the exit I succeeded in escaping at a moment when she was not looking. Arriving at our cubicle I hid from her pursuits with a bad conscience. After some time she came again but I pretended to be asleep, and Dr. Schreiner sent her away.

One day a girl, Erika Fröhlich, turned up at our place. She was twenty years old—a simple, innocent country girl—and had come because of a sore finger. When she saw the mess in our place, she immediately started clearing up without asking for permission. We were surprised to see how much she accomplished, and asked her if she had relatives in the camp. No, she said, she was all alone. So we asked her if she would stay with us.

At the end of April dysentery began to spread. The most seriously ill were taken out of the various halls and laid in rows before the door of our dispensary where the floor had been cleared for them. Almost a hundred were soon lying there on planks or on doors taken off their hinges, or even on the bare cement floor, some of them only half-dressed and without blankets. In the opposite hall about fifty women were lying in a partitioned space nursed by a deaconess, Sister Bertha. She took their temperatures and accompanied Dr. Schreiner on his regular rounds.

On our side, as on the opposite one, everything was remarkably quiet. The patients seemed to be only barely conscious. On April 28 we carried out the first dead. Chaplain Klein and I laid them down beside the sentries like a bag of game. Their places were at once occupied by new patients, most of whom were much too weak to leave their place and simply relieved themselves where they were lying. The condition of the floor was indescribable. I could only jump from island to island, as it were, to get to the individual patients, or to reach our cubicle and throw myself on my bunk for a moment, burying my face in the overcoat.

Not all our patients were suffering from dysentery. Other afflictions came up, aside from the enormous number of women with venereal diseases, whom it was almost impossible to sift out. I was particularly sorry for one old man whose bladder I had to drain every day with a thick cannula—in the absence of a catheter—which of course could not be cleaned. He thought it wonderful and thanked me every time very warmly.

One evening a man was brought to us who was bleeding from his wrist. Two weeks before he had cut his arteries; the wounds had festered and one of the arteries had opened again. By the light of a small wax candle I made an incision above the wound and ligatured the artery with the only thread I could find. The man bore up with everything without stirring. He had been brought up from the cellar by two young army doctors who had managed in this way to escape from the cellar themselves. They hoped to be able to remain hidden with us, and not to be taken down to the cellar again. What they told us about that place made us realize that we had not yet seen the worst.

Meanwhile, I had managed to rid myself of my three weeks' beard, which lifted my spirits considerably; washing was still out of the question, because we were not allowed to waste a drop of water. Dr. Schreiner finally succeeded in persuading a Russian officer, who had come to him from time to time as a patient, to permit water to be brought to the camp. Consequently, twenty wretched men pushed a sewage cart out of the camp gates to the nearest pump which was about seven hundred yards away. It took them several hours to return with their load, but in this way the camp got at least a few hundred gallons of water.

April 29

The number of dead has increased so much that the Russians, from an instinct of self-preservation, have started a sort of fight against the spread of infection. Schreiner was appointed medical director of the camp and was made responsible for practically everything else. By midnight we were supposed to have moved the sick from all the halls into the second floor of a huge barracks —if we did not bring it off some of us would be shot. Holter who acted as interpreter translated this to us in a dutiful tone with a slight touch of humor. Schreiner listened to the order with equanimity, but told the Russians at once that, due to the great number of patients, an exact carrying-out of this project would be out of the question. Their reaction was a howl of indignation, which, however, did not intimidate us. The consciousness of being at their mercy gave us a certain feeling of superiority. Shooting people could really no longer have much attraction for them, and they would besides have nothing at all to gain by it.

The first thing we did was to inspect the place assigned to us, and we discovered that the Poles who had occupied it before had no intention to clear out. Their removal to another barracks had to be expedited by the Russian sentries. They had left the place again in a condition, to which we had long been used. With improvised brooms and a little water, the worst of the filth was scraped off and carried down in buckets, the drains being choked up. Around thirty men, still fairly strong, among them some former medical orderlies, were mobilized, and with their help some four hundred patients dragged upstairs in the course of the evening. In the gathering darkness we could distribute them in the empty rooms only according to their sex and not, as intended, according to their diseases. Again they were lying on the cement floor, except for a few who had been brought up on planks. So their situation had not in the least improved. On the contrary, it was even more drafty up there, because some of the windows had been smashed or carried off by the Poles.

Towards midnight the rooms were sufficiently filled that the Russian officers who had constantly hustled us were satisfied and left us in peace for the rest of the night. In the smaller rooms stood a few iron bedsteads; into the first one, next to the entrance, the four of us from the dispensary moved by order of the Russians, and made everything draftproof for the night. Holter had scrounged from somewhere a quart glass of sugar, probably from the Russian kitchen. We did not ask him where it came from, but let our portions trickle down our throats at once. Our helpers and some colleagues were lying in the rooms next to ours. In a small adjoining room Erika was sitting with a young woman who had been delivered of a dead child in the dispensary and had been kept there.

The night was very quiet. As our kidneys functioned now only when we were lying down, we had to go frequently out into the corridor where the pails were standing. You could hear nothing there but the soft groping and shuffling of all the people who were also looking for the pails. And we were grateful that it would still be dark for some hours.

April 30

In the morning the dead were singled out. Several persons had died in the corridor; one was sitting, dead, on the pail. The rest were not easy to pick out, because even the living reacted very slowly, when we talked to them or nudged them. Eventually, about thirty-six dead, all men, were piled up several feet high in the washroom. The women held out longer. Many of the dead were almost naked, their clothes having been appropriated by others for protection against the cold. Very few have any identification papers left and they will not be able to keep them much longer, so eventually nobody will know who has died here.

As for me, I have given up any independent thinking. I follow Schreiner's directions and function as well as I can. There is no longer any question of doing anything properly; we merely help one another and now and then save a person from the worst. For however much we try to do something, we are in no position to judge if we have done any good or harm to our fellow beings. Although the sick have been separated from the crowds, they are even more uncomfortable than down in the halls. Fortunately the majority of them are so weak that they hardly know what is happening to them. We doctors have already become co-workers in the death-mill of the camp, whether actively or passively makes no difference.

In some mysterious way Erika has made friends with the Polish woman who distributes the food. She has probably discovered some ailment the woman was suffering from—she has an unfailing instinct for this sort of thing—and has given her some pills. Now she spends her time running about, carrying, hidden under her jacket, one can of soup after another for us and her other charges. We no longer ask her any questions and let her do what she likes. She has taken a second woman into her room, who is near giving birth to twins.

All day long new patients were brought in, and there has been friction with the Russians, who disapprove of everything. One commission after another turned up, including women in uniform. We don't know where to hide from them.

As it has been impossible for quite some time to find room for all the patients on one floor, some hundred men have had to be put up in the loft—an ordeal for all concerned. It blew and rained through the open windows and the holes in the roof. When it was almost dark, I went up there once more and found them lying in all directions, on top of one another. heard here and there faint, meaningless talking, and felt the sparks of life fading everywhere. Some of them were definitely dead. I removed their overcoats and jackets and covered others with them.

From time to time I seem to hear a voice asking me: "What exactly are you doing here?" Yes, what am I doing here? What are we all doing? But it is useless to go on trying to find an answer. What we do here is no longer a doing in the true sense of the word; we are only now and then permitted to do something. And as I turned around in the door before leaving the loft, my arms lifted almost of their own to bless these unfortunates— doomed to death.

Later at night, the first twin was born, assisted by Erika and myself. Life goes on—as people say so sensibly.

May 1

We did not notice much of the first of May except that some loud-speakers were blaring more than usual into the neighborhood. We still see bomber squadrons flying in a westerly direction. Apparently Pillau has not yet capitulated. How in the world do they still manage to hold out?

It's raining in torrents. Down below in the yard the Frenchmen have been lined up to be transported to their own country, via Odessa—quite a roundabout trip! Two of our helpers, who have passed themselves off as doctors which did not, however, help them much have joined them, hoping to get out of the camp in this way. As they do not know a word of French, we have advised them from our window to act deaf and dumb as much as possible.

The people in the halls are getting more and more weak. A rumor has got about that charcoal is good for diarrhea, and we see them everywhere hunting for bits of charred wood to eat.

A Russian medical student had got permission from the camp

commandant to go through the cellars with one of the German doctors. I was chosen for this job and took Röckert with me, who carried a box with bandage material and medicaments which had gradually been found. We knew more or less what to expect down there and had no illusions about really being able to help.

The cellars of all the barracks are crammed with people, about four thousand men and women, many of whom are interrogated every night by NKVD officials (Soviet People's Commissariat, which was subordinated to the political Secret Police). The purpose of these interrogations is not to worm out of the people what they knew—which would be uninteresting anyway—but to extort from them special statements. The methods resorted to are extremely primitive: people are beaten up until they confess to having been members of the Nazi Party. But the result is almost the opposite of what most of the people probably expect, that is, that those who hadn't been party members would come off better. The authorities simply assume that, basically, everybody has belonged to the Party. Many people die during and after these interrogations, while others, who admit at once their party membership, are treated more leniently. In any case, it is by now only a question of the lower ranks, because the higher ranks have beaten it in good time or have committed suicide. A fairly large batch of these so-called "party members" is shipped daily to Insterburg or Gumbinnen, and the vacant cellars are filled up again with men and women from the halls. This is done in the following way: a Russian and a Pole appear in the halls with a list of German names in Russian script, which both call out, one after another, in a hoarse voice. Not one of the names can be recognized. Frequently they are not names at all but some sort of designations which have been copied from the collected identification cards. All the same, a lot of people answer to them, hoping to be let out of the camp in this way. As many as were on the list are then taken out and brought to the cellars. Once there nobody takes any interest in them for the time being. It is purely accidental that some of them are later interrogated, sometimes three or four times, some not at all.

The very first cellar the guard opened for us had recently been filled again. Three men staggered out into the corridor and were pushed back again with the butt of the guard's rifle, with difficulty, however, because the cell was too small and the door could only be closed by pressure. The people had been standing there for three days, waiting to be interrogated. At the sight of us a pandemonium broke out which left me helpless. It was impossible to deal with individual requests. As far as I could gather, the usual senseless questions were being reiterated: Why were they here, and for how long? They had no water and hardly anything to eat. They wanted to be let out more often than once a day, and so on. I asked myself what sense my being here made at all. The guard got fed up with the screaming. I had just enough time to call out to them that they must think out their most urgent requests before my next visit and let a spokesman report them. Then the door was slammed shut into their faces.

To prevent a similar scene in the next cell, I quickly thought up a few introductory words. These gradually became a kind of formula which I reeled off in a loud voice every time a cell door was opened. It went more or less like this: "People, be quiet, otherwise I'll have to leave at once. I am the doctor. We are going to try and get those of you who are most ill out of here and into the hospital. Who has blood in his stool?" "I, I, I!" rang out from all sides.

"No, that won't do. Attention, please! Who speaks for himself can't be considered. Who is so sick that he is a trial for the others? Choose a spokesman for next time and have everything ready." This made matters easier. The more serious cases were quickly listed, but whether we can really get them out is another matter. If only they would be better off in our hospital, I thought; any way it was colder there. Perhaps it would at least make conditions better for those who were left behind in the cellars.

In some of the cellars I found people I had known before; that is to say, I recognized them only when they whispered their names to me—the attending physician of the children's hospital and other doctors that I knew slightly, and Pastor Leidreiter in a military overcoat. Their confinement here was just as accidental as my relative freedom. It was possible that they even took me for a protégé of the Russians. Some of them had already established some order in their cells, and we could at least leave them some bandaging material and a few medicaments. A longer conversation with them was impossible, because the guard kept on interfering with his: "*Davai*—quick, quick!"

A group of cellar occupants was just being led out and taken to the fence, surrounding the camp, to the constant shouts of "quick, quick!" A couple of holes had been dug there and two boards put across each. That was all. In addition, in most of the cellars, there were pails standing, brought in from the yard by the prisoners.

A great number of them have dysentery so badly that they can no longer get up. In their case we are always faced with the problem whether it is worthwhile putting them on the list, or if they will be dead anyway in another few hours. We have started appraising people like cattle. We know that if we put too many names on the list, they will not let any people out at all. We feel as though we are constantly pronouncing death sentences, more so because people think, of course, that the hospital must be heaven. Moreover, I have the greatest difficulty trying to convince them that I am not God Almighty. They are still under the impression that they have been wrongly imprisoned and then neglected. They haven't done anything wrong, after all! What is to become of their families, if they are kept here? They will be glad to work for the Russians, and I must tell the camp commandant so.

Some of the cells are less crowded, and I can move around and make contact with individuals. One seedy little man hung on to me and implored me to report to the camp commander that in one of the barracks there are eleven Italian old masters, which were taken from him when he was there. They are worth several thousand marks, he said, and should not be left there, because of the dampness, or they will be a loss for the Russian State. Although I am touched by his anxiety, I think his last argument is going too far, especially at the moment, and in my heart I congratulate the Italian masterworks on their fragility, which prevents them from representing their money value at an important place, while millions of living human beings are rotting in oblivion. I hope these paintings will find a useful end as substitutes for window panes or as fuel in a stove.

Some of the cells are occupied only by women. It is almost a relief. Their behavior is a great deal more intelligent and practical than that of the men. When the first of these cells was opened, I saw at once that I could save myself the usual speech. The women were sitting back to back, distributed over the floor like a mosaic. At the sight of us, one that I knew—Nurse Waltraut from the mental hospital—stood up, and we greeted each other from a distance. She gave me the most important details: two elderly women and a younger one, lying next to the door beside the pail, can no longer get up without help. The others, sixty-nine in all, are in slightly better shape. They do not give in as quickly as the men. As I was about to leave, the nurse made a sign, and all the women sang a cheerful song. I am constantly amazed at the things people find the strength to do. Where order reigns within, outward help can find a starting point. The little we can do is not useless here.

It was not possible for us to go through all the cellars on that day. Only my felt boots kept me upright, and I was glad when the guard finally stopped us from going any farther. But I had hardly reached my bunk when a Russian came for me again. Chaplain Klein was taken along, too, and we returned to the cellar. We were stopped before a door at the end of a corridor and expected to be locked up ourselves.

A pitch-dark, windowless cell opened before us, sloping to the back. In front of us a few human forms, blinded by the light, were moving on the floor. The Russian made us go in. It was obviously a cell which had been forgotten. We drew one body after another out of the darkness into the light. There were fifteen men, and we examined them as quickly as possible. Seven were dead, and there was not much life left in the other eight. We were allowed to take them with us to the hospital. Four of us carried them out, one after another, the living and the dead.

For two days we were left in peace with our patients; then came the next upheaval. A high medical commission turned up to inspect the hospital, and, in fury about the conditions here, stormed around the building like a herd of elephants, as if they would have liked to trample down anyone who could still walk. We doctors were to blame that a regular hospital service had not been organized long ago. What a pigsty! And the Germans were still claiming to have culture! No chloride of lime even! And the cupboards still lying around everywhere in the barracks could have long since been used as beds! Worst of all, we had no office with lists and medical case histories of the patients! We shuddered when we thought of their probable idea of a regular hospital service. It was useless trying to explain to them the reasons it had been impossible for us to make all these praise-worthy arrangements. They were not concerned with reasons, but only with conditions, they themselves being solely responsible for the sanitary arrangements.

Schreiner was given the latest orders: this place was to be evacuated in the shortest possible time, and everything moved into the three floors of the opposite barracks. Moreover, all the necessary installations should be taken care of, or else we doctors would be shot—the usual refrain. Faced with Schreiner's difficult situation, I should probably have thrown in the sponge at this point, but he still has enough reserves of strength to comply with these new demands. In the first place we had to procure an enormous number of workers from among the internees, which was, of course, possible only with the help of the Polish bullies. For it was not only the problem of occupying the building, which the Poles had lived in up to the last moment and had left in the usual condition, but also of much other work, such as building latrines, installing a sort of field kitchen to boil water, and carrying over water as well as bedsteads and cupboards from the other barracks, to which we had not had access before.

There is a blank in my memory concerning the events of that day. In retrospect, I have the feeling as though my only worry was not to be conspicuous and to have always some chloride of lime at hand. Six large barrels of this were suddenly at our disposal. Chloride of lime was the charm with which we could brighten the grim faces of our tormentors. Whoever throws chloride of lime about shows that he is not indifferent to Russian culture.

I cannot say, therefore, how Schreiner finally managed to get everything done. In any case, after dark, we settled across the road, on the ground floor in a room just large enough for our four cots, which could only be reached through an adjoining room, in which we planned to establish our "office." Quite near us Erika has moved in with the two women in childbed, one of whom had given birth to her second twin two days after the

first. Giese and Röckert have settled opposite us, separated only
by the central corridor. They guard the washroom which we
have decided to use as our operating room. About twenty medical
orderlies have been taken on as nursing staff, which also includes
many women from the cellars, among them a few trained nurses.
The cell with the singing women has been completely evacuated,
and Nurse Waltraut has taken over one floor of the so-called
surgical department.

The greater part of the block became, of course, an isolation
ward, through all the floors, including the loft and the cellar;
the sick coming from the cellars are to be housed in the cellars
here too. The cellar windows have, therefore, to be cleared of
the earth, once shovelled against them as an air raid protection.

Standing at a window I started a conversation with one of the
men engaged in this work. He was the owner of the big farm
near Rauschen which had impressed me by its undamaged condition when I passed it two weeks before. Less than a year ago
Goerdeler had stayed with him, and later, after July 20, the
Gestapo had looked for him there. We talked of these events
which a few months earlier had concerned us more than the
advancing Russians. Now they seemed like happenings in another life.

Seven doctors are at work in the isolation department;
Schreiner and I were in charge of the internal and surgical cases.
Schreiner has gladly surrendered his position as medical director
to the eye doctor who knows a smattering of Russian and is not
entirely dependent on the Polish interpreter when making his
daily report to the commandant. The house had been divided
into two sections from top to bottom by cupboards on the corridors. With the permission of the commandant, all sorts of
bedsteads, mattresses, pallets, and cupboards have been collected
from the other barracks, unless those were occupied by the Russians, and distributed over the whole house. Many patients are

now lying in upturned cupboards which, singly or pushed together like a fortification, have been placed in the middle or in a
corner of each room. The majority continue to lie on the floor,
and all of them are still suffering from the cold, because the
windows can only be gradually reglazed or filled in with cardboard.

A special squad has been formed to collect supplementary
material. They are even allowed to drive, under escort, into the
town and fish out of the ruins anything that is somehow useful.
We even get bandaging material and medicaments from the
recently opened Russian pharmacy. The leader of the squad is
a certain Schäfer—as I am going to call him—a tall young fellow,
not bad-looking from a distance, who was probably a soldier
but now wears civvies. It is not worthwhile enumerating the
stories of his past with which he used to regale his astonished
audience. But he is an expert in everything, good at organizing,
and knows to perfection how to wheedle the Russians, so his
usefulness cannot be denied.

On May 8 we heard that the war was over. The loudspeakers
blared even more penetratingly than usual. In the halls some
dubious German soldiers were holding forth about our libera-
tion from National–Socialism and the blessings of Bolshevism.
Outside the commandant's door a luxuriant floral arrangement
had been set up—from where in this desert? Otherwise we
noticed very little of the final victory. The official food situation has not improved. There is still nothing to eat but porridge, and once in a while some dry bread which is brought
in sacks. The hospital has, of course, the considerable advantage
over the rest of the camp; we can personally get our rations,
prepare and distribute them. In addition, patients and personnel
are given a tablespoonful of sugar daily.

Our main trouble is still the cold. In the first half of May we
had storms and rain almost without interruption, and at night

the temperature was still mostly around zero. Most of the deaths at that time were the result of lowered body temperature, and took place without struggle, and were soundless. The movements of the patients became feebler from day to day. Although they still spoke when nudged gently, we were relieved when at last the day came to remove them with a light conscience, and to place them in the cellar on the mound of dead who are buried daily; there are many waiting for the vacant places.

The only warm spots in the building are the kitchens, one of which has been installed on each floor. Iron ranges and stove pipes have been picked up in the barrack yards. The pipes are led through the windows and the holes stopped up with cardboard. Anything combustible is used as firewood. Most of the time the whole room is full of smoke, particularly on the windward side; but the warmth makes up for everything. Moreover, we can now make the bread eatable instead of breaking our teeth on it. It is soaked in water and afterward toasted. All other food has to be wangled surreptitiously. As a spread on our bread we used Vitamin-B extract out of a big can which the indefatigable Erika had found, opened, on a rubbish dump. When Schreiner and I went scouting through a barrack block which had just been evacuated, we discovered in the former lecture room the remains of some semolina, flour, and rice, which had served as material for an object lesson. We were as delighted as children at this unexpected booty.

The fence surrounding the camp is open in several places and the gaps are only superficially guarded. In spite of that hardly anyone thinks of escaping. What we have heard of the town does not tempt us to go there. Anyone who shows up on the streets is grabbed and taken off to work or to another camp. As for running beyond the town limits, we all lack the courage and strength.

A few days after our move, Giese, Erika, and I buried the

twins near the camp fence; fortunately they had soon died of the cold. Giese read a text from the Bible and said a few words. The burial of the other dead takes place in a very different way. The young Chaplain Klein to whom this difficult office had been assigned, because he is, in the opinion of the Russians, obviously an expert in burying, never tells us anything about it, although we are living together. When I asked him cautiously if he felt equal to saying a few religious words on such occasions, he waved my question aside without a word. Once he lay on his cot for two days without speaking, and Giese had to take his place. Later Giese described to me the proceedings almost in the form of a confession: In the field back of the camp, near the fence, an oblong hole was dug, into which the dead were flung, fifty to sixty every day, mostly naked, because their clothes were used as bribes for the men from the halls to do the digging. It is the only possibility to do without the Polish bullies. As the men are all very weak, it takes them a whole day to dig up the heavy clay, and if one of them collapses, it is difficult to persuade his comrades to carry him back after work, for the burden of one's own body is heavy enough, and you actually risk your life with every added exertion.

One day the guard was reinforced and the fence repaired. We were not allowed to move more than about fifty yards from the house, only as far as the latrines. The reason for this: two dentists had escaped, using their last strength, to avoid their impending interrogation. But they did not get very far. They were tracked by dogs and trapped in the crematorium. The older man who had climbed into the dome and lost his way was shot down. The younger one was taken back to the cellar.

This incident was the occasion for the commandant to come to us late at night, and to call all doctors and nurses for a meeting. Assisted by an old Polish interpreter armed with a crutch, he gave us a long lecture on the uselessness of running away.

It wasn't, moreover, in the least necessary, he said, for nobody need fear the interrogation, which was only concerned with statistical investigations. If you gave the right information at once, nothing at all would happen to you. We couldn't believe our ears. Was it possible that this man, who had been living all this time in the middle of the camp, had no idea of what was going on there? That night after night people were beaten to death, only because they told the truth? In the dim candlelight I tried to form a clear picture of him. His outward appearance did not in the least conform to that of the other Russian officers we had seen. He looked like an old British colonel, tall and thin, truly distinguished, with an expressive face and a definite air of kindness. I just could not believe that he was lying as shamelessly as the others. At the end of his speech, he enlarged, in addition, upon the state of our nerves. National–Socialism must be, after all, a very emotional matter, he said, to have unbalanced people to this extent; otherwise it wouldn't have been possible for so many people to fall ill and die.

When he had finished, I felt an impulse to answer him, more for his sake than ours, for undoubtedly he could not change anything in our situation even if he wanted to. But he had shown himself so humane that you could not listen to his misconceptions in silence. I, therefore, asked permission to speak and realized only while speaking, that I was no longer mentally alert enough to make the situation clear to him as we saw it. With a friendly nod he took his leave, promising to visit us again some time. We looked after him with some emotion, wondering how such a man could stand the general atmosphere here. That he should be the commandant of this camp makes its conditions appear still more grotesque.

It is ghastly to see the intensity with which every thought and action of those who can still stand is centered on their own dwindling lives. These tortured beings have turned into horrible caricatures, grayish amphibians, covered with the remains of their former passions as though with wet fungi. They babbled so incoherently that often you do not know whether to laugh, to cry, or to get furious. But in the end you can only be silent and tell yourself that as long as your stomach still has a chance to snatch a mouthful here and there, you have no right to criticize.

But we, too, have come down a peg or two and have got into the habit of shuffling our feet. We hesitate before taking a step, for our blood pressure is so low that, theoretically, we should not be able to stand upright. When we walk upstairs our legs become numb and our ears feel as if they were plugged up. The skin of the outer and inner surfaces of my thighs has become insensitive to touch. The whole body sensation has changed: I often feel like floating. I can only think properly when I am lying down and use any opportunity of stretching out to make my next decisions. The kidneys do not function except at night, and the pail is the most important object in our room.

Of all the doctors in the camp I personally have the least exacting work to do. In my so-called surgical department the question of treatment comes up very rarely. What the patients need is food and warmth, and as I cannot procure either, I feel my medical activities to be more or less a fraud. It is mainly their sufferings that gives me the right to work as a physician and to enjoy the resultant privileges. I have tried out a number of methods to prolong their lives, but cannot say that these attempts have been successful. Most of the men die of facial erysipelas. With the women, a sudden terrific pain in the basal joints of their toes is the most excruciating concomitant symptom of hunger and cold. The feet of one woman turned black and fell off. Fortunately, we at least have drugs.

The only moment of the day when I feel that I am doing something useful is when I'm distributing cod-liver oil. We have received a whole barrelful for the preparation of a remedy against the itch. Since then the whole house reeks, of course, of cod-liver oil because something or other is fried in it on every kitchen range. I, too, have secured a few quarts, and go through the wards twice a day to put a spoonful of it into each patient's mouth. As I dislike cod-liver oil, and distributing it, therefore, has no temptation for me, I have taken on the job myself. Nevertheless, the greed with which the people expect me is hard to bear; the gaping mouths, the grunting and smacking of lips—a sound recording of this would horrify the world.

The hardest task for me is making the rounds through the cellars, which are permitted every three or four days. There I am powerless. The irresistible Nurse Hedwig who can even impress the Russians with her voluble tongue and gets by everywhere, comes for me, full of energy and initiative. In the cellars I gladly let her do the talking. She distributes medicines indiscriminately, which we have made ourselves with a great deal of water, delivers popular lectures on the general situation, and gives instructions to the right and left. Sometimes I am not sure she is still in her right mind, but in the camp she is irreplaceable, and anyone who has survived, will remember her with gratitude. That she is almost a skeleton does not seem to worry her.

The operating room is by far the quietest place. My two helpers, Giese and Röckert, who live in the adjoining room, are working there, keeping an eye on the bandaging material. Fortunately, we cannot operate, because we have no instruments; we can only do some unavoidable minor surgery. If a leg has to be amputated, we do it with a garden saw. Neck carbuncles are lanced, and the many swollen legs covered with sores are bandaged. Very annoying is the vermin. Many people are so covered with lice that they look quite gray from a distance. But they are just as afraid of the delousing, because it means that they have to part from their clothes and later cannot find all of them. Besides, some patients died as a result of the procedure, if not at once then later on, due to the great change of temperature, to which they are exposed.

Sometimes Russians, too, come to us for treatment. They are not really allowed to do it, but come secretly, and always leave some food behind. Our greatest help is a young Russian woman who came once and later sent for me several times. She told me that her three years in Germany have been the happiest of her life. When the Russians came, she went through the same things as all the other women, and now she has caught the disease. Here in the camp she is forced to live with one of the guards. This means that she has at least more than enough to eat, like the German women who are detained in the billets of the other guards. When I saw her in her place she insisted on giving me a real good meal, and then gave me half a pound of margarine to take with me. The latter became the occasion and foundation of our first banquet, which took place at night.

Only when darkness has fallen on the many and varied worries of the day, we can breathe freely at last. At dusk, when it is still just possible to recognize a printed word, I go to the operating room where my two helpers are awaiting me. We read the Bible lesson of the day according to the Watchwords which I still have with me. In the darkness a few words are exchanged now and then, words which cannot be said during the day, expressing a quest for the meaning of all we go through here together.

Before we go to bed, Erika usually has a surprise for us. The margarine came most timely on the same day when she had successfully begged a few potatoes from a Russian. There was potato soup at midnight for eighteen people—an exciting feast in pitch darkness. Erika sat in the kitchen crying for joy; it was a memorable day for her.

The Russians have assigned a female supervisor to our hospital, a small, hunchbacked, very dark woman, from whom one is never safe. She has been trained in a primitive method of disinfection and is an expert in her field. Chloride of lime is the only means of diverting her attention for a time from the worst of our offenses. In the first days she was very strict with us, especially when she discovered that we had posted no night watchmen. But she soon had eyes only for the notorious Schäfer, and her conversations with us mostly end very quickly with the words: "Go to work, send for Scheffair!" He seems to have a special appeal for her, and is now the coming man in the hospital. With a few pieces of furniture, he has set up a private establishment and lives there with a woman who displays the same dubious characteristics as himself.

Among Schäfer's friends are two fellows who are employed in the so-called special work, in other words, they earn better food for themselves by denouncing daily a lot of people for having belonged to the Nazi Party, or for other offenses. One of them is often hanging around our place and likes to talk with us. He claims to have been a very early member of the Communist Party and probably would soon be appointed mayor of Königsberg. The other man's nationality is not clear. Both are in the service of the NKVD and seem to have the run of the place. Wherever they show up, you can be sure that a certain number of people are taken out in the evening by the guards for interrogation. Afterwards the unfortunates are brought to the cellar, or back to us, in the middle of the night, beaten half dead. These two have hundreds of victims to their credit.

One day they organized with Schäfer and his lady friend a major raid on all the wards, undressed all the patients, robbed them of their last usable belongings, and beat many of them with clubs. We were quite prepared that it would be our turn next. But their laundry basket was filled, and after having divided their spoils, they made off for the time being. As they are officially appointed spies, we can do nothing to defend ourselves; the guards only laugh, and our own physical strength is no longer sufficient to cope with them. We should have to kill them at once in that case, something we have, of course, seriously considered. (I shall never forget the moment when the worst of the two came to me to have a few teeth extracted and made me give him a shot of novocaine.)

But the reaction of our camp commander was quite unexpected. The eye doctor had managed to report the incident to him, and as a result the two were forced to return their loot and were sent into the cellar, while Schäfer was left to our jurisdiction. Although we could have got rid of him easily, he was let off once more by the eye doctor. Hardly was he out of this scrape, when he came to me and offered me a raincoat which he had probably kept back from his swag, reminding me that I had always wanted one. I took this opportunity to tell him what we all thought of him, which did not prevent him from offering immediately the same raincoat to the eye doctor. He hasn't a shred of conscience. (Later he kept many people in suspense, and then disappeared from Königsberg. I sometimes wonder what became of him.)

Among the so-called personnel of our hospital are several unusual characters, too; among the women, Wanda—as we call her—is a special case. She impressively introduced herself in the early days at the camp. Once, when we were sitting in our partition, she rushed in, with a determined stride, made straight for me with a piercing look in her eyes, and showered harangues upon me in a sharply accentuating voice, without giving me a chance to interrupt her. With unmistakable pride she told me that nobody could beat her record in regard to rape; she counted up to a hundred and twenty-eight times. Unrepeatable details followed one after another in her description. I failed to under-

stand why all this was showered exclusively on me, and saw
Erika looking at me with pity. My colleagues were almost bursting with laughter. At last we met with a downright caricature
of that devilry! The outburst had a relieving effect on her. At
the end she looked triumphantly around her; at least she had
still sufficient "pep." We harnessed her to the nursing service,
regardless of unforeseen episodes which she might still be involved in.

How many and various sick and dying persons have passed
through our hands! I shall always remember, for instance, Pastor
Lubowski, who had to live as an outcast under Hitler because
of his origin, and fell into the hands of the Russians as a sick
man. When we took him into the hospital, he was in a miserable
condition, but we put him back on his feet sufficiently for him to
take care of the medical records which the Russians had ordered
us to keep. Then his life was suddenly ended by an attack of
pleurisy. I remember, too, the old man who was brought to
us from the cellar and was so covered with lice that you could
compare him only with an ant hill. I carried his fur coat on a
pole to the loft to air it. In an almost inaudible voice he told
me that he had been director of the Cranz and Samland Railroad, and was, therefore, terribly afraid of the interrogation. I
was not to tell this to anybody, for heaven's sake! An hour later
he was dead. It often happens that people die immediately after
arriving at the hospital. Tension has kept them alive until then;
as soon as they relax, they pass away peacefully.

Not till halfway through the month did May at last remember
spring. Dandelions are out, and their leaves have become very
popular as salad, for our food still consists mainly of porridge,
although it has gradually become somewhat thicker.

May 20, Whitsunday

For the first time the sun has shone all day out of a cloudless sky. The commandant has given us permission to hold a church service. He even showed a personal interest in it, and asked the interpreter if he might be allowed to attend it himself. Of course, there was no God, and in Russia people became priests only to be exempted from work. Was it the same in Germany? Our interpreter had answered, that it could happen but in general was not the case, because God was definitely against idleness—an argument which the unbelieving colonel had promptly and sympathetically confirmed. But when, after all, he did not show up at the service, we concluded that his interest did not count for as much as we had assumed.

Sunlight and warmth flooded through the two wide open windows into the operating room. The walls were covered with fresh greenery, and right and left of the altar table stood a few tall sprays of laburnum in full bloom. Even a crucifix had been found somewhere. Our nursing personnel had managed to put on clean clothing, it was a festive sight! About a hundred people pushed their way in. We had written out the hymns on slips of paper and distributed them. Pastor Reiss, who could stand only with difficulty, had taken on the liturgy, whereas Giese preached the sermon. For one hour we were released from any earthly burden. Afterwards, when the room was emptying, I chanced to see the commander outside, sneaking away from our windows. I wonder if he had been standing there all the time. What unhappy people—these conquerors!

Entering our sleeping place still lost in thought, I started back. What did I see? Sheets on all four beds! My three friends were standing beside them, radiant with delight. We did not ask out of what dumps Erika and Waltraut had fished these riches;

their kind of eyes could discover something where nobody else would think of looking. We just ate our noon meal of porridge, and then lay quietly and blissfully in the red and white checkered sheets. The door to the next room stood open, and we could see the beautiful laburnum sprays. "Cloven tongues like as of fire." It had truly become Pentecost.

Even our tongues seemed released from the spell which had bound them so long. That same evening and also on the following days Giese and Klein held prayer meetings on several wards where people had asked for them. I myself had summoned up courage again to talk to the patients on a text from the Bible. In the cellar of the dysentery department the ward nurse—not trained but a woman with a warm heart and great strength—had arranged a small table with two candles on it, and set up a crucifix. I cast a gigantic shadow into the room. The darkness made speaking easier for me, and the Gospel of the rich man and the poor Lazarus provided a fitting text for many of those, who were lying now on bare boards, had formerly been wealthy people. I told them that God did not intend to punish them, but in His goodness turned the rich man, while he was still alive, into the poor Lazarus, to give him the chance to behold His Glory and to open his heart to it. When I later walked through the rows, I found two of the men dead.

In the first days of June somebody told me that a visitor from "outside" wanted to see me. What could that mean? It was certainly a trap! Who would have come into the camp voluntarily? Already a few days ago someone had slipped a letter to me through the camp fence, a letter from an unknown person. Reluctantly I went downstairs—there stood Doktora, unchanged, in a neat dress and in much better shape than we inmates of the camp. She had somehow discovered that I was in the camp and had forced her way through the guards.

It was not easy to take up the threads after all that might have happened after we were separated. She was so ethereal, no longer quite in this world. At first I did not know what to say. We sat for a while in the open, on a fragment of wall, in the sun. She came from the Treasury building, where the rest of the doctors and patients of all hospitals and part of the nursing personnel had been assembled at some time. What had happened until then, she passed over with a smile. (Six weeks later, after her death, I read about it in her diary.)

At present, about a thousand patients are lying in the Treasury building, which has become the main first-aid post. Doktora herself has a ward on the third floor and is still together with some nurses from the municipal hospital. Since they were in the Treasury building, they have been given peas, bread, and some sugar to eat. But they have also hidden other foodstuff and are, therefore, rather well-off. The general atmosphere is, however, unpleasant; the house is full of spies; nobody trusts anybody; everybody tries to play up to the Russians. Doktora feels it is her main duty to help those to escape who still have enough strength, for she considers the further development of our situation hopeless. For others she can still think very realistically. She stayed with me and my friends for a while, and we ate the pancakes she had brought us.

Three days later she came for the second time, and again I couldn't believe my eyes when I saw her coming. She had a rucksack with her—my rucksack—filled with the things which had not been discovered in her cache between the pipes of the burned-out engine house. She had salvaged everything, taken it across to the Treasury, and now brought me all my belongings, in case I should have a chance to escape. I could not imagine how she had managed to pass the camp guards with it. At first, the sentry had refused to let her pass, but at her urgent request took her to the commandant. They had wanted to confiscate the rucksack, but she handed it over so readily, that they allowed her to take it with her after all.

I unpacked it piece by piece. My friends were quite envious when they saw my smart trousers. At the bottom of the rucksack a strangely heavy small rubber cushion came to light. Doktora had used it as a pillow, she said, but thought it better if I kept it with me in case of an emergency. An emergency? I could not imagine what she meant. I took the thing in my hand and turned it around—it rattled a bit. I looked at her inquiringly, and she nodded. I stole a look at my friends to see if they had noticed anything. It was my Russian Kommissar's pistol with the fifty cartridges. I groaned under my breath. Where was this going to end? She was like a child playing at the edge of a precipice.

She told me later that the pistol had created much excitement after I had parted with it. Although it had never been used, the fact of its existence was enough. Doktora had casually asked a colleague whom we knew well where it might best be hidden, whereupon he almost became frantic and reported it at once to his chief. The latter implored her for heaven's sake to get rid of it and was still scared after Doktora had reported to him that she had disposed of it. I took the so-called pillow but, taking no risks, I hid it in the wall of the loft.

Doktora told us what was going on in the town. A kind of hospital for contagious diseases has been set up in the former mental hospital, under the direction of Professor Starlinger, who seems to impress the Russians. But he has a lot of trouble with an old fat nurse, well known to me, who has found favor with the Russians because of her remarkable corpulence, and is regarded by them as a marvel. She uses this unexpected advantage to tyrannize unscrupulously over her unfortunate countrymen.

After the entry of the Russians, almost the whole personnel of the military hospital, where we had worked, had been removed from the mental hospital, including Brother Martin and Doktora's sister. Nobody knows exactly what has become of the wounded. Some have been taken along, the majority have probably perished. Many are said to have been shot straight away.

The major disease in the hospital for contagious diseases is a fever resembling typhus, whose nature has not yet been determined. Already a great number of people have died of it. So far there have not been any cases of dysentery. Not long ago fifty of the older nurses and Professor Joachim were turned out of the Treasury and sent to Insterburg. Some of them had returned on foot after days of horror. Professor Joachim who had held out so long hanged himself in Insterburg behind the barbed wire.

Doktora comes almost every day now to give us the latest news. It looks as if they are interested in me at the Treasury, because they are short of surgeons. They are said to have tried unsuccessfully to get me out of the camp. I am in no hurry, for Doktora's reports about the events at the hospital are not very tempting. In the camp we are at least sure of one another. Doktora would love to stay with us.

At the end of May another female major arrived at the camp to replace the former supervisor who had left on private business, which had something to do with looted carpets. The new one is her exact opposite, quiet and friendly, almost pretty, rather shy— again an occasion for all sorts of conjectures. We persuaded her to take us for a ride into the town to search for medicaments in various places among the ruins. She ordered a truck, and we drove at a crazy speed down the Cranzer Allee with its undulating surface. One of my colleagues disapproved of my hat, which I had picked up somewhere on the road during my involuntary round trip through the Samland: "Really, you can't go to town in that!" I could not believe my ears. The town! A grandiose rubbish dump! And I, a little dung beetle, which had just been run over by a steam-roller and could not yet grasp that it was still alive. But the old ghost is stalking again, prescribing to the Herr Doktor the kind of headgear he has to wear when he goes to town. Life seems to be one unending joke.

The town is really an incredible sight. Your eyes no longer attempt any reconstruction, but are overwhelmed by the entirely transformed landscape. The sight confirms so much, and you can hardly believe that there are people still capable of regarding this obvious judgment of God as a horrid accident.

The East Prussian power plant near the Northern Railroad Station, where Bode's hospital had been in the fortress days, is still fairly intact on the outside. (It was blown up later.) Inside, everything, of course, has been ransacked time and again. When I was searching for objects we might be able to use, I came upon several corpses still lying on their mattresses in the knee-deep rubble, and everywhere my imagination found clues to realize the capture of this military hospital. In Bode's former room the walls are torn out. In one corner I found the red-rimmed glasses out of which we had been drinking his supposedly last Martell. Nobody has been able to tell me what has become of Bode himself. I cannot imagine him still alive among the Russians.

My search among the ruins of the municipal hospital was far more rewarding. I had slipped away from the others in order to go alone through the cellar and inspect our caches. The walls were so black with soot that the light of my small candle was almost swallowed up. I climbed over indefinable rubbish—there were certainly many dead still lying about—and felt with my hands for the places where closets had been built in. Most of them had been torn open; but one had not been discovered and was full of the most wonderful things: ampullas with dextrose, morphine, bandaging material and—a special surprise—castor oil which can be used for frying. I packed everything into a waste basket and put the bandaging material on top as camouflage. Then we drove back to the camp. Passing the Dohna Tower I saw Doktora picking flowers on the rampart of the fortress. She was obviously on her way to us.

At the beginning of June conditions had become quite relaxed. We had fewer patients, for some of them were taken daily to the Treasury, and very few new ones came in, because the camp was gradually being broken up. Many internees were taken to Insterburg, where apparently a camp for Nazi Party members existed. Others were simply turned out onto the street, having suddenly become uninteresting. The cat-and-mouse game goes on.

We who were left behind often have nothing to do. Sometimes we sun ourselves in the open windows, reflecting upon our conquerors. Several of them are still on duty to guard the building. They walk up and down or sprawl on arm chairs which they have placed in front of the doors for this purpose.

It is very amusing to watch them bicycling, which obviously still has the fascination of novelty for them. Wildly ringing their bells, they tear up and down the street, preferably through the puddles, of which there are many because all the drains are stopped up. When the water splashes high, they shout for joy. Many of them have never seen bicycles before and only slowly dare to ride one. They are afraid of anything unfamiliar. Trusses, for instance, scare them; they tear them off the patients, hold them to their ears, try to break them, and, if they don't succeed, fling them high into the air. They evidently think that they are secret radio transmitters.

They are completely insensitive to noise. Some of them stand all day in the garages, honking all available horns. In their billets the radio blares non-stop far into the night. Electric lights also have to be as glaring as possible. All the rooms are wired at top speed, and where there is still glass in the windows, they shoot holes into the panes to lead the wires through. We are baffled again and again how rapidly they discover the simplest method of attaining their purpose; for them only the next moment exists, and everything must serve it, even if what they ruin in the process is something they might urgently need at the next moment.

What constantly bewilders us is their total lack of any relation to things which, to us, are part of our life. You finally give up thinking of them as creatures like yourself, and slowly assume the attitude of an animal trainer. This happens quite automatically; for even before you yourself become conscious of your behavior towards them, you experience their remarkably prompt reaction to any kind of resistance. To show fear is the worst line to take; it obviously provokes them to attack. On the other hand you can achieve a great deal with effrontery. The most stupid tactic is to play up to them. We often watch with a certain malicious relish the inefficacy of such attempts by our fellow countrymen. The Russians have no use for such practices, and though they use people like that for their own purposes, they openly despise them.

It is their singing that reveals to us most clearly that they come from another world for they suddenly form a community and carry us, the listeners, away with them into an immeasurably remote sphere. At that moment at least, they are still living there, and their life here is as unreal to them as a circus, to which they have been taken. When they return there, all their experiences here will seem to them like a crazy dream. It is perhaps the reason why it does not occur to them to regard us as people like themselves, and why our claims on their humanity meets with hardly any response. The fact that they drive cars, can shoot, listen to the radio, and are frequently trained to the same tricks as we, is not sufficient to create a living bridge from one human being to another. Of course, it will not always remain so. They will soon become accustomed to the new environment; we know how quick they learn. The excitement of the circus will blow over; but then they will also become useless for the purpose they should answer. They will be discarded and replaced by others, with whom the dance will start again. It is not exactly fear which you feel at this thought, but helplessness, as if you are lying under a heavy wet blanket.

Compared with this uniformity, the diversity of our own countrymen is all the more evident. We are constantly amazed at the difference between one human being and another, which is not so noticeable under so-called normal conditions, when there are written and unwritten laws, which most people observe. But here in the camp, beyond the reach of law, all human qualities stick out glaringly. The fact of being seen by others is no longer a reason for not doing what one likes. Everything is permitted, perhaps because nobody is there who can forbid it. And you really wonder if education and mores might not be peacetime luxuries only.

Meanwhile the camp is gradually shrinking in size. One day I was left alone with a few nurses and medical orderlies, and the last patients, about fifty, who are still to be interrogated, should they ever be able to stand again. The other doctors and patients have been transferred to the Treasury or to the Elizabeth Hospital, which is still partly intact. Schreiner is going there, and, to his regret, Schäfer, too, this time as an architect.

Except for Erika, Chaplain Klein is the only member left of my little group. We have little to do and have decided to read something together. The Bible suggested itself at once, but, as a Catholic, Klein would probably first have to take a short leap to step with me into the Old Testament. We started right at the beginning, and found it immediately reassuring that the light had been created independently of the heavenly bodies. Therefore it would not perish together with them as Mephisto claims. Evidently it uses them only as camouflage.

The medical supervision of our hospital at this time has been assigned to a woman we had learned to appreciate at the beginning of the camp period. A tall, lively, good-looking woman from Riga, whom I am going to call Natasha, introduced herself at first as a nurse, but let herself later be called Dr. Natasha. When I first saw her, she passed us on the stairs in a crowd, and exchanged a few quick words with Schreiner. I asked him who she was. He knew only her first name and said we should try and keep in touch with her. Several times during the following days, she sent us something from her meals or asked one of us to come and get it. I went to see her once, and was allowed to sit for a while in her room and begin to eat. She lived in a barrack room with her two children, ages six and three years. Her grandmother had been an actress. Since the fall of Riga in 1941 she had been living among the Germans, and her life was probably in danger for that reason, but we did not talk of that. She did not know much about medicine, but could handle a hypodermic syringe, which belonged to her, and which she successfully used to cure the Russian officers. They could stand rather big doses, and if they felt really weak and dizzy afterwards, they were all the more impressed by the effect of the medication. She has accumulated large quantities of ampullas and pills and always finds cases where they are useful. She has also invented a kind of massage which her patients like.

Once she even consulted me. One of the dreaded NKVD bosses ran a high temperature and demanded to be cured as quickly as possible. When we entered the room the radio was going full blast. His cap tipped to the nape of his neck, the man was sitting at a table, behind a bottle of vodka, in a cloud of tobacco smoke, and coughing at the top of his lungs. Before him was a pile of pills of every kind, red, yellow and white, which he was supposed to take in a certain order. He asked me if it would not be better to swallow all of them at once, because he might then be cured more quickly. I took a closer look: there was no sublimate among them, the others would not do him any harm. A few looked like sleeping pills, and I wangled these out of him or Natasha respectively. On the whole, I agreed with Natasha's treatment. I advised him to take the rest of the pills at intervals. When he asked me if massage would do him any good, I said that it certainly would not do him any harm— he seemed to have the flu. Natasha was rather pleased with my professional advice; but when her patient was not well next day, to be on the safe side, she gave him a few more shots. These were, no doubt, helpful too.

It was certainly no easy game which Natasha has to play in the camp, but she plays it with courage, and we benefit from it as well. On our last day in the camp, she has even become my chief, and I do not at all begrudge her this little intermezzo in her make-believe game. We made the rounds on the wards together, and the patients were delighted with her. Fortunately, she is moderate in the matter of prescriptions. When I was finally transferred, I felt quite easy about leaving the last patients under her care. She has more opportunities to help them than I, and she will also make use of them.

Our departure from the camp was so informal that I smuggled the whole of the collected material of our dispensary onto the truck. Somewhat earlier Doktora had taken the pillow with the pistol back to the treasury. I had wanted to leave it behind, but she had insisted on carrying it out of the camp under her arm, like a handbag. The sentry had been letting her pass for some time without stopping her. She found it more difficult to part with it than I did.

Just as we were leaving, the commandant appeared on the scene, and took leave of us very warmly. When the camp gates closed behind us, he was still standing there, looking after us. We almost felt like waving to him.

· 5 ·

GERMAN CENTRAL HOSPITAL
Mid-June to Mid-October, 1945

We were the last to arrive at the Treasury. I had been there a week earlier, accompanying patients, and had three hours' time to have a look around the building, one of the few still intact. It has only been damaged on the yard side by a heavy bomb at the same moment the heaviest bombs had fallen on us at the municipal hospital. Captain Temme, M.C., had been among those killed on that day. They had just moved in with the main first-aid post, after the post office at the main railroad station had been destroyed by artillery fire. Bothmer himself was hit by a bullet the next day in the gateway of the courtyard, when the Russians were marching in.

The reception room is to the left of the gateway, and there I found Second Lieutenant M. C. Brichzy still in uniform. He received me very kindly and gave me his dinner, two platefuls of gray pea soup, a typical East Prussian dish, the only food they had been given these last six weeks. The kitchen is next to this room. The courtyard is overcrowded with patients waiting to be admitted; even those brought from the camp first have to settle down on the ground outside. The house is overflowing, and the number dying is smaller than the number of new arrivals.

When I walked through the building I found a great many nurses with whom I had worked in the Fortress days, and also many former patients. All of them had mask-like faces and moved around very slowly. To my surprise, the liveliest among them was the dentist from the Samaritan Hospital, who was again able to work and had set up a dental ward. He drew me into his room and handed me a meatball, made from horsemeat, which one of his Russian patients had given to him. He warned me earnestly against his assistant, a genial-looking young man, one of the most dangerous of the spies. In any case, I should be very careful of everything I said in this house.

This was my first impression at our reception at the main entrance, when we finally moved in. A tall, gawky girl was standing in the doorway, looking me up and down. I gave her a slight push in order to get through the door with my box of medicaments. She seemed about to speak to me, but I took no notice of her and made my way towards a woman I knew, who was sitting on a trunk in the lobby. She had noticed the little episode at the door, and warned me of this person, who was in the service of the NKVD and was dreaded by all alike. Because of a big, ugly operation scar on her neck, she had obtained a certificate attesting that the Russians had freed her at the very moment the Nazis were trying to cut her throat. Armed with this document she had free access everywhere and terrorized everybody.

I looked around the lobby and thought that even as a waiting room it was not very inviting. Although there were flowers on a table and a few stately chairs from the assembly hall standing around, I was conscious of more than one pair of eyes appraising me. I felt like an object in a store window to which the price had not yet been affixed.

To my surprise I was given a small room on the top floor. Dr. Hoff, whom I had known at the municipal hospital, had occupied it before, but had recently been sent for by the NKVD and had not returned.

I found Giese and Röckert, my two loyal friends, rather at sea.

They had not yet discovered any place to settle down, and during the three days they had been there had been given food only at their urgent entreaty. They helped me to find a safe place for the pharmacy, and later brought their luggage into my room. It is tolerably cool there, in spite of the broiling heat outside. A chestnut tree lifts its canopy of leaves and countless flowers just above our window, and we look into a green world.

Suddenly a heavy thunderstorm developed, and for several minutes we sat like Noah in the Ark under a downpour of rain. When it was over, Doktora came to take us on a round of inspection through the building. But we had hardly reached the large window at the end of the corridor, when we were stopped by an extraordinary sight. Down below us, against the black background of the passing storm, lay a whitely shimmering sea of ruins, lit up by the evening sun. In the midst of it rose the split tower of the castle like an exclamation mark; and above it, in rare perfection, a rainbow arched like the Gate of Heaven over the desert. We held hands. When the apparition began to fade, we turned and went back to our room, unable to speak after this impressive experience. "Shouldn't we read the watchwords?" Doktora suggested. I took the book out of my baggage and handed it to her. She opened it at June 13 and read: "God said, I do set my bow in the cloud, and it shall be for a token of a covenant between me and the earth." She did not read the following verse. We bowed our heads in silence and seemed to hear the angels of God ascending and descending.

Next day I was put in charge of the men's surgical ward, so called because the patients there suffered from wounds in addition to their other troubles. A deaconess from the Samaritan Hospital was my ward nurse. In the operating room downstairs on the yard side is constant activity, consisting almost exclusively in operating on festering wounds. The surgeons working there are old Professor Ehrhardt and Captain Ody, M.C., from Bothmer's hospital. Dr. Rauch has also started working again, having recovered under Erika's care in the camp, from the hardships of the walking tour through the Samland. Dr. Keuten who had, until recently, been working alone, is critically ill with typhus, and so is his wife, also a doctor. Two deaconesses, Sisters Lydia and Martha, are acting as surgical nurses.

K., a medical orderly in the operating room, told me that he knew the exact place where Bothmer was buried. I made him take me to the spot and decided to exhume the body, which was probably only lightly covered with earth. I wished to give my friend a proper grave, for I could not bear the thought that this man was lying somewhere, quite nearby, under the surface of the ground, while I was running around here taking life seriously. Giese came to help me. First we searched the loft of the house for something to serve as a coffin, and found a narrow cupboard which would do. Then we went to work with our spades. In the communicating trenches dug into the embankment above the railroad tracks during the Fortress days, several hundred dead from the time of the Russian entry, were lying one on top of the other, covered lightly with earth. The orderly marked out the place exactly—here the head and there the feet, barely eighteen inches deep. However much you might have known about this sort of thing, you never got used to it. From here to there, you think—it might be, considering his height, and there would be the scar over his eye and the mortal wound—it should be possible to recognize him even after two months. On April 8 he had been shot in the gateway. The Russians had invaded the building and ordered the doctors and the nursing personnel to line up outside. Then came a German counterattack. A rifle bullet tore his chest open. When it had later become possible to attend to him, he asked to be handed a mirror and showed them how to patch him up. They did their best but the attempt failed, and he died two days later.

We found the digging very difficult. He was probably lying much deeper. I remembered our standing together, at night, three months ago, only a few yards from this spot, and the cranes flying over our heads. It is good that there are moments which can be exactly defined; they are the hooks on which to hang the tangled threads of our life.

While we were still digging, I was suddenly called away. The entire Treasury Building was to be evacuated at once, and I had been selected to go as advance guard to the new shelter assigned to us: the remains of the Samaritan Hospital. Giese did not feel like continuing with the digging alone, and raised a small mound over the marked spot. Meanwhile I started with the first of the trucks which were loaded with bedsteads and mattresses. The Russians had allowed us twenty-four hours for the move. Anyone who was not over there by that time, would be left behind. Fifty trucks would be driving several times back and forth, transferring all the equipment and about a thousand patients.

Late that afternoon I was unloading in the yard of the Samaritan Hospital, together with Erika, several nurses and a few men; when I turned my back, the trucks disappeared with the men who were supposed to help us. I stood there alone with the nurses. We scattered quickly over the house to get at least an idea of the place before it was dark. The nurses had worked there before and soon found their way around. The newer part, built of concrete, is almost still intact; only the upper floors have been hit here and there and the roof has been ripped open in several places. Otherwise nothing is left, of course, for the place has been empty since the evacuation on April 17, except that some Russians have apparently slept in the cellar. There we found the usual sofas with their leather coverings torn off. Every window is broken; the doors have been taken off their hinges and left lying about the corridors. All the drains are clogged, and the electric wires and waterpipes, in any case pointless now, have been torn out of the walls. We gave up racking our brains how we are to live here; like everything else, it will happen somehow; we will live to see it. For the moment, the heavenly evening sun compensated for all the impossibilities in store for us. We did not even hurry to drag all the things upstairs. Tomorrow the whole narrow yard will be chockfull of them, and they will perhaps push themselves upward on their own. The little strength my nurses still have will not go very far anyway. They settled down on the floor of the third floor and Erika joined them. On the fifth floor, where my men's ward is to be, I looked around for a room for myself, and found it, far back at the end of the corridor—unsuitable for patients, but more or less meeting with my personal needs. I marked it at once and barricaded it.

Next morning things really began moving. To avoid having to reason out how to arrange everything in the right order, I just tackled what came in my way. Beds, furniture, and patients came pouring in indiscriminately, covering the whole of the premises. During the morning the Russians worked with us and things were not too bad; but in the afternoon they just hung around on the stairs and in the doorways and laughed at the chaos. As usual we took comfort in the thought that this, like so much else, would be over some time, too.

One of the seriously ill patients lying on stretchers on the floor of the packed entrance hall caught hold of my leg as I passed him. I was horrified to recognize a man I had long ago believed to be dead. He had been on the dysentery ward at the camp and was called for an interrogation every night. Each time he returned severely beaten, because he had refused to admit having been a Blockwart. One night they called me to see him; he seemed to have an intestinal obstruction and was already so ill that an operation, even had we been able to perform it, would not have helped him. I gave him morphine. Immediately afterwards he was sent for again. I pointed out his condition, but it was useless. Giese and I then asked to be allowed to at least carry him, but the guard refused our request. We were, however, permitted to accompany the unfortunate man, who was kicked ahead by the guard. The Kommissar took no notice of our explanations either; on the contrary, he became furious when he heard that we had given him morphine. Then the man was interrogated once more. Standing outside the door, we heard him collapse several times under the blows. We waited, expecting that we would also be taken in and called to account for the morphine, but the man was simply kicked out again and down the stairs. Not till we were alone with him could we carry him back. I had not forgotten the expression on his face when I saw him more clearly at daybreak; it had been a mixture of hatred, impotence, and greed of life. He had even shown me a photo of himself. Nothing was left of the fat, self-satisfied face but the eyes, and even they had been popping out of his head from fear, fury, and emaciation. In the afternoon we had sent him by ambulance to the Treasury and reported him to the Russians as dead. Professor Ehrhardt then operated on him after all, but had been unable to remove the intestinal obstruction. And now, three days later, he is still alive and has survived the second move. He is a mere skeleton but refuses to give in. It makes me shudder to look at him.

Towards evening the whole street was blocked up with patients and pieces of equipment. Across the street, Doktora is moving into one part of the former municipal hospital; she has been, unfortunately, put in charge of the tuberculosis department. With the nurses assigned to her, she is untiringly dragging one bed after another up to the second floor, while her patients are standing around without lifting a finger, among them one or two veritable devils who are probably not sick at all, but are gadding about everywhere, acting as informers for the Russians.

The drudgery went on for another whole day. Then the patients were accommodated, and the first dead buried in the cemetery of the Altrossgärter Church. Meanwhile the Russians sent us a lot of glass which made it possible to glaze some windows. I moved into the top floor with my one hundred seventy patients, and am living with my two good friends in the corner room. Erika has taken over the small anteroom, to keep a watchful eye on us. We are happy to be living so high up, and are beginning to breathe freely again.

June 1945

About 1,500 people have found shelter in this building, a thousand patients and at least five hundred persons, male and female, as nursing personnel. Many of them had never had any experience in nursing, but are making every effort to retain contact with the hospital, because it assures them more protection and a better chance for survival. Outside they are at everybody's mercy, and for this reason we can hardly discharge any of our patients. Having no home, they can only expect death from starvation on the road. Therefore we try, as far as possible, to fit them into the machinery of the place. Actually, the need comes up only rarely, for nearly all those admitted as patients do not show any improvement and die after a shorter or longer period. Every day thirty or forty dead are carried down in the morning, wrapped in blackout paper, and piled up beside the back gate. From there they are gradually brought in a two-wheeled timber cart to the ground beside the destroyed Altrossgärter Church, where, under the supervision of Pastor Leitner, they are buried in common graves.

The two floors at the top constitute the surgical wards, as they did before. My men, 170 to 180, are right at the top, the women one floor below. At first they were in Dr. Ody's charge but he was suddenly removed by the Russians and sent to Wehlau. His place has been taken by Dr. Rauch, who has, meanwhile, more or less recovered. We work side by side in the operating room, or relieve one another occasionally, and are extremely busy all day long. We have sufficient space, the outer walls having remained intact, and also enough instruments, medicaments, and bandaging material from the ample supplies which have been stored in the town. But what use is all this, if we cannot give the people anything to eat. They have pulled through somehow, longer than might have been expected. But after all, there is a limit to starvation.

Nearly all the people brought to us are in the same physical condition: skeletons above, heavy watersacs below. Some can still walk to our place, on shapeless swollen legs, and sit down in front of the door, where many others like them are lying on improvised stretchers or on the floor. When their turn comes, they often give some trivial reason for their coming, for instance a sore finger, for they can no longer feel their legs. This becomes evident when we put them on the operating table and slit the greasy, glassy skin from top to bottom with a knife, without their reacting at all. Each time we wonder whether there is any sense in amputating their legs, or whether we should not rather let these people die as they are. Usually we decided on the latter course.

This death from starvation is a strange way of dying. There is no sign of revolt. People give the impression that their actual death is already behind them. They still walk upright, we can even speak to them, they will reach out for the stub of a cigarette —more eagerly than for a piece of bread which they can no longer chew—and then, suddenly, they collapse like a table which stands firm under the heaviest load until the additional weight of a fly breaks it down.

Aside from these legs, we primarily treat malignant, often extremely malignant, phlegmons, among them many neck carbuncles, sometimes stretching from one ear to the other. If they are teeming with maggots, we consider this a good sign, for then there is some hope they will heal.

Even the women are beginning to show signs of lowered resistance. Many we know from the camp days have passed through our hands again—mere shadows of their former selves. The most distressing thing about them is often their talk, completely unrelated to the actual misery, as though our common experiences these last months were mere delusion and not brutal reality. A woman of forty, held together only by the mask of her former coquetry, asked me shortly before she collapsed where she would get now her compensation money; she had worked long enough in the office of the Gauleiter, she said, to be entitled to it. Only gradually did we discover her real reason for coming to us. She had been lying for ten days in one of the garden lots, eating nothing but unripe red currants. Now her bowel was blocked up with seeds. The procedure necessary to free the passage was almost fatal for her.

Occasionally, however, we have normal surgery to perform, for which we wash according to rule, and which gives us the uplifting illusion of still being authentic surgeons. We have mostly cases of incarcerated hernia, of intestinal obstructions caused by the twisting of the shrunken mesentery, and occasionally an appendicitis. Aside from these cases we see others which hardly exist any longer, for instance, gangrenous stomatitis (noma), in which the affected part of the face falls away after a few days, together with the jawbones, teeth, lips, and cheek, leaving an enormous hole.

In addition to the men's ward I have taken over the surgical care of the children's ward, a particularly difficult and depressing task, because we know that the children are even more cheated than the rest of the people. Every day the Russians give out a certain amount of fat for them, with which we might have been able to keep some of them alive, but it never reaches them; it is diverted at the last minute and somebody else hoards it for himself. In the very first days I had an encounter with a woman working on the children's ward, and we came almost to blows. She is a downright friend of the Russians, and we are powerless against her. She is also not the only one of her type. On the contrary, we are surrounded by other shady creatures, informers of every age and degree of dangerousness who make their living by betraying their fellow countrymen to the NKVD. For this institution, strangely enough, makes use of traitors even here, although it can dispose of us without any talebearer. But a semblance of justice probably has to be kept up somehow. Or else it is considered expedient to demoralize as many people as possible by accustoming them to betrayal. In any case, we always shudder when certain people turn up on our ward, ransacking the rooms of the patients and taking notes with the greatest effrontery. During the night, one or more unfortunates are always taken away and never seen again. It is difficult to size up these people as to their former civil occupation, except for a man, named Schmidt, whom we know to have been active in the SD, the Secret Service. How is it possible, I often wondered, that these devils are not murdered? But would I myself have the guts to do it? Did we not continue to look on patiently, always hoping that the cup may be removed from us?

Our kitchen has been installed in the Frischbier School, a building opposite the back gate. Twice a day our soup, made alternately of oatmeal or turnip parings, is fetched from there in pails and tin cans. In addition, we each get a spoonful of sugar and a kind of bread which tastes of paraffin and contains a great deal of water. People scrambled for this duty, because several well-fed compatriots are working in the kitchen, and there is sometimes a chance of picking up an extra morsel. For that reason they gladly carry the heavy pails up to the fifth floor. They are not so keen on carrying down the full latrine buckets which are emptied into the nearby ruins. But even for that duty we can always find some people.

At first our water was drawn from the Castle Pond, which was full of dead men. Then the news got about that water could still be pumped from a hand pump in the yard of the lemonade factory, not far away. From then on people were lining up there at all hours with containers of any type. If, by chance, a gap occurs in the line, those newly arriving waited until a group has formed again, because single individuals are easily attacked. It is the same as with jungle beasts at the drinking pool. Down in the factory cellar are still a lot of barrels with lemonade extract, which nobody bothers about because of its lack of nutritive value. Also a bath tub stands there, in which I sometimes have a furtive wash.

As we can't, of course, subsist on the regulation soup, every free moment is spent in the search for food. The early morning is the best time for it, because there are fewer Russians around. At five A.M. Russian time—three by ours—when the sun is just rising, Erika and I leave the house. In the municipal hospital, across the street, Doktora is already waiting to join us. Usually we roam the suburbs of Karolinenhof and Maraunenhof. In the weed-grown gardens there, we can pick as many red currants as we want, and the thick bushes provide enough cover. For this reason, a large number of people have taken up their quarters in the little summer huts standing in the lots. We trade with them, swapping some of our beet soup for their red currants.

After the garden lots it is the turn of the deserted houses on the Cranzer Allee. Although they have been ransacked over and over again, you can still find here and there a potato or something else to eat. What we always bring with us in great quantities is orach, which grows everywhere like a rank weed, and which we eat at every meal.

These excursions are often emotionally disturbing, not only because of the constant awareness of possible danger lurking everywhere, but also because of the tremendous contrasts. The race course especially fascinates me. There was a time when it was the highlight of our life. We always arrived there in a festive mood, to look enthusiastically at the horses, to see people and to let ourselves be seen. How beautifully everything was kept and organized! You leaned on the fence, chatted with an acquaintance, nodded to someone, followed another with your eyes, and felt on top of the world. And now I lean on the fence again, in a canvas jacket, frayed trousers, boots I had found, without shirt and socks, watching a small group of cows, grazing between the old hurdles and guarded by a Russian sentry. Had one of them come near enough, I would have tried to get some milk. All around me nothing but weeds, rubble, and ruins; only heaven remains the same—I wonder to which of the two realities I actually belong.

Our hospital owns some cows, three to be exact, which produce between them seven quarts of milk. They are guarded by Professor Urbschat, specially appointed to this duty, and occasionally assisted by other unemployed university instructors. It is not an easy job, for the cows are, of course, greatly coveted in spite of their leanness, and one day one of them, the best milker, became the victim of a robbery. Two men pulled her into a cellar and cut her throat but were frightened away by the shouts of the guard. Next day we saw a light yellow, soft, indefinable object floating in our communal soup, on whose nature we speculated for a long time, until Giese suddenly declared that it must have something to do with "Herr Pastor sin Kauh." (Pastor Stachowitz, institutional director of the Samaritan Hospital, is considered by the Russians as the owner of the cows.) Giese was right; it was the udder of the slaughtered cow.

Otherwise we have no meat as a rule, although seventy pounds of it is officially delivered to the hospital several times weekly. As it mainly consists of the heads and feet of cows, complete with hide, hooves and horns, it is obvious that none of it reaches the patients.

The two remaining cows give three quarts of milk between them, which trickles away somewhere. The supervisor of nurses in our hospital is supposed to have some of it every day. She is sick in bed in a cubicle next to the dispensary, calmly and graciously meeting her end, having successfully protected many of her nurses from the worst during the most terrible days.

From my ward on the fifth floor an iron staircase leads to the flat roof, from which I have a magnificent view over the ruined town and the surrounding countryside. We usually go there late at night, when all is quiet in the building, and relax in the infinite peace we can enjoy there. Nobody besides us makes use of this opportunity. We take chairs with us and read together something that gives us food for thought or lifts our spirits, or talk about matters, which we cannot discuss in daytime with all the people crowding around us, or are lost in contemplation of the sky, along which wild ducks are sailing in long files, and one-half of which remains light all through the night at this time of year.

We are not short of reading matter. Everywhere in the deserted houses books are lying around unnoticed. Only a few have been carried off and thrown away again, and ardent booklovers have been able to set up considerable libraries in their quarters.

We are kept busy enough during the day, either by Russians suddenly descending upon us for a raid, or by the constant intrigues going on between single groups in the house. Or windowpanes may come flying around our ears, because some large building nearby is being blown up. At other times we are involved in dramatic human reactions. For instance, a demented woman had been put up above the tuberculosis ward across the street, and her screams created a disturbance for the whole neighborhood. She suddenly managed to escape from the bare room in which she had been sitting, climbed out of a window, more than six feet above her, to the roof, which itself began only far above that window. There she sat at a giddy height, on the small railing above the gutter, leaning forward, her hair hanging down, and singing at the top of her voice whatever came into her head: hymns, popular hits, Hitler songs—a weird potpourri. Finally the Russians got fed up with this exhibition and were about to shoot her down, when Doktora and the delousing orderly set to work. We saw the two of them climbing out of two different dormer windows and move from the right and from the left along the railing toward the runway, Doktora armed with a syringe. How easily and assured she moved at that height! She was evidently determined on skirting abysses. To everybody's surprise the woman let herself be pulled inside again through a window.

One day we were ordered to report to the police. A number of us were assembled and, led by a Russian, marched through the streets. After we had crossed the whole town, it turned out that we had been going in the wrong direction. We then described an enormous half circle, passed the upper pond, went through Maraunenhof, and finally came across the fields and over a level crossing to a military barrack, standing suddenly before us. Several grim-looking officials were sitting there with the usual, yelling female interpreters, prepared to make mincemeat of us. Convinced that this was just another trap, into which you walk out of sheer stupidity, I slipped out of the ranks with one or two others and disappeared with them into an overgrown garden, where we awaited further developments. The screening of our comrades took hours. They were neither given papers nor were their names registered. They had only been shouted at. The whole affair had obviously been got up, as usual, for the entertainment of the NKVD.

July 1 was a radiant Sunday. Doktora came across and persuaded me to come with her to Preyl to explore the region. Barefoot and otherwise rather poorly dressed—someone has made me trousers out of two towels—we did not attract any attention and got safely out of the town. The countryside was unbelievably deserted; we walked for an hour without meeting a soul. At the edge of the fields we picked cornflowers and decided that we should come here with scissors when the grain was ripe, to cut off the ears. The large pond which had formerly provided Königsberg with drinking water had been drained. Russians were standing in the middle of the mud looking for fish.

The house of my relatives has been burned down, except for a part of the foundations and the basement, in which a couple of women were clearing up. We got no answers to our questions. The stable buildings still exist, and I was tempted to look around and see what had happened to the part where formerly the race horses were kept. The moment we entered we were stopped by a Russian and led with considerable pride to the commandant who had moved into the rooms of the trainer above the stable. I produced my empty briefcase and begged for some potatoes, after which he released us. Where the garden used to be, we found a Russian cooking his porridge over two bricks. He kindly gave us some of it, and we sat down at the edge of the pond to eat it. Opposite us, on the hill in the forest, were the family graves. We went up there to see if we still could find them. They were unharmed and partly overgrown by potato haulms which had sprouted out of the German defense positions. Although the potatoes underneath were very small, we filled the briefcase with them.

Suddenly Doktora started crying. I was deeply alarmed, for I had never seen her do this before. The mosquitos were bothering her, she said, and she implored me to leave the forest with her as quickly as possible. I felt that there was something else behind this, but I could not get more out of her. When we were back on the road again, she seemed to feel better. We also visited the Warglitten farm, which the Russians were apparently running again, and were given a lift in a Russian wagon, going in the direction of Königsberg. We got out in Juditten, where Doktora again tried to see her house, which was still standing and was occupied by Germans. When she entered it, she was physically attacked and had to flee.

On Wednesday she came into the operating room and asked me to have a look at her neck which was itching terribly. I found a large number of lice which had bitten their way deep under the skin. When I told her, she broke down. I tried hard to calm her, while Dr. Rauch helped me to cut away the hair and expose the spot. Although she calmed down gradually, she was so changed from then on that I was at a loss what to do. Her vitality must have been exhausted long since, I thought, and she was going around among us as if she was dreaming. Only her obedience to our Lord's command to love gave her the strength to be an example to her fellow workers and to take care of her patients, who all rely on her so fervently.

Next morning I was called across to see her, because they could not rouse her from her sleep. On her table was a note saying that she had taken some sedatives, for she had not been able to sleep for several nights because of the terrible itching; they should wake her only if it was necessary. We let her sleep. Although she would never have taken her own life, I knew how glad she would be to pass away in her sleep. But when her condition remained unchanged in the evening, everything was done, almost over my head, that should be done in such cases. I could not feel anything and went about my daily chores as if the whole matter was not my concern. Perhaps I was already inwardly dead, because I could not summon up any ambition at all.

On Friday night her heart stopped beating. The patients of the tuberculosis ward brought a coffin from Kalthof, where, they said, there is a whole warehouse full of them. A German soldier, who works in our building, brought me a wooden cross he had made. We wrote her name on it with the dates of her birth and death, and on the back of it we wrote the closing words of the Holy Scriptures: "Amen. Even so, come, Lord Jesus."

Her grave is where they all lie, beside the Altrossgärter Church. I found in Doktora's Bible, as a bookmark, a small notebook in which she had written down her thoughts on certain passages from the Bible, and indirect references to the happenings after the barrier had been broken down. "Russia—and I once wished to go there. Now it has come over me." I read the words again and again, like a bequest. And I heard distinctly through her words those others: "These are they which came out of great tribulation and have washed their robes and made them white in the blood of the Lamb."

All through July I took long walks alone when I had no work to do. I rummaged through cellars and gardens, and brought back a number of useful dishes and jars and occasionally flowers, once a beautiful blue clematis plant with innumerable flowers. On these walks I often came upon people, both dead and living, who had collapsed on the road. It was not so easy to get the living to our hospital and each time meant a special determination. Never had I been so often reminded of the parable of the Good Samaritan as in those days. It was humilitating enough, for in most cases the rescue work proved to be easier than I had expected.

In the cellars I sometimes came upon Russians too. Once, after my eyes had got used to the darkness, I saw one before me leaning against the wall. He did not move and put his fingers to his lips. There was no doubt that his life was threatened.

Erika never tires of providing us with food. She is no longer in the least afraid and always tells us stories about nice Russians with whom she has talked. One of them has promised her potatoes, and she is firmly convinced that he will keep his word. (He did, but somebody grabbed them from him when he turned up and refused to give them back.)

Cooking is done in the room next to ours. A sergeant has put up a tiled cooking stove there which he has taken apart elsewhere; and although he declares that he does not understand anything about such things, the pots and cooking vessels of at least twenty different parties are simmering day and night on the range beside ours. Erika often has to wait for ages before she can get near the range.

Far away from us, in the ruins of the Hans Schemm School, are thousands of capsules lying among melted glass: narcotics and drugs for heart and circulatory diseases. I discovered them on a scouting trip on foot with Erika, who had been employed as a domestic help near there for a year, and wanted to see if she could still find the family somewhere. When we returned, our pockets were full of medicaments, and I made the children playing around in the neighborhood promise to collect more of them for us.

A few days later I set out in a little cart, which the hospital has been allowed to use, to get the stuff. Old Nurse Ida accompanied me, and we stopped first at the surgical clinic in Drumm Street, where we had worked together at the end of January. Although six months of wild confusion had passed, Nurse Ida hadn't the slightest doubt that she would find what she had hidden there at that time. And she was right: out of a wide crack next to the side entrance she pulled several large pots of ointment, a good deal of bandaging material and several cans of alcohol and benzine, much to the surprise of the people of the outpatients' department now installed there. We loaded our booty quickly on the cart and left before our right to it could be disputed.

Many dramatic events had taken place in this clinic, too, since we left. As Doktora had told me once, when she came to see me in the camp, my former Czech orderly had practiced dentistry there on a large scale after the arrival of the Russians; that is to say—the Russians had him crown their healthy teeth with gold from the looted rings. He was said to have grown so rich on the remainder of the rings, that a Russian murdered him for that reason.

Every time we walk around in the town, we do not look for medical supplies only, but also for bedsteads and mattresses; for my walking patients, five persons merely camouflaged as patients, have banded together to go and get these things and distribute them on the wards. We have particular designs on the ruins of the castle. They are guarded by a sentry, which seems to us proof that there is still something worth looking for.

One morning at 5 A.M. everything was ready. My scouts reported that the sentry had left his post. We broke in at once and found, in a large room to the left of the gate, several boxes with bandaging material and other useful matter, enough to load our cart several times. Some heavy boxes, bound with wire and addressed to Moscow, we regretfully had to leave behind. We took only one picture, packed and marked "Brueghel," with us as a curiosity. When we got back to the hospital, we discovered that, unfortunately, there were only hundreds of small pieces of wood in the box, which could not be fitted together again. The picture had probably been hacked to pieces with an axe, and then laboriously collected again. In the afternoon the sentry returned to his post before the castle gate.

Not far from us, on the other side of the Königstrasse, Professor Starlinger was working as director of the so-called hos-

pital for contagious diseases, to which the Yorckstrasse and Elizabeth Hospitals belonged. About 2,000 typhus patients have been
assembled there. They are lying two to a bed, the children four to
a bed. We have heard a great deal about the place, but for a long
time I had not felt much inclined to go there, until one of the
spies on the tuberculosis ward informed me that Starlinger was
at the head of a clique which intended to do away with me and
several other people.

I found the professor in a sort of monk's cell, lying on a narrow cot, a table with books by his side. I could not believe my
eyes—he was holding in his hand the very book I had been trying to find: the third volume of Bismarck's *Thoughts and Recol-
lections*. This led at once to a conversation which I much enjoyed,
in spite of the differences in our viewpoint. I did not mention
the silly rumor which had brought me here, neither did I ask the
professor if he really had typhus, as the notice on his door said.
Perhaps it was only a trick to get rid of the Russians for a while.
After an hour I left him, feeling extremely stimulated by our
meeting. The whole get-up of the hospital has a certain style
about it. In spite of some odd particulars, it is the expression of
an almost reckless will to establish order, and, thinking of the
chaos in which we are drifting, I felt immensely cheered up.

When I left the building, I ran into the dreaded corpulent
nurse, mentioned earlier. I had known her from the Fortress days
when she was still quite harmless. "Come and have tea with me!"
she called, and I accepted her invitation. Right in front, next to
the entrance of the hospital where she could watch everything
that was going on, she had appropriated two rooms with the
help of her Russian major, and had fixed them up with the furniture left by the director of the mental hospital. Although I
knew every piece of it very well, she referred to the whole equipment as being the dying bequest of her late brother. But out of
sheer greed for her tea and a rasher of bacon, an inviting sight

in the background, I kept my mouth shut and put up with all the humbug until I had attained my object.

Near the Elizabeth Hospital is a pond, lying in the open and surrounded by high ruined walls resembling pieces of stage scenery. The water of the pond is fairly clear, and occasionally I take a dip in it. You are completely alone there, for people are no longer living in this area. Only once did I meet two children, who had also come to bathe. They jumped into the water, dipped, and spouted mouthfuls of water like fountains. It is a mystery to me where they have got all that energy. I called out to them that they should not swallow any water because of the danger of typhus. But they would not listen and only shouted: "O nuts! What does it matter of what we die. We'll not survive anyway!"

Going to the barber shop on the ground floor of our building is always rather exciting. It is the rendezvous place of the spies, and the mirrors and pieces of broken glass there have been arranged in such a way that, on looking up, one always looks into watchful eyes.

Towards the end of July my strength began to give out. I felt completely exhausted, could not breathe properly or stand for a long time, and always had to hold on to something for a support. It was nothing particular, but one day Schreiner turned up, alerted by somebody, and took me across to the Elizabeth Hospital. There I just stayed in bed, and did not care any longer about anything. I was wrapped in infinite peace. Of the two Catholic priests who were lying beside me, one was down with typhus, whereas I suspected the other was only in hiding. We looked out onto the white walls of the chapel and heard now and then faint singing. I let go completely. Schreiner looked after me; Professor Starlinger came and examined me; Sister Raphaela was a perfect angel.

After two weeks I felt much better and could begin to make myself useful around the house. The Sisters had been lucky not

to have been turned out completely nor to have had a fire; there
fore, they still have many things which are no longer available
in other places. Just before the Russians came they had flooded
the cellar, so that the canned food was at least preserved; they
had even managed to hide a cow in the upper floors for quite
some time. All this was due to their good team spirit and also to
the absence of traitors in the house.

At the end of August Schreiner disappeared. A Russian whom
he had cured of the usual disease had agreed to take him with
him. Sister Raphaela and I were the only people who knew
about it. Unfortunately, you can't say goodbye to everybody,
however much you would like to. The Russian had promised to
take him as far as Stettin; how he would go on from there we
had not the slightest idea. But, meanwhile, more than one person
had cleared out, even doctors, and we had only heard of a few
being recaptured.

I was moved into Schreiner's room. Brichzy was living next
door and doing medical duty. Second Lieutenant Ott, who had
belonged to my group in the military hospital, and Pastor Gross,
who had been a patient with me here, came over occasionally in
the evening from the hospital for contagious diseases to play skat
or chess with us, or to take part in a nocturnal banquet of potatoes which had been given to us by some Russian patients. In
one corner of the room stood a roll of canvas six feet high, which
we sometimes unrolled for fun. It was a special piece of loot, a
large oil painting from the assembly hall of the Treasury, which
Brichzy had quickly cut out of its frame when we were forced
to leave there. Although it represented, in spite of its gigantic
size, nothing but a poor little forest scene with a small pool in
the foreground—probably a symbol of our future impoverish-
ment—its sudden disappearance had extremely worried the Russians who had tried everything to discover where it was. Later
on it served more than one purpose: Erika was buried in one half

of it, and rucksacks for escapees were made out of the other half.

At noon I often went up to the roof and sunned myself. It would soon be autumn. Crows were flying over the dead city and I wondered how to catch them. Perhaps in lime traps, but they would not enter them so early. In the winter they would, but no, we would not and could not live through another winter here. People were already dying anyway. And besides the cold and all the months in which nothing was growing, not even weeds— it was unthinkable.

In the middle of September Erika, a victim of typhus, was brought to us at St. Elizabeth's. She was very ill, delirious for days, her pulse irregular. Whenever I went to see her, she had delusions, warned me against false friends who were out for my life, and implored me to escape. It was agony to see her in this condition. Fortunately, she has a bed to lie in and the Sisters take good care of her, doing all they can possibly do.

I returned to the German central hospital again, where Dr. Keuten, now recovered from typhus, had taken care of the men's ward during my absence. For a long time, he and his wife have been in danger of their lives on Schreiner's ward in St. Elizabeth's, for days almost pulseless, until they slowly began to improve. Meanwhile, two other young doctors died of typhus.

Shortly after I had taken up my duties again, Dr. Rauch came down with typhus. He was not moved but remained in his own room. Our wards, too, are so full of typhus cases that there is no point in isolating them. The only advantage is that the Russians avoid us more and more. They come up to the fifth floor only in cases of emergency and leave again very quickly. Dr. Keiten has taken over the women's ward. Giese is down with diphtheria. Our surgical nurse, Martha Wolf, died of typhus and was buried in the courtyard of the hospital. The delousing orderly, a young, husky German soldier died, too. And so many others I had known! It is impossible to name them all. Half of the Protestant pastors who had stayed in Königsberg were no longer alive; I believe that only five are left. Two of them, who have always been close friends and were living together, once came to see me: Pastor Beckmann and Pastor Müller of Haberberg. They have made definite plans to restore the church services and have got as far as seeing the town commandant on this matter.

By the beginning of October I again felt strong enough to risk a return visit to the two pastors. They are living in Ponarth, in one small room, and are looked after by a woman pastor, Pastor Sendner. They are doing a great deal of visiting and holding services. But people hardly dare to attend them, because they run the risk of having their last possessions stolen while they are not at home.

The walk to Ponarth is never without a hitch. On the wooden bridge behind the Cathedral Isle, the only bridge left over the Pregel, a sentry is posted, who is very reluctant to let you pass. Besides you have to clamber over the embankment of the main railroad station, because the underpass has collapsed. Teenage boys from Russian families, living in Ponarth in great numbers, are always lying there in ambush to attack the women struggling to get across the railroad tracks. For this reason people have to band together for mutual protection on this walk. I always carry an iron rod with me, which I brandish to the right and left.

October brought us cold and rain, and our hospital looks like an enormous gypsy camp. A smoking stovepipe sticks out of every other window. Fresh troops have arrived in the town again, and attacks and acts of violence are on the increase. Every now and then shots are fired into the windows of the hospital.

For some time reports of eating of human flesh had been received. It is impossible to wonder about it or to get excited. How shocked had we been, not so long ago, when we heard the same thing reported from the camps for Russian prisoners of war in our own country! We presumed that only Asiatics were capable of doing this. Now it was the turn of the Russians to be upset about us. Poor Dr. Rauch was their particular victim: they ordered him to do post-mortems, exhumations, to give expert opinions on pieces of meat and other ghastly matters. We were especially grateful to him when he gave a lecture on the so-called "edematose disease," in the course of the educational lectures ordered by the Russians. After the first speaker had nervously hemmed and hawed about the subject per se, Dr. Rauch demonstrated this disease, which the Russians and their friends had found so particularly interesting, on the corpse of a young girl, exhibited and described all the organs and tissues with dignified calm and knowledge of the subject, and, turning to the Russians sitting in front of him, ended with the words: "Give them enough to eat, and this disease will disappear of itself."

The rumor which had been circulating for weeks—that we would very soon be transported to the west—became in the last days more substantial. Swedish ships were said to be on their way to take us aboard, and what was more important for us, the people from the western part of the town would be the first to leave and then the rest with the inmates of the hospitals. No wonder that this news ran like wildfire through the suffering populace. And as people can never resist adding something of their own imagination, soon they knew exactly how big the ships were, what they looked like inside, what you would get to eat on board, and other details on which our primitive wish-dreams could thrive. In Pillau, where the ships were expected, the Red Cross had already set up a camp. And as the transportation to Pillau would take place under international supervision, we did not have to be afraid that the Russians would deport us to some other place.

Every day freedom became more tangible and, although not one of the earlier rumors had been confirmed, people started parting with their last reserves in order to survive in the inter-

val before their departure. The last woolen jacket was swapped
for six potatoes, the only overcoat for a can of meat; and many
objects, until now carefully hidden, came to light. The crooks
made the best of this new situation and offered cans filled with
mud and leaves, so that people, who had walked into the trap,
almost went out of their minds when they opened them.

Meanwhile winter was definitely coming on. Rain fell in torrents and the days became shorter. In the evenings, when it had
become so dark that we could no longer recognize our patients,
we met together in the small corner room where Giese and
Röckert were still living, and where the light of a small wax
candle created an almost homelike atmosphere. We only missed
Erika who was still critically ill. After we had separated, I always
liked to visit Dr. Rauch, who had a high temperature, and could
tell fascinating stories in which fact and fiction blended imper-
ceptibly, that I could listen to him for hours. His thoughts, too,
revolved round our departure, and one evening he described to
me thirteen ships, aboard which we would start our voyage in
a day or two. But in his opinion they were not at anchor in Pillau—they had already reached Königsberg, and I ought to be
able to see them from the roof. Finally he asked me to look out
for them first thing next morning and then report to him.

I always enjoyed climbing the iron stairway to the roof. Up
there I felt as free as a bird that needs only to spread his wings
to leave all the misery behind. Moreover, when I climbed up to
the little cabin on top of the elevator shaft, I had reached the
highest point in the whole area. It was true that the harbor could
be seen from there. Far away in the west, at the edge of the field
of ruins, glittered a strip of water. But however hard I tried I
could see no sign of a ship. How could it have got there anyway?
We knew that the entrance into the harbor was not yet navigable.

Dr. Rauch received my report with a tolerant smile. He thought
that I had not looked properly; some effort was needed, it was

not as easy as that. I promised him to go and look again later when the weather had cleared up, and distracted him meanwhile with the latest reports from the hospital for contagious diseases, where they had already started to work out plans for the transportation of their 2,000 typhus patients. Two men, who claimed to own a radio set, were giving running information on the position and internal arrangements of the ships in question. Professor Starlinger had asked the doctors to settle in good time who was to share the two-berth cabins with whom.

My own feelings were strangely divided. On the one hand I gave myself up, in spite of all my doubts, to the same illusions as the others, if only to avoid thinking of the winter; on the other hand, the ground on which we were living was so packed with the dead that it almost hurt me to think that our dilemma might now be solved in a happy fashion. How could we face the people we would meet, when they would ask us about those we had left behind? We should simply have to keep quiet about the sufferings of those who had died, in order not to blush from shame under their reproaches. I could hear them ask: "How is it that you have returned and even want to live? What kind of people are you? You have probably kept yourselves alive at the expense of the others!" How could we answer such accusations? I could hardly see any possibility of starting a new life without betraying the dead.

But then came a day which upset all these deliberations. On October 18, towards evening, just as I had finished the distressing round of visits, our friend Paula appeared, very excited, and whispered to me in passing: "Herr Doktor, you must get away; they are going to arrest you tomorrow. I just heard it by accident; I hope nobody has noticed it, otherwise I'll be in for it. Get everything ready; I'll come again when it is dark." She disappeared quickly and I looked after her and felt all that former energy, long since written off, come to life again. To be free once more from our gravedigger's duty, to stand once again on my own feet! I had looked forward to this moment for such a long time that now I could hardly believe it. I packed a few things in a hurry and took them over to the Gray Sisters in St. Elizabeth's. Then I told my two faithful friends. I would have loved to take them with me on my "leap into the dark." But they could not make up their minds so quickly, and still hoped, moreover, to get out legally.

When it was dark Paula came back again and told me all she knew. She had happened to hear a Russian asking to have my name spelled out, so that he could arrest me next morning. The man who had betrayed me was a man from whom I had frequently got some medicaments, which he had collected in a drawer. I knew that he was an informer, and though we had always been on good terms, I could well believe that I was on his list. But what could have moved him to deliver me up to the NKVD at this moment? Never mind—this time I was deeply grateful to him.

I had no doubts about Paula; she had been very attached to Doktora, and would go through fire and water for me. We had known her for a long time. During the last days of the Fortress period, she had shown much energy in tackling any difficult job in the municipal hospital. On the second day of the surrender, she had robbed the Russians of one of their horses, slaughtered it, cooked it, and fed the patients with it. Then she got very sick, but recovered under the care of Doktora in the Treasury. As she behaved and dressed in a fashion so that nobody knew whether she was a man or a woman, she was more successful than anyone else in leading the Russians by the nose. Everything she cadged as a result was for the benefit of those she loved. She often brought us food, and for my sake she had taken care of two young men, lying very sick on my ward, whom I had put up in a small room by themselves. I urged her once more to take good care of them.

I spent the evening with my two friends. They read to me from the last chapters of the Bible and gave me, as a farewell present, a picture they had cut from a book on Raphael: the angel delivering St. Peter from prison. Then I slept soundly, without dreaming, until it was morning.

When I woke up, everything outside was gray and shrouded in mist and rain. The few trees, still standing in the courtyard, were dropping their last leaves. I dressed without making a noise and went out into the corridor. Dr. Fincke, who had shared my room for the last two weeks, looked at me in astonishment. I hesitated for a moment, but then told him quickly what was up. I would have felt like betraying him had I not done it. In the corridor the dead of last night were lying outside the doors to the wards; they used to breathe their last most easily in the early morning hours, without any struggle—all that was lying behind them. Only a few were left for whom I still had hope, among them the two young men in Paula's care. Life was running entirely "between the lines."

The surgical nurse on the lower floor was already up and working. We exchanged a few words and I told her, too, that my time had come to an end. She understood at once and kindly wished me good luck. I did not wish to incriminate anyone else; by the time they learned of my flight, I should be far away.

When I left the building it was almost too light; but without any baggage I would probably attract no attention. And also the rain helped to veil everything. May God be with you, all you dear and dreadful people living under this roof! How many of you are still going to be among those who are carried away daily through the dark back gate, the few steps to the ruin of the Alt-rossgärter Church, and then to the left to the spot where, since

June, 5,000 inmates of this hospital had been buried in mass graves.

In passing I took leave of Doktora's grave. She had always wished to walk once more on secret byways across the East Prussian countryside, more for the sake of those roads than for the journey's end. If she had still been alive she would have walked with me now.

In St. Elizabeth's, Erika, out of bed for the first time, met me beaming with joy, steadying herself along the beds. "Look, Doctor, how well I can walk now," she called. "Yes, for your first time you are doing very well," I agreed. But then I had to tell her the reason why I had come. "Oh, that's wonderful!" she said; "I'll get dressed immediately—we can start in ten minutes." It was useless to tell her that she could not possibly walk that day for miles. "Don't worry," she said, "if I have the will, I can do anything." What should I do? As long as I had known Erika, she had sacrificed her life for others in an unparalleled way. Never had she wanted anything for herself. I had to let her go with me as far as her strength would last. It was madness, but I knew that it would be a fatal shock for her if I refused her offer. Was she, too, not already standing on the other side of the boundary which made a return hardly possible? So I agreed at the risk of wrecking the whole undertaking.

Sister Raphaela, to whom we could safely confide our most secret plans, brought my rucksack, in which she had packed more food from a secret cache. Brichzy also put in an appearance, and we waited a long time for Erika. Meanwhile, a messenger arrived from the central hospital, young Frau Passarge who was working on my ward as a maid. She had been sent to tell me to hurry, for the Russians had arrived and were looking for me.

It was almost ten when we were ready to start. Much too heavily dressed in clothes inherited from the dead, and heavily loaded as well, we set out at last. Erika had to lean her hand against the ruined wall as she walked—it was a grotesque flight. People watched us from their windows, shaking their heads. There was no doubt how it would end. Somewhere by the side of the road Erika would break down. Everyone was used to it; people were lying everywhere. I could only hope that it would happen within the town limits—there might at least be a chance that somebody passing would help her get back. A small cart, taking patients from Schönfliess to the hospital, came that way every day.

We moved at a snail's pace through the moth-eaten city, and met only a few Russians. None took any notice of us. Once again the rain was our ally. Our first major difficulty was the crossing over the Pregel: a Mongolian sentry was posted in the middle of the bridge. We had nearly passed him when he called us and asked for our papers. We showed him a chit, on which our discharge from the hospital was written in Russian, and gave one of the suburbs as our destination. He was satisfied and the next moment we were able to dive among the uniform, skeletal houses on the left bank of the river. Even there people still seemed to be living at the end of long alleys which melted away in the ruins, like wings of a stage.

At the next rise in the road Erika had to stop. She sat on a stoop, gasping for breath. I must be patient, just for a moment, she said; she would soon be able to walk on. A van drawn by two tired horses stopped in front of us. Three old men were loading parts of sledges and wagons on it, which had been lying around at the side of the road since the exodus. They took Erika on the van, and stopped every few steps, while I helped them to load the junk as best I could. This work wore off my scanty strength, and my hope to get out of the town that same day became smaller and smaller. The only advantage was that we attracted nobody's attention.

In the neighborhood of the Friedländer Gate the street became more crowded; a few almost undamaged houses were standing there, and Russian troops were busy turning out the people who had made them their temporary homes. It had happened to them again and again for the last six months. They were allowed to take with them as much as they could carry; the rest had to be left to the soldiers, who were moving in. No sign of emotion showed in the almost frozen, masklike faces, and to a person who had not himself experienced to what low level human beings had been gradually degraded, it must have seemed quite natural to treat them like cattle. Now they were standing on the street: women whose age was difficult to determine, clothed in sacks, their legs and feet swollen to deformity and wrapped in rags. There was nothing left for them but to move into the huts of the garden lots, now for winter. The Russians had meanwhile lost all interest in them. Perhaps they would stay here only temporarily. Probably there was no peace for them either.

When the street left the town in the direction of Löwenhagen our van turned left; it apparently belonged to a farm where the Russians had concentrated people for agricultural work. We got down from the van and continued our way on foot. My plan was to get as quickly as possible to that part of East Prussia which we had heard had been ceded to the Poles. It would probably be easier for me to go underground there. I had been told that the Polish sector began immediately after Preussisch Eylau, but nobody knew for certain. In any case, I thought it advisable first to proceed in a southerly direction. In Eylau we would have to be careful not to end up in the detention camp. As far as I could judge, it was the principal danger point.

In the middle of the suburb of Schönfliess Erika's strength finally gave out. She dropped down on a heap of stones and could not get up again. Once more the dead weight of human misery pressed down on me like a wet sack. Was this not worse than murder? I was almost on the point of turning back and facing up to the consequences when a Russian approached us. I thought he was going to arrest us, but he only asked the way and walked on. For a short while I stood waiting, fully prepared to yield to the extreme fatigue of my heart. But meanwhile Erika had pulled herself together and said, almost like a command: "Now you must go on, Doctor, I only wanted to see you out of the town. Remember me to the people and tell them they should search their hearts, so that what happened to us will not happen to them too."

While she was speaking, it suddenly came to my mind that I had been haunted for days by an old, glorious song: "And if you don't stake your life in the strife. . . ." I had rediscovered it only recently by chance. What was left for me to say or to protest? What was I waiting for? Wasn't an angel already standing between Erika and me? Slowly I began to walk, at first reluctantly, then faster and faster. Once I looked back—there she sat, upright, waving to me. It looked like a gesture of triumph.

· 6 ·

GRASNITZ
October 19, 1945 to January 20, 1946

October 19, 1945

Before me the rain-wet road to the south. All at once I felt
fresh energy in my deadly tired bones and my feet moved rhyth-
mically of their own accord. "On, on! ere your courage fails you!"
It is in this mood that a man runs into life, the incredible miracle
when God gives him another chance, after he has died many
deaths. Soaked to the skin, the rucksack pressing on scrawny
shoulders, both shoes competing in chafing the feet—what
could stop a man who was heading for freedom? But slowly,
slowly, for Russians were coming my way again. "Go on, my
dear, they don't look at you!"—these and similar magic words I
muttered involuntarily to myself, while my free stride changed
into a weak-kneed limp. They passed me. I had been lucky again;
but I should have to keep up this mimicry in my bearing and
gait for quite some time, because men of my age were nowhere
at large hereabout. If I did not want to attract attention, I
would better walk in the middle of the road. Back roads would
certainly not be advisable in the daytime. A car was approaching,
this time from behind, which was more unpleasant. But fortunately they drove at such speed on the smooth road that they
would probably hate stopping. The same thing happened time
and again. Russian cars raced past me from both directions. Perhaps they really did not see me.

Gradually the town receded farther and farther behind me. The countryside was completely deserted. In the fields to the right and left unharvested grain, dripping wet, stretched as far as the eye could see like a gray-green felt blanket. Bomb craters in the road, mangled trees, military vehicles in the ditches, burned out villages. For a short while I took refuge from the wind and the rain in a dilapidated house. Something stirred close to me. I heard noises and discovered some ragged people with three children standing around half asleep. They scrutinized me with hostility. Apparently, they had tried to get out of Königsberg and were caught here by the Russians who prevented them from moving on. Now they could neither go forward nor backward. Their last food had been a few potatoes, which they had been allowed to take from a truck stopping here a short while ago. I did not ask what they had had to pay for them, because I could guess from the manner in which they spoke of this incident that obviously the women had had to foot the bill. Who in the name of Heaven can still find pleasure in such ghostlike creatures? If this is to continue, there will be no peace for anybody.

The next place I reached was Wittenberg. Even there I did not at first detect anybody, until turning round a corner, I saw several parked cars. It was too late for me to dodge them, for at the same moment a Russian appeared who was evidently searching the empty houses. Again my sang-froid served me; I limped on with difficulty and stopped beside the trucks. They were full of captured German soldiers who came from a camp near Tapiau. For the last three days they had been driving around to look for potatoes and were now on their way to Preussisch Eylau. The guards had not found anything here either and were climbing on the trucks again. One of them looked across at me: "What sort of a guy is that?" I heard him say. I played a bold game and asked him if he would give me a lift to Preussisch Eylau. He motioned to me with his hand and I got in. Before we started, the drivers tossed the stubs of their fags, rolled in newspaper, to the prisoners who had been waiting for them and caught them eagerly. They all seemed to be on the best terms, provided you did not draw any comparisons with earlier times.

Secretly, I had a good look at my scrubby compatriots to find out which of them I could perhaps take with me should a chance of escape present itself. Unfortunately, they were all too weak and their shoes would not have lasted. They plied me with questions while we were racing at a crazy speed across the waste land, but I answered evasively. There was no point telling them more than they knew.

Eylau came in sight. A turnpike. At the entrance to the town the truck stopped abruptly and the guards climbed down and conferred with the sentry. I pointed to one of the empty houses as being mine, and they let me get out and go into it. At once, I ran out by the backdoor, and was soon out of sight, running behind trees and shrubs along a narrow field path into the open country, through wire fences and hedges, past a small manor farm, and then to the left through tall grass until I came to a hidden ditch which gave me sufficient cover. For the time being I was safe.

At a stone's throw from my hiding place a road ran westward. The rain had stopped; it was beginning to get dark. I took out my little book with the watchwords to write a few notes into it. The text for the day was: "And Noah found grace in the eyes of the Lord." How infinitely comforting to feel protected. While I was writing my notes, my motor column rolled past. They probably had not been lucky here in their search for potatoes either. With a grateful heart I watched them leave. They had helped me along a good part of my way. Then, with a great rushing sound, growing louder and louder, a flock of starlings, thousands upon thousands, flew over my head; they rose, fell, and were soon lost to sight over the forest in the west. Slowly the cloud bank parted and single stars appeared in the gap. A milky light told me that soon the moon would appear. Again there was a loud noise on the road. From the direction of the forest came a wagon full of drunken Russians at a furious gallop; one was hanging over the side, another shouting and flogging the horses. When they were gone it was night.

I got up and sneaked like a drowned cat through the tall grass, crossed the road, and wriggled on the other side through a tangled rye-field to the nearest rise in the ground. The moon had suddenly come out completely, and the whole region was now lit up far too brightly. A sandy country lane with a few willows here and there led me on. But then I had to turn left again through old standing grain, meadows, and reedy ditches, for I did not want to lose my southerly direction.

Soon I could no longer ignore the fact that it was growing increasingly lighter in front of me. Could it already be the Russian-Polish frontier? Nobody knew what it looked like. I imagined myself crawling through barbed wires in glaring floodlights. But when I came nearer I saw that it was only a brightly lighted village which I could avoid. A brook wound between elder and poplar trees, and I found the bridge, then turned directly to the right, leaving the last houses far to the left. All the same a dog had noticed me; it started barking and came nearer. We both ran through wire fences and paddocks. While I was running I took the surgical knife out of my briefcase and threatened the dog. It finally turned back. Behind me, in the village, shots were fired, but I had reached the forest.

After a brief pause to catch my breath I kept on trudging the muddy forest paths. The moon was shining between the trees and made the reedy grass glitter like silver. Where the wood ended I hit upon the highway which extended across the whole country, recognizable from a distance by its ancient trees. I could see from the stars that its direction was just the one I wanted to take, but, not wishing to run into the arms of a sentry, I thought it better to go across country. This meant walking through desolate fields, water courses, fences and hedges, and later on along slippery field paths, past solitary farms and abandoned villages. Nowhere a sign of life. Just as I was passing a deserted settlement my legs gave out. I stopped in front of one of the small houses, reconnoitered, looked for footprints—there could not have been anybody here for a long time. The moon was hidden again. Rain squalls raced up the bare hillside. It must have been after midnight. The wind rattled in the rafters. When I opened the door of the cottage something collapsed inside with a big crash. There was a shambles of boards, broken glass and paper. I lay down on a door, which had been taken off its hinges, and tried to sleep; but it was impossible. The shutters banged incessantly in the storm, and the garden gate creaked on its hinges. In the darkness I could not see anything, and expected somebody to come in at any moment. I could no longer bear staying in this depressing place, even its name unknown to me. Although the signposts still existed, the letters had faded out.

Slowly I found it more and more difficult to keep my balance. The mud was ankle deep, and the water had formed large puddles in the roads. Probably all the drains and sewers were choked up. I was on the verge of despair when I noticed that I had lost my briefcase with some dry bread in it; I loathed having to walk all the way back to look for it. Fortunately, I soon found it under the last signpost, which I had tried to decipher with the help of a match. I was so overjoyed that I took a long swig from the canteen that Sister Raphaela had filled with delicious lemonade.

Soon I was drawn back to the main highway, which I had kept in sight. Nearby whitish spots shimmered through the morning mist—no doubt, a large place. Slowly I drew nearer, all the time expecting to hear a sentry move. I heard the welcoming rustle of old trees, then, suddenly and ghostlike a church clock in the town struck three. Cautiously I crawled on my stomach across the road, where I discovered a large, freshly painted signpost. Gradually I deciphered the Russian letters: LANDSBERG. Landsberg! I could hardly believe it. I could not have hit it better, because the road to Wormditt forked off here. I knew the place well. And there was also a second post bearing Russian letters: WORMDITT. It was too far for me today, but the direction was the one I wanted.

Inside the town something was stirring. With a loud rattling, which echoed from invisible walls, an antiquated steam tractor advanced slowly and passed me on the highway. I squatted on the marshy ground next to a small meadow, where I discovered several rows of potatoes. I dug up a few and put them in my briefcase, wondering who might have planted them in this spot. Certainly nobody in a position to harvest them, or they would have been taken out long ago.

Apparently the Russians did not often drive to Wormditt. The road looked almost untraveled. All the better for me—I was no longer capable of walking through the fields. Quite unconcerned about the noise my shoes made, I let the soles crunch on the paved road. The moon was now very low in the west. The cloud bank from under which it would appear at any minute grew more and more light. Another few steps and I started back in alarm. A black monster barred my way. For some minutes I waited in breathless suspense, but nothing moved. I walked cautiously around it to get to the bottom of the mystery from the side, and saw another black colossus standing close behind. Then it dawned on me that they were two heavy tanks, shell-battered long ago, and now standing there like frozen elephants. But even so, I could not pass them without feeling my hair standing on end. After some time the same sight, then the road was free.

Later I passed a village with fairly intact houses, standing far apart on both sides of the road under old chestnut trees. I took off my shoes to avoid making any noise and carried them in my hand. Neither man nor beast stirred. But then I saw two little red flags on a garden gate—it was the Russian guardhouse. The sentry should have seen me for quite some time. Why didn't he come forth from under the tree? He was probably in the house and asleep. After all, who would be wandering through the night?

After another few miles a road branched off to the left. Hanshagen. Two miles, the signpost said. The name sounded promising, and I decided to get there before daybreak. I found it more and more difficult to walk. The tendons at the back of my knees were creaking and would not stretch. Up another small hill and then the road finally ran down into a quiet village.

October 20

Hanshagen, my salvation. No Russians in the village. The command post was in Petershagen, quite some distance away. Now and then they came over from there to rummage about in the houses. Some time ago Poles had turned up but had disappeared again. Only a few women and children were living here, most of them unrelated. Some of them had grouped themselves into families. Others had been detained on their flight, and some were stragglers who had happened to join them. Not one of the original inhabitants was left.

I was lying in a real bed which belonged to two old women living in a house somewhat off the road. My wet things were drying over the kitchen stove. In the front room, facing the village road, they carefully watched to see if any Russians were coming. After I had left my observation post in the loft of an empty house, they had received me so unhesitatingly and kindly that I hardly needed to be afraid of betrayal. My hostesses were occupied with the cleaning of mushrooms. They told me that

mushrooms were unusually plentiful this fall, and that at present
the whole village was feeding on them. The people here certainly
did not look as undernourished as those in Königsberg.

Now and then I heard a scratching noise above me. "Are they
rats?" I asked. No, they had two chickens hidden in the loft. I
almost could not believe that there were still chickens. The last
one I had seen was half a year ago at the very moment it was
killed. After chasing it around for a long time, a Russian had
thrown himself flat upon it. I wondered what tricks the two old
women had used to manage the survival of their birds up to now.

At noon they gave me a meal of mushrooms. Afterwards I
tried to sleep, but I could not. The stress had been too great.
Only towards evening did my limbs become slightly relaxed. I
kept my knees in a stretched position as long as possible, so that
they would not stiffen when bent.

At nightfall I got up and dressed. My clothes were almost dry.
Fortunately, the Russians had not been in the village that day.
I contributed to our common supper some dripping out of a
screw-topped glass—it represented my emergency ration. We ate
our mushroom dish near the stove, and the two women told me
about their past experiences. When the Russians arrived one of
them broke her femur, and the other took care of her. They
had remained together since then and had had no news of their
families since they had been forcibly separated.

I told them a little about myself. Meanwhile the room had
become flooded with light. The full moon looked over the roof
of the barn and was rising in the cloudless sky. I hurried to get
going, although I hated to leave this warm refuge. Before parting we gave thanks to God for His mysterious ways, and when
I left the house the two women were kneeling beside their chairs.

A stormy night. The moon raced through white wisps of
clouds. The treeless road to Wormditt seemed endless. In Frauendorf I heard chains rattling and a dog barked. I walked as fast

as possible. Everything was quiet in the houses. Later the road ran under trees and the ground was already covered with yellow maple leaves. I trudged from stone to stone, from tree to tree, counting my steps, and having to lie down more and more frequently. I knew that I would not get far that night. Only the cold forced me to go on.

The next village looked very suspicious. I waited until a cloud had covered the too bright moon, took off my shoes and walked noiselessly along the narrow lane between the houses; I could almost touch the windows on my right and left. And then I again saw two little red flags on a tree. Somebody only needed to look out a window to see me. The way these people slept was ridiculous. Go on, go on, you must not get weak! Perhaps the whole village was holding its breath until I had passed. Where the village ended, the road made a wide turn to the right, and I was in open country again. There the fields were also lying waste, but in some parts of the meadows someone seemed to have made hay. Close to the road stood a few ricks, no doubt from last summer.

Then I came through a wood, the first time in the course of this night and of the journey up to now. At last I could proceed without caution, because there was enough cover to the right and left in case danger should threaten. Slowly the distance to Wormditt became shorter. I was determined to get there before daybreak. When at last I turned into the avenue of trees which I knew terminated at the town, a light, early morning mist was in the air. And finally the railroad station emerged on my left.

I left the road which ran under the railroad line, because the underpass seemed too precarious, and walked along the embankment until I came to an empty shed beside the tracks. There was no light in the station and nothing suggested that trains were running. Nevertheless, I thought it advisable to keep away from it. A deep gravel pit, running for a few hundred yards beside the tracks, brought me safely to a spot where I could cross the tracks without any risk. Now I was on familiar terrain. The forest—a miracle that it was still standing. A whole era must have gone by since I had last been here, just after Christmas, 1944.

October 21

By the time it was light I was sitting in the main stand under a spruce tree whose branches drooped to the ground. I had filled the gaps with other branches. In front of me was the railroad line to Mohrungen, without any tracks—a fact I noticed with satisfaction, because there would be no train running through this lovely forest for a long time.

What a radiant autumn day! Most of the trees in the main stand still had all their leaves. I picked a few edible mushrooms and ate them raw with sugar and dried bread. In a strange way I felt extremely happy. During the last part of the journey my misgivings had already vanished. Someone seemed to walk ahead of me and to watch over my way. It had started at dawn when I had seen a dark object in my path which rather scared me. I was about to dodge it when I heard a voice saying quite distinctly: "Go ahead, but do not get alarmed when you see beside the bush in front of you a dark pool, from which some wild ducks will fly up at once." And then I walked up to the bush confidently, twenty or thirty steps, saw the pool and the ducks flying up—it was no longer a surprise but the fulfilment of something which had happened before. Afterwards I walked on like a person who looks into a picture book, printed on transparent paper, and knows before turning the page what he will see on the next. Although we may experience our times like a disconnected sequence of harmonies and dissonances, there is nevertheless a melody hidden in them. God alone knows it and anticipates the last note when He intones the first. And sometimes He lets us sing with Him for a short while.

For the afternoon I had chosen another spot and lay down there at the edge of a plantation of young trees, gazing into the deep blue autumn sky. Gossamer floated past me, jays flew from tree to tree, golden leaves were falling. And this was Poland now? I was thinking of all those whose homes had been here only a year ago. What wouldn't they give to be here with me, even for a moment!

In the evening it became cold. I could hear voices from far away. Children marched along the highway, singing a strange wild war song. I waited until the sounds had died away toward Wormditt, and then set out on my third night of wandering.

Near the Oberheide railroad station I took the road to Mohrungen. This time I walked still slower, and the forest seemed to have no end. The long bridge across the valley of the Passarge, of course, no longer exists. A winding road, worn out by tanks, ran down the steep slope to the river, climbing up again on the other side. The railroad bridge, although rather shaky, was still there and apparently used by pedestrians. I stopped in the middle of it and sent many silent questions downstream with the waves. What would it look like now, where this river meandered through forests and parks? Were the beautiful old houses still standing, houses in which generations could grow up in peace and cultivate the soil? It was hardly conceivable that they could have withstood the bulldozer of war. And would it not be the same with the region from where the river originated? How many did I know who had lived there and loved their homeland! Now this stream of life was flowing through a devastated country, which probably none of the old eyes would ever see again.

The next railroad station, Sponthenen, had been destroyed by fire. Walking became more and more difficult; in fact, I could no longer do it. At a bend in the road I sat down and began examining my bag, because I definitely had to discard some of my ballast. While doing this I unexpectedly pricked myself on the point of a sharp knife. I was bleeding profusely and this pepped me up considerably. I packed everything together again and went on until the defiant tower of Liebstadt rose in front of me. To the right, on the other side of the river, I saw a faint light; otherwise all was dark and quiet in the town. Many houses were in ruins, others still standing. On one of the latter two little red flags—all this drifted past me as though I would dream it.

Once beyond the town I had to make a decision—my bag or myself. The tendons at the back of my knees were on the point of breaking. I sorted out some heavy objects, which had been intended for barter, and the greater part of my surgical instruments as well, and left them lying on the grass. The blades of the knives glittered provokingly in the moonlight. Whoever found them would be delighted. But it was worthwhile: walking had become much easier.

Around midnight I arrived at the spot where the road branched off to Ponarien. Surrounded by its fence, the old signpost was still standing on its triangle of grass—exactly as before. For quite some time I debated if I should try to get as far west as possible, or if I should turn off here and see if my sister and my brother-in-law's house was still standing, and what was going on there. It was not very far from here—less than an hour's walk, and I might not have another chance. All around me the grass and the leaves glittered and sparkled. I ran my hand over them —it was hoar frost. It meant that I should look for a place to sleep; moreover, my curiosity was too great.

Before the village of Royen the road turned to the left toward the forest. I noticed footprints of women, and in the fields the first signs of cultivation I had seen since leaving Königsberg.

At the edge of the forest a field had even been plowed. Ducks flew up from the carp ponds in the paddock, just as they used to do. I made a last stop at the tall beech tree on the road to Hermenau, wondering if ever before anyone in my situation had leaned against its huge trunk. I felt certain that it had given confidence and hope to many a man without his knowing it.

A silvery moon. Close to me, in the avenue of chestnuts, single leaves, frozen stiff, detached themselves from the branches, brushed one another with a scraping sound and fell to the ground. In the silence of the night I seemed to hear pigeon-like nightbirds rustling in the tree tops and I kept trying to spot them.

It was not far to the manor, only a few steps. I hid my bag in the shrubbery of the head forester's lodge and advanced cautiously under cover of the old trees. Wide tracks indicated that people were driving here with thick rubber tires. I was prepared for a sentry. But even here nothing stirred, neither man nor beast. The houses to the right and left of the gateway stood there as in the past, and back there—good heavens—the old manor house, wide, white, and completely intact. And the park was there too, and the mirror-like surface of the lake behind the trees. I seemed to hear a mocking voice: "What more do you want? Isn't everything in perfect order?" Oh, never had there been such an enchanting night, not in a hundred years! It was only difficult to realize that you had to behave like a thief.

I did not risk knocking on a door, but looked around for an observation post. In doing so I came upon two red American tractors, evidently the originators of the wide tire tracks. The smithy behind them was not locked. I glanced at the forge, but unfortunately there was no fire, not even to warm my hands. I sat down on the anvil and waited.

After a short while I was roused from my nap by a slight noise. I jumped up and pressed myself close to the dark wall.

A footstep before the door; it opened noiselessly. A man with a black beard stood outside in the moonlight. He hesitated for a moment and then shot a question into the darkness—in German! I moved away from the wall and came forward. He retreated a step, looked me over carefully and quickly grasped the situation. Inside the smithy I explained to him what had brought me here. He told me that I occupied the customary seat of the night watchman, who had apparently not waited to be relieved but had gone home earlier to his warm bed. The tractors belonged to the Poles who had been farming here since last summer. The manager of the estate lived in the manor house. I had been lucky not to have run into him, because he had planned to stalk a wild boar tonight near the big beech tree.

The general situation was very bleak my informant said. He himself was not from here, but he could not escape because his wife and his six children had also been detained here. He had grown a beard to look older, and this was the reason the Russians had not carried him off to Russia as they had the others. I asked him about the man whom he was supposed to relieve, and heard that it was Preuss, an old family servant. "What! Preuss is still here? Can you take me to him?" Cautiously we sneaked up to his window and tapped on it several times. The shutters were opened and there was Preuss standing in his nightshirt, his hair snow-white. A wave of warmth flowed from him to me. He opened his eyes wide in surprise, when he recognized me. I ran quickly for my bag in the shrubbery, and then I crept into his warm bed with a feeling of indescribable gratitude.

October 22

It may have been around four in the morning—Preuss and his wife had moved a little to one side of the bed to make room for me—when Preuss told me roughly the following: "On Janu-

ary 23 the Russians came. They robbed us, of course, of everything and were after the women, but otherwise the first three
weeks were not too bad. Then came the Kommissars and rounded
up all the people of the neighborhood, questioned them and took
the younger ones with them to Russia. Frau Gräfin [my brother-
in-law's mother] stayed here and at first was treated quite well.
She even managed to protect the girls many times. Then the
Russians ordered her to clean their rooms. That, too, was not
the worst. But being dragged around on the roads was too much
for her. She got sick when all that started. Near Reichau she
refused to walk any further, and they shot her there in a small
wood. Somebody wrote on the backboard of a sledge, lying there
in the ditch: 'Here lies the countess from Ponarien.'

"The evening before the Russians came, Frau von Stein [my
aunt] and her daughter arrived here on foot from the Allenstein Gestapo prison. She wore her convict's clothes and trousers,
and the Russians did not pay any special attention to her. They
only asked her 'Man or woman?' Her daughter was carried off
and we never heard anything of her again. Frau von Stein stayed
here and looked after the cattle, first here and then in Reichau.
Eight of us men lived there with her in a cellar. On the fifth
of June, in the early morning, she disappeared. She wanted to
try and get home. Since then we have heard nothing. She may
still be there. Later they let us come back here. The few Poles
who are here now want to start farming. We have always had
something to eat, at least potatoes. Nobody has actually starved.
But during the summer nineteen people died of typhus. I am
keeping a diary about everything. One forgets so quickly, and
later nobody will ever know what really happened."

He also asked me about my sister and my brother-in-law.
The Russians had told people here that they had been caught
while escaping and had been brought into a camp, my sister
to Hohenstein and my brother-in-law to Russia. I told him that

none of this was true. Both had got through to Holstein. I had, of course, heard nothing of them since. Preuss told me that they had both left on horseback when the Russians were almost in the village. By that time it had been much too late for the trek, and a few people, among them the forester, had finally got away on foot. In the beginning Preuss himself had been harassed by the Russians, because he refused to tell them where the "gold" was buried. Even among our own countrymen had been some unpleasant customers who had tried immediately to ingratiate themselves with the Russians at the expense of their fellow beings. But they too had soon been carried off to Russia.

I spent the day in bed to nurse my aching legs, and even slept for a few hours. Nobody had noticed my presence. The blackbearded man had kept his mouth shut. But I could not stay any longer without endangering the people here, and I was firmly resolved to walk to Grasnitz the following night and to look for my aunt there. The thought of seeing her again made me quite restless with happiness and anxiety.

After a good meal of potatoes and bread I was on my way around half past ten. It was another radiant, glittering moonlit night. Just behind the head forester's lodge a herd of wild pigs trotted leisurely across the road, their black backs gleaming like silver. Here, too, everything seemed to be in perfect order. I passed through Reichau and turned right onto the highway. Several times I caught a glimpse of the Narien Lake until the road turned to the left in Willnau where no guards were to be seen; I felt increasingly confident. I had plenty of time, the whole night for a distance of less than fifteen miles.

Slowly I crossed the magnificent Tomlack Forest, making frequent and long stops. When the road came out into the open again, it ran downhill in a wide curve, bypassing a small round lake which lay like a mirror at my feet. On its far side were two farmsteads, thatched with straw, and overhung by silver-gray willows. The ridges of their roofs were bathed in moonlight.

Gallinden, another straggling village, lay before me. When I was in the middle of the village, a shadow detached itself from a dark doorway and stepped out in front of the white wall of the house. As there was no way out on either side, I calmly walked up to him. He was an old, gaunt man in civilian clothes and carried a shotgun. I asked him the way to Locken and pointed to the Red Cross on my left arm. He did not understand my gesture and looked at me with suspicion, even with some alarm. Evidently he was alone on guard duty. I made a few vague gestures and simply walked on. He was not sure if he should arrest me or not, ran for a while beside me but then dropped behind. I made as long strides as I could until I was out of his sight, and then ran to the end of the village where I hid behind a haystack in case he should follow me. But nothing happened and I soon walked on.

To be on the safe side I avoided Brückendorf. Beyond it, the road to Locken was covered with newly fallen leaves, which crackled at every step as if I were walking on parchment. Just as I passed by Ramten a single shot fell quite close to me. I thought it might be better if I walked at the side of the road, so that I could take cover in the bushes if necessary. Later I took a short cut on a field path which swerved to the left before Locken, and then joined again the road to Biessellen. Lights were burning in Locken and I could hear loud voices. It would soon be morning.

Worleinen was badly damaged. Again parts of wagons and sledges were lying along the road, and the trees showed marks of the impact of shelling. I suddenly had the feeling that I was being followed. I hid in a bush beside the road and heard hurried footsteps nearing. Two men passed, pushing their bicycles. I followed them at some distance. On my left I could see the

Eissing Lake, and the first flush of dawn on its surface. The sawmill seemed to be deserted.

Again the road crossed the Passarge, now far upstream, where, hidden under linden and alder trees, it flows from one lake into another. I should have loved to walk from here to Grasnitz, a twenty minutes' walk through the forest; but very likely my aunt would not be there but in Langgut, the next village on the road, which formerly belonged to Grasnitz. I decided first to look for her there.

There were lights in Langgut, and the farmyard was alive with many voices. There was no point in hesitating too long. I walked along the back of the first laborer's cottage and rapped on each window. The first two figures who appeared drew back at once when they saw me and did not show up again; but the third, a young woman, stayed put, looked me over, seemed to recognize me, put her finger to her lips and opened the window. I had seen her eyes before. "Is Frau von Stein here?" I asked. "No, she is in Grasnitz. But do not go through the farm, because of the Polish soldiers; better go around by the sawmill—nothing can happen there. She lives in the gardener's cottage."

And so I walked back to the mill again, along the lake and through the forest. I was so excited that I started running, and my legs almost gave out. The thought that after all that had happened, I should find a human being who belonged to me was like a foretaste of meeting in Heaven.

One last stop for breath. The first rays of the rising sun flashed up over the lake. The avenues of chestnut trees were hanging like golden bridges from the forest up to the hill which was my objective, still hidden from my sight by the old linden trees on its slope. But then I arrived and saw to my great surprise the undamaged manor house on the hill. Deeply moved, I walked up the wide paved road, past an empty Russian sentry box with a turnpike, and stopped in front of the gardener's lodge.

Once more I drew a deep breath before I opened the door and entered the room. Three women were sitting at the kitchen table. For one moment we looked inquiringly at one another, then one of them jumped up, and we were in each other's arms.

End of October

Heavenly security! Up in the attic my aunt had fixed a guest-room for any emergency with furniture she had pulled out of all the dump piles in the neighborhood. I stayed in bed and rested my feet, while she came up from time to time to bring me something to eat, or to sit at my bedside and tell me about the events of last summer.

As I had heard before from Preuss, she had bolted from Reichau in the early morning of the fifth of June and walked to Grasnitz. A nail in her shoe had made her journey quite painful; but she had not dared to take off the shoe to see what was wrong, because she was afraid that she would not be able to go on. When she arrived here, she found most of the old tenants alive, and had been warmly received by Fräulein Jokuteit, her former housekeeper, who was living in the gardener's cottage with the gardener's wife and two eighty-year-old spinsters who had formerly belonged to the household of my aunt. Moreover, they had taken in a stranger, whose frostbitten feet had prevented him from walking on when the Russians arrived.

The other people had not known at first how to treat my aunt. They were probably not too happy that she had returned because, under the pressure of circumstances, a certain *modus vivendi* had been established between them and the Russians and Poles, which now seemed to become a problem by her sudden appearance. For that reason they kept aloof. But slowly they had become used to seeing her around. She went to work with the other women and received, as they did, flour and a quart of skim milk. At first she had to work in her own house, where the commandant was living with a certain Frau Schmidt whom he had brought with him from Pomerania. She had started immediately cleaning in a manner which Frau Schmidt did not like at all. In any case, she was soon dismissed. Meanwhile the couple had moved to Langgut, and the manor house was unoccupied. Nothing but an enormous wardrobe had been left. Everything else was lying on rubbish piles, or was scattered in the neighborhood. Some of the furniture was still standing in a shed in Langgut and was gradually used by the commandant as firewood. He always insisted on chopping it up personally.

The Russians had farmed here until summer. In June, hundreds of dead cows, lying around everywhere, were dragged off and thrown into the ponds until they overflowed. Then they harvested hay and grain. Meanwhile the Poles had taken over the management of the estate. At first nothing reasonable had been done; but when it started freezing, they finally began to dig up the potatoes. Up to then all the women had been sent into the forest to gather mushrooms for Warsaw. They liked doing it because it gave them a chance to gather other matters for their own use. The mushrooms, which were still plentiful, had been piled up in a shed, several yards high, and had been left there to rot.

In September my aunt had been in Januschau once to try to get news about my mother. She boarded a freight train to Deutsch Eylau and walked from there. Arriving late in the evening, she spent the night under a tree in the avenue and went next morning into the village. There were only Russians who took her into their house, gave her something to eat and wanted to keep her there to work for them. She managed, however, to get away, to run straight back to Eylau and board the next freight train. In the forest near Jablonken she had to jump out of the train because a Russian attacked her. She reached home in the evening with a sprained ankle.

My aunt had no complaints to make about the way the Poles treated her. They had beaten her once, and it had not been pleasant. But otherwise all her experiences until now had been a "picnic" compared with the six months in the Gestapo prison in Allenstein. Besides, how beautiful was old Grasnitz this fall, more beautiful than ever! Incredible the colors! And the game was not shy at all. Only recently a wild pig had come past the house with her young, and had stayed for quite some time in the grass under the window.

As for myself, my aunt thought it would be best if I stayed here for the time being. It would be managed somehow. The Poles possibly would be glad to know that a doctor was nearby. There wasn't one in the whole neighborhood.

My aunt did not know anything about her family. She had only heard that people had seen her husband and her two daughters in a camp, and that they had sent her greetings. Her sons had been on active service when the war ended. We gave up torturing ourselves with conjectures about the possible fate of those we loved; for the moment all we needed to be happy was our being together.

After two days in bed my feet were almost all right, and I could put on shoes. My presence here was not yet known, for neither the commandant nor the Polish soldiers, stationed in Langgut, had made inquiries about me; but, prepared for any surprise, I kept in the background and stayed at home while the women went to work in Langgut as usual.

When I came down in the morning, I always found the floors of the room and kitchen scrubbed, the barrel filled with water, the stockings worn the day before, darned, and breakfast on the table. After breakfast I stayed alone with old Ili, the totally confused survivor of the two spinsters, and tried to make myself useful. I chopped wood, carried up water from the small creek some thirty yards further down the hill, and boiled potatoes—everything strictly in accordance with my aunt's directions. It was important to remember how and when the fire should be kindled in the kitchen stove, how many pieces of wood should be put in for the baking of bread, not to throw out the potato water, needed for the soup, and many other matters which had proved to be necessary for keeping ourselves alive.

Towards evening I went out to meet the women coming from their work. Every day I walked a little farther, because in the long run my presence here could not be kept a secret forever. Each woman brought home two baskets of potatoes from the harvest. We emptied them in the cellar in two different heaps, strictly separated according to their quality, in order to introduce some variety to our daily menu. Then we ate supper at the kitchen table: potatoes and a kind of pumpkin soup, while the wet stockings were drying by the stove.

During the last days of October the villagers were in great excitement about rumors of a transport to the west. Nobody knew if it would be advisable to apply for it. These transports involved hardships and dangers. People were not allowed to take anything with them and were moreover stripped to the skin and robbed more than once on the way. The journey, by cattle truck, would in any case last several days, if not weeks, and there was no possibility of keeping warm or getting anything to eat. Besides, there was no guarantee that you would really arrive in the west. You might even end up in one of the dreaded labor camps.

For all these reasons my aunt thought it wiser to wait for a while. Nevertheless, we decided to try and get some information about the particulars of the transport, and, therefore, we walked the three miles to Biessellen which was on the railroad line. On our way there across the forest we came upon two poaching dogs which had just mangled a roe deer. We succeeded in chasing them away and tied the deer to a tree, to be picked up on our way home.

In Biessellen we first called on an old couple called S. The wife was well informed, thanks to her knowledge of Polish, and warned us urgently against applying for the transport. After she had given us something to eat, we went to the Polish registration office. I did not go in but hid nearby. My aunt went into the barrack and came out after some time, accompanied by a Polish woman who was talking to her excitedly. They came to my hiding place and I was introduced to the lady, known as "Doktourka," a former nurse who had taken it upon herself to attend to the sick in this region. When she heard that I was a physician, she wanted me to come to Biessellen and assist her. I gave an evasive answer, for I could not yet see how this could be done. In any case, my existence couldn't be concealed any longer now, and I was curious how all this would work out. On our way back we took the poached deer with us, to be shared with those who, like us, had seen no meat for ages, for want of "connections."

At the beginning of November the rumored transport actually left. Trucks drew up suddenly, and those who had applied had to get in. We later heard that several hundred people had assembled in Osterode, and also heard that there had soon been trouble. In any case, we were glad not to have been among them.

After the village had calmed down again, the women went back to work. In spite of warnings, an order was issued to cart the good potatoes from the field into the empty cowbarn where they were piled up to the ceiling. As they would inevitably freeze there, the women did their best to carry away as many as possible, semi-officially, into their own cellars. For the same reason we secretly made a small private potato pit on the Fünf-lindenberg. Before sunrise we dug an oblong hole and filled it with almost a ton of the choicest potatoes, put straw and earth

on top and slightly camouflaged the whole. Just as we had
finished, two Polish soldiers walked along the ridge between
the fields. They hesitated for a moment, apparently puzzled,
but then walked on.

That same evening three soldiers came in a very rickety cart
to take me to Langgut. I went with them quite calmly but was
much relieved when I heard what it was all about. Frau Schmidt
had, for obvious reasons, taken something that had not agreed
with her and wanted my advice. The Poles didn't attach great
importance to the matter; they even brought me back in their
cart.

The fact that I had been consulted in such a casual manner,
encouraged me to move around more freely. I established my
contact with Doktourka and besides visited sick people in the
surrounding villages. Soon my day was organized: I was in
Biessellen in the morning and saw patients in the small dispensary set up by Doktourka, received a meal at noon, and
then visited patients in the villages on the left and right banks
of the Passarge. I gradually became known and was allowed to
go my way unhindered. Even the dreaded militia consulted me
occasionally, which, of course, considerably strengthened my
security.

All the same, this period, too, was not lacking in elements of
suspense (uncertainty) to which our small and vulnerable
existence was exposed. When we separated in the morning, we
never knew for certain if we would see each other again. I
walked down the steep hillside, across the footbridge of the
creek from which we drew our water, to the forest and then
along the shore of the lake upward until I came to the highway. There I had to be careful, because Russian troops might
be passing. Leaving the forest I followed an overhead power
line for one and a half miles across a field, which brought me
directly to the house of the old couple S., who had received my

aunt and me so kindly when we first visited them. They would see me coming from some distance, and always had something warm for me to eat—sufficient reason for remembering them with gratitude.

In a house beyond the grade crossing was the recently set up dispensary with two additional bare rooms in which stood a couple of primitive bedsteads. In the cellar below Doktourka had stowed away the remnants of a German army medical depot, which not only met our own needs but also those of the pharmacies in Osterode and Allenstein. Among our patients were a few cases of typhus, both Polish and German; they were nursed by two girls from the neighborhood who had had typhus before. Aside from these cases we occasionally had to admit casualties: Poles who had burned the frontside of their bodies when distilling schnapps; an elderly German found half-starved beside the railroad tracks, probably having fallen or pushed out of a transport train taking soldiers back to Russia; a young Pole who had a fight with some Russians between Osterode and Allenstein, was shot through the chest and flung out of the moving train; a nice Polish soldier who had broken his leg below the knee and wanted to be treated by me. His case had been quite a problem for me, for I had nothing with which to immobilize his broken leg properly. After I had failed to fabricate something out of straw bottle-covers tied around with strips of paper, I asked one of his comrades to find plaster somewhere. He drove to Allenstein and came back in the evening with a paperbag full of cement. With this I was able to make a slightly more solid, fairly immobilizing bandage. Unfortunately, the patient was transferred, so that I never learned how the improvised cast stood up and, particularly, how it was later removed.

Most of the walking cases who came for treatment were women and girls, all with the same horrible symptoms of a disease before which we were helpless, because there was not yet any possibility for a proper treatment. We gave them a kind of pretended treatment, more to our mutual consolation than with any hope of success.

At noon I got a regal meal—considering the circumstances— usually consisting of potatoes and some canned food sent from America. Afterwards I started on my rounds of the surrounding villages, trying each time to extend the radius a bit farther. Never before did I have a chance to get acquainted with a countryside and its people as well as at that time, and, as a doctor is usually welcome, there was always something especially stimulating about these walks.

On the right bank of the Passarge, in the so-called Ermland, a much larger number of people had remained than on the left bank. They were, without exception, Catholics, could speak some Polish, and probably believed that for this reason they would stand a better chance with the Russians and the Poles. But they had become just as poor as all the others. Only from the fact that you could still see a few young men, could you conclude that on this side of the river a certain camouflage of a person's nationality was possible.

Some families still had chickens, others a few goats. One or two privileged people owned an old horse, but otherwise there seemed to be no cattle left. Many hiding places had not been discovered for a long time. One woman with three small children had even managed to hide her cow for several months; she had walled it up in a room, and it could only be reached through a window. Another woman with small children had kept a milking ewe for a long time between a door and a cupboard, until it betrayed its presence by bleating. Pigs had also been kept for a long time in the cellars.

Even people had been hidden. Only recently a woman had brought her newly-married daughter up from the cellar where she had hidden her since January, not even telling her own sister. This summer, in another village, the Russians discovered two girls and carried them off, whereupon their desperate mother had betrayed the whereabouts of all the other girls still hidden in the village.

Even here there had been no lack of traitors; but most of them had not been motivated by despair, as in the latter case, but rather by an unsatisfied lust for revenge and by other impulses which, in times of chaos, break forth, uncontrolled, out of the darkness of human nature. Almost every village was marked by the destructive effects of such an evil spirit. Many persons carried things so far that even the Russians tired of them and put an end to their activities in some way or other.

I had a curious encounter with the wife of one of these individuals, the mother of many sons, some of whom, in fact, served in the German army. I had been invited by an old man, who enjoyed a high reputation as minister of the East Prussian "Fellowship in Prayer," and talked with him about the predicament of the village, mentioning in the course of our conversation the monster, of which I had heard by report. The minister became suddenly evasive and tried to talk about something else. At first I did not understand his reason and reverted to my topic with great insistence, until a woman who was sitting with us at the table, all at once said with a deep sigh: "You are right, that was my husband."

Among the people I visited were some who had returned from Russian prisons, partly from camps in East and West Prussia, but also from those in Russia itself. Most of them were candidates for death. Two elderly men, brothers and co-owners of a big farm close to the Passarge, had come back from Russia by a margin of a few hours and probably with the same transport, completely wizened and in a stupor. One of them died after a few days, the other a month later. A young woman who had returned from a camp in the Arctic region was in the same condition. She could still sit at a table and you could talk with her. Completely cool and hard she described everything she had gone through, and especially what she had suffered at the hands of her own countrymen; it sounded like somebody talking who was already dead.

On some days my rounds also brought me to the villages on the opposite side, farther west and north. The people there were all Protestants. I found some children who had not yet been baptized and seized the opportunity to make up for this neglect. The ceremony was always connected with a little celebration in which the neighbors participated, too. On these occasions I often pondered over the nature of baptism as a sacrament and over our strange attitude towards it. Very characteristic was the answer of a woman to my question whether her two-year-old child had been baptized: "No," she said, "he's been vaccinated but not baptized."

Encouraged by these small celebrations, I decided to hold devotional services on Sundays in the empty little church of Langgut. The first one took place on All Souls' Day with the commandant's permission and under the supervision of an armed sentry. I said that we should on this day abandon for once our thoughts of the dead and the missing and listen to the words of God who wants us to think of life and of those left to us, and with whom it has been granted to us to live together. And that we should be grateful for all that, undeservedly, we were still allowed to call our own. Many women had come from other villages, and they begged me to hold services there too.

On Sunday afternoons my aunt and I explored the surrounding countryside, partly to enjoy our outlawed state and partly to add some variety to our diet. In addition to all the dried mushrooms, berries, and tea herbs stored by my aunt, we helped ourselves to a few hundredweight of turnips from a deserted field in Worleinen to make syrup, and we also experimented with lupines and similar plants, in which nobody took an interest. We got firewood for our stove from the forest and coal, illegally, from the cellar of the manor house which nobody had discovered yet.

On one occasion we took a good look around the manor house, the door of which had been fastened only with a nail. Nothing was left in it but a few antlers and an enormous wardrobe, probably ignored because of its size. Everything else had been used as firewood long ago, or was scattered in the houses of Germans and Poles, where I found it when visiting the sick. Time and again I found shirts with my relatives' monograms on the bodies of my patients.

In the last days of November we acquired a new lodger—the former chauffeur, Gross. After his release from a prison camp in Graudenz, he had turned up one day in Biessellen. On account of his bad physical condition and also because of our lack of means of transportation we had first kept him there in our small "clinic," and took him home only after he was able to walk a little. He recovered very quickly, used to go fishing, and was finally commissioned by the commandant to look after the damaged sawmill and do his best to get it going again. We put him upstairs in my room, and I moved down to my aunt's room, which we shared with old Ili who rambled incessantly about the times at the turn of the century when she had lived as a governess in Vienna, apparently in the house of very prominent people. She was forever preparing to alight from some carriage, getting entangled in the bedclothes and falling forward onto the floor. Sometimes she made very vehement remarks, and we heard her say, "Lord, thou hast been our refuge for generations and generations," and immediately after, "Pleasant refuge, indeed!" In spite of all the trouble she gave my aunt, we sometimes could not help laughing at her.

The women continued to go to work in Langgut. They now

had to cart the huge pile of potatoes, lying frozen and rotten in the cowbarn, back to the field to be stored in a pit. They could no longer be used as food, and handling them was extremely dirty work; but they were at least used for making alcohol, and two hundred hundredweight of wheat had been procured with great difficulty for this purpose. As this wheat now was stored in a granary with a leaky roof, the work had to be done in a great hurry. The still was put into operation as well as possible; but when things had progressed so that the mash could ferment, the outer wall of the still fell out, and the first big barrel emptied itself into the Passarge.

I often visited patients in Langgut. On one of these occasions, in the house of the new manager, I ran into a high-ranking Polish officer who had evidently come to inspect the soldiers stationed at the farm. When I entered the room, he looked up and eyed me suspiciously. "Who's this?" I heard him ask. "The doctor," answered the manager. "Papers?" he shouted at me. If you only knew, I thought, that I am immediately going to run twenty miles or more to some place where you will never find me. Meanwhile I dipped calmly into the breast pocket of my canvas jacket, pulled out a scrap of paper which happened to be there and offered it to him. This was sufficient. He waved it away and was no longer interested in me. To my great relief I could go.

When I was visiting Polish families they usually gave me schnapps to drink and also something to eat. Most of them were extremely poor and lived in bare rooms which were not sufficiently protected against the weather. Members of the militia and of the secret police, called UB, were better off, having more means of obtaining food, and occasionally they gave me good things. Once the commandant of Locken sent his carriage for me during a snowstorm. He had an abscess on one of his tonsils and would have liked me to stay with him for a few days. I stayed one night, but next morning succeeded in convincing him that he was much better. After long pros and cons he sent me home again with his horses. Moreover, he gave me some money, eggs, white bread, stockings, and a shirt to take with me, the shirt bearing, as usual, my uncle's monogram.

I owed my good relations with the dreaded UB mainly to the Doktourka. Right at the beginning she once gave such a dressing down to three armed men, who apparently wanted to search me, that they slinked off, half dazed. She also did her best to "polonize" me and kept asking me if a Polish name had not perhaps played a part in my family at some time or other. Finally I gave in and told her that before the Thirty Years War the name "Mgowski" had occasionally come up in connection with my own. She was overjoyed and handed to me, some days later, a kind of certificate in which I found myself, to my great surprise, listed as "Jan Mgowski." Unfortunately I lost this interesting document on one of the later occasions when I was being searched.

Sometimes I could bring home considerable booty. Once it was thirty pounds of wheat flour from the grain mill, when Polish soldiers had called me to come there as a doctor; another time I got a live chicken from a family which was down with typhus. The flour was especially welcome because Christmas was approaching. With the chicken, called Lorchen, we became very good friends.

For a long time Doktourka had planned to introduce me to her friends in Allenstein and Osterode. One day she quite boldly took me with her to Allenstein. For fourteen zloty we could take the early morning train, consisting of three freight cars. When we arrived in Allenstein, the sight of what was happening at and around the station made me at first rather nervous. It was swarming with Russian and Polish military personnel and nondescript individuals as well, who usually followed them, having something to sell or just hanging around. Again I felt as if I were transported into deepest Asia, and noticed that Doktourka too was anxious to get away from this place as quickly as possible. Only a part of the town had been destroyed; the greater part seemed to be completely intact and was densely populated by Poles.

We visited St. Mary's Hospital and met a doctor and several cigarette-smoking nurses, with whom Doktourka carried on an animated conversation. In the meantime I visited the seven German nurses who were leading a shadowy existence on the top floor, and were not allowed to do any nursing.

Three days later Doktourka took me with her to Osterode. I had to carry bottles of alcohol, ether and other liquids from her dispensary, which were intended for the pharmacy. I felt rather unhappy about this expedition, for I did not at all cherish the idea of becoming better known among the Poles. On the other hand I welcomed, of course, the possibility of seeing Osterode under feminine protection.

The town was pathetically destroyed, and fewer people were around. Near the office of the County Commissioner I could see a greater number of people standing around, and a few bicycles and horse-drawn wagons as well. We called on the so-called district medical officer of health, at present the only doctor available there, bartered a few things at the pharmacy, and did some shopping for our dispensary and Doktourka's household which was beginning to flourish. We also visited the five Catholic German Sisters, who had stayed behind in the rectory, and to whom I could bring greetings from St. Elizabeth's in Königsberg, their motherhouse. On our way back I had to carry a lot of things, including a bag of bones for our kitchen.

The train service between Osterode and Allenstein was rather complicated, because the Russians had removed the second track on the whole line. Only two passenger trains, one of them consisting of cattle cars, were running daily in either direction; but even these had difficulties getting through, because the line was constantly blocked by freight trains coming fully loaded from Berlin and travelled back empty. On these trains, ten to fifteen of which were said to pass through daily, the Russians transported to the east everything they had dismantled in Germany, either packed in crates or loose. The crew was frequently German, guarded by Russian sentries, and sometimes I had a chance to talk with the men, when the trains stopped at Biessellen. I also gave them letters to various addresses in Germany, hoping that one of them would reach its destination. It was out of the question for me to get away on one of these trains which were repeatedly searched during the journey. Nevertheless, I did hope that some day it would be possible for me to use this chance, for I longed to see my people again and did not want to get stuck here indefinitely.

The Russian guards frequently used the stops at the stations for quick, private looting. Once I watched one of them panting toward the train, carrying a sofa on his back. Since the engine with the car for the personnel had meanwhile drawn out of the station for quite a distance, he had to tramp about four hundred yards along the embankment in deep snow. But hardly had he reached the car when the train slowly moved back, so that he had to carry his burden all the way back again. But even this was useless, for when he reached the car, dripping with sweat, the train started so suddenly that he had no other choice than to dump the sofa and jump on the train. That we watched similar scenes with a certain malicious glee was perhaps understandable in our situation.

The Polish signalmen had anything but an easy time under the Russians. If something serious happened they could only save themselves by disappearing for good. One morning, for instance, the scheduled train from Osterode collided in the darkness with a Russian military transport train, and several people were critically injured. The furious Russians wanted to arrest the guilty switchman but he had bolted, not without having warned his brother in the village, who had therefore preferred to disappear too, being rightly afraid that the Russians would take it out on him. Escaping was no big problem, because hardly anyone had possessions other than what he was wearing. And the danger of being pursued was relatively small in a countryside unfamiliar to the Russians.

Shortly before Christmas the problem became acute as how to get some fat, a bottle of oil, or something of that kind. Finally I took my old briefcase, stuffed a green velvet dress into it, which had belonged to one of my cousins and had been found by us in a rubbish pile, bought a ticket in Biessellen and boarded the train to Allenstein.

When I got there, I squeezed myself as inconspicuously as possible through the mob at the station and arrived safely at St. Mary's Hospital, where the nurses gave me a few tips. Then I went to the market to try my luck with the dress. The market was held on two narrow streets, not originally intended for this purpose. In spite of the cold weather, the hustle and bustle, the cries of the vendors, the standing around, bargaining and pushing reminded me of a visit to Sarajevo in summer—everything seemed so remote from the Allenstein of old times.

Besides there was actually nothing worth trading for. What I saw were mostly matches, onions, remnants of material, wooden clogs, and old garden tools. But as soon as I pulled an inch of the velvet dress from my briefcase, a large crowd of interested persons gathered around me. Everybody tried to pull out more and finger the material. I slowly moved backward to the booth of a woman selling matches, who looked trustworthy, and furtively pushed the case over to her. She disappeared with it under the counter to examine the dress undisturbed. It was no longer anything to boast of, but I did not really want to get more for it than the price of a bottle of oil, that is to say, six hundred zloty. But the woman did not want to invest so much money and handed the dress and the case back to me. I was immediately surrounded by the mob. Suddenly a very energetic woman, who had apparently watched the scene from her window, came out of a house, pushed back the people and drew me into her entrance hall. We went upstairs to her apartment, and she disappeared with my case to try on the dress. The apartment was very nice and had evidently belonged to a doctor. I was astonished how decently the woman had managed to establish herself here under the existing conditions. Very soon she appeared again, wearing the green dress which was much too tight and too short for her, besides being threadbare in several places. I could not help laughing; but she did not resent it and told me in fairly good German how she had come to live in Allenstein. She was the wife of a doctor who was at present busy somewhere else, and she apparently wanted to keep his position here for him, although she did not seem to be too sure if he would come back to her at all. She, too, found herself somehow on the fringe of existence, as we all did.

I put the dress back into the briefcase and went down onto the street again. When I passed by the woman who sold matches, she beckoned to me and quickly bought the dress for five hundred zloty. Still having some Polish money, I could now buy the longed-for bottle of oil. It dated, of course, from the German period, like every harmless article which could be bought in these countless little stores.

Christmas came nearer. On my walks through the forest I gathered beechnuts, some of which I scattered again at my aunt's request. "Whenever you have beechnuts," she said, "throw a handful now and then on the Fünflindenberg; we have meant to plant it for a long time." We kept the rest for baking, and having oil and a lot of flour, we were well supplied.

During the Christmas holidays I held services in several places; on Christmas Day, in Rapatten, in the house of a family who had put their large room at my disposal. When I read the Christmas story and saw before me all the touching people, I had to pull myself together not to lose my inner balance. Afterwards my aunt and I visited people in the village and listened to their stories. Although they had all suffered the same, it seemed to do each of them good to talk about his or her personal experience. All of them had seen their husbands and young sons, and frequently their daughters, dragged away; and although there was really nothing left to loot, they were still exposed to occasional raids by the militia or passing Russian soldiers. As the latter did not stop searching for buried treasures with long, pointed iron rods, the villagers had buried empty pails in many places near their houses to spoil their pleasure, and had thought up several tricks to put the looters on a wrong scent. As they were always ransacking the tidy-looking spots, such corners were carefully arranged in the houses and useless objects hidden there.

The winter was fairly mild. At times there was deep snow, and the tracks of game tempted us to contemplate a hunting expedition, all the more so because nobody ever went into the forest except ourselves. "You really should be out hunting something," my aunt said, "otherwise you'll get bored stiff here." I asked her how she imagined I could do it without having guns. But we have, she thought; one of the old men had mumbled something about a carbine, supposedly hidden near the icehouse. It could only have been under the thatched roof of the icehouse itself. When it was dark we went there and found two guns and ammunition for them. With utmost precaution, we took one of them home to clean. Then we hid it again.

The following day was foggy, which made it possible for me to go on a real hunt. It was a short walk to the forest, and once I was there, the probability of meeting anybody was very small.

I had decided that if I shot at all, it should be either a red deer or a boar, and only then if I was sure not to miss it. But darkness fell before I had a chance.

Next morning I stationed myself at a predetermined spot in the forest, and my aunt walked towards me through the tree plantation known as the Rosengarten, to drive any possible game in my direction. But the wild pigs that were in it broke out to the side, and again I had no luck. Anyway, we enjoyed the feeling of having gone out hunting together at least once in these hard times.

But even without a gun these walks through the forest were a joy for me of which I never got tired. Just at that time of the year, when the beech trees had lost their leaves, and their trunks stood out like columns against the background of snow, I was drawn away from the path again and again to run leaping down the slopes to the crystal clear mirrors of the lakes in whose dark depths the fish were drawing their circles. Every day we felt deeply that this was a short interval of grace, granted to us.

Friday, January 11

When I arrived in Biessellen, I was told that the UB had been looking for me, and apparently for a serious reason. As I was not conscious of any reason to bolt, I went straightway to the guard room, where they were somewhat surprised at my voluntary appearance. I asked them if anybody was sick or for what reason they wanted to see me. Confronted by at least fifteen armed men who were more or less drunk, and some of them half-naked, I did not feel very comfortable. They eyed me for a while with contempt, and then informed me that I was not allowed to hold any meetings. When I asked them the reason for it, they gave me no answer, but let me go.

Saturday, January 12

Rain fell in torrents. I found a note from Doktourka in Biessellen telling me to go immediately to Osterode to assist the "district doctor" in an operation. This sounded hardly possible, because I knew that neither an operating room nor surgical instruments existed in Osterode. Soaked to the skin, I climbed on the
engine cab of the train to Osterode, where I cautiously made my
way to the doctor's house. My colleague received me with a
heartwarming friendliness and asked me to act as his substitute
for the next four days, because he had to attend a course of lectures in Allenstein. There was, naturally, no question at all of
an operation. But chance would have it, that just at that moment
a young Polish tractor driver was brought in, who had been
accidentally shot through his right upper arm by a friend. They
had been sitting side by side on the tractor when the other's automatic went off. The bone was shattered, and we had to find a
way to transport him to Allenstein, to have his serious injury
properly treated. As there was no other train running that day, I
dispatched his distressed friend to find the only car available in
Osterode which belonged to the militia. In the meantime I bandaged the arm of the patient provisionally. He clung to me, im-
ploring me to drive with him to Allenstein and, to my great surprise, I discovered that he came from Finckenstein. But he did
not know if the castle was still standing, from which I concluded
that it had been burned down. It was all the more likely as it was
the most beautiful of all the manor houses in East and West
Prussia.

I got a very good supper at my colleague's in Osterode, after
which we had to wait another few hours, because the militia
had taken a drive. Late at night the car finally drew up—one of
the short American motor trucks with a flat nose. We put the

injured man aboard and drove at top speed on the winding road via Jablonken and Dietrichswalde to Allenstein. When we drove through the forest of Grasnitz I tried to jump out, for I had nothing to do in Allenstein, but the Pole would not let me go. He had been sick several times in the car; I had been the victim of his predicament. At about one o'clock in the morning we pulled up in front of the second hospital in Allenstein, were received by cigarette-smoking nurses and put the patient to bed in a smoke-filled room. We were supposed to drive back at once, but apparently had run out of gas and were forced to spend the rest of the night in Allenstein. The drivers knew of a warm place, so we drove to the control plant where we settled comfortably on three tables next to red-hot radiators. Under the light of a glaring lamp my two companions were soon fast asleep; but it took me longer, for I had been in wet clothes for the last twenty four hours and did not dare slip out of my wetpack because it was safer to be prepared to start at a moment's notice.

Sunday, January 13

There was a light frost and the roads were slippery. One of the drivers set out to look for gas. Around ten o'clock he found some and came back for us. We drove across the whole town and stopped in front of a house from which three open milk cans full of gasoline were carried out and put on the truck. The tank was also filled, and six more people got in who wanted to be taken to Osterode. This time we drove via Hohenstein. Although the way was longer, the road was much better, and it was, of course, necessary to drive again at a mad speed. After all, what was a car for?

We raced across desolate countryside. After a little while we sighted Hohenstein, again totally destroyed as it had been in the First World War. The Tannenberg Monument, its front and rear tower blown up, drifted past us like a bad dream. Then came the forest, where the road was still more slippery than in the open country. From under the closed top, I could only look out to the back, but suddenly noticed with alarm that the road inclined increasingly. We started skidding, first to the right then to the left, then again to the right, there was a crash, the rear of the car lifted, we shot forward and finally landed, soaked in gasoline, in the top of the overturned car. The top had surprisingly stood the shock. As I had been prepared that something like that would happen, I was the first to crawl out, the others following me one by one. No one had been hurt. Our truck was lying helplessly in the ditch, its wheels in the air. Beside us, on the road, stood a passenger car which had evidently been the cause of our accident, because we had been forced to leave the middle of the road to let it pass. One of our passengers got into it to drive back to Allenstein. He had a stiff leg and nobody knew how long we would have to wait here until help came. We alone would not be able to set the truck on its legs again. After we had taken a nap for half an hour, a truck like ours appeared coming from Osterode, as usual at a mad speed. We signaled to it from some distance, it braked, skidded, and we jumped from the roadside into the forest. The truck made a 180 degree turn, struck a tree with its rear, and stopped short. After the first seconds of fright, the crew, members of the Polish militia, poured forth torrents of abuse on us. They shifted gears several times, the truck turned around and off they went.

Not long after this, a peasant came driving from the opposite direction. When he saw us in the ditch, he tried to stop, but his miserable horse slipped, lost its footing and remained lying helpless on the road. After countless attempts by the peasant to get it up, our united efforts brought it to its feet, and the man drove on very cautiously.

By now I was chilled to the bones in my rain- and gasoline-

soaked clothes, and I tried to get away. Slowly I walked along
the road as if I only wished to look around the next bend; but
when I was out of sight, I quickened my steps, for I wanted to
be in Grasnitz that evening, if possible. At the crossroads in
Hohenstein I came upon a sentry, but as I was walking east, he
did not become suspicious. I turned north, passed through Manchengut where I paid a short visit to old Skibba, whose daughter
had come back from Chelyabinsk in a hopeless condition. Again
I had to listen to her descriptions of the terrible behavior of her
own countrymen toward one another there. In February eighty
girls had traveled in a cattle truck for weeks across Russia, without food and water, and the truck had not once been opened all
that time. Many were dead when they were let out. For those
who survived the misery continued—just as we had seen it in
Königsberg. (The girl died four weeks later.)

Before I left, I was glad to hear that the old minister of the
Fellowship in Prayer had held a service there that day. Thank
heaven that the militia at least allowed him that. Later when I
was almost in Biessellen, I became suddenly suspicious. A one-
horse shay passed me from behind, the driver being the commandant of the militia in Biessellen. Seeing me, he hesitated for
a moment, but then drove on without taking any further notice
of me. I had the feeling that something was brewing, but I arrived safely in Biessellen where I got some coffee in our dispensary. In bright moonlight I walked on, making a slight detour
across the field to inspect our potato pit, found undisturbed, and
arrived at my aunt's house about ten in the evening.

Monday, January 14

Early in the morning I was in dry clothes and on my way to
Osterode. I did not want to let my colleague down. Moreover, I
had the feeling that my days here were probably numbered, after

having attracted the attention of wider circles. My plan was to get through to the west before obligations could tie me down in this region for an indefinite time.

My aunt accompanied me across the forest. The time we had spent together seemed to us like a chapter from a cherished children's book. Now we had to say goodbye. New snow had fallen during the night. We saw fresh tracks of red deer and wild pigs. I felt once more the powerful presence of my homeland. A short word of farewell—then I ran off and reached Biessellen just in time to jump onto the train to Osterode from the wrong side.

First of all I visited the five Catholic Sisters who received me very kindly. The youngest of them was ill, and the Catholic priest had just arrived to give her Holy Communion. When he heard that I was a doctor, he pulled up one trouser leg to show me a wound which would not heal. I bandaged it and gave him directions for further treatment. Then he put on his vestments to go to the patient, and the other Sisters followed him with reverence.

I left my rucksack with the Sisters and walked with the usual precautions to the hospital where I was meant to replace my colleague. Situated outside the town, the hospital was outwardly well preserved. They were cleaning inside, and a German deaconess who took part in the work, quickly showed me the building. To my astonishment I discovered parts of our Insterburg X-ray equipment, which we had sent here a year ago to save it from the Russians. It had been useless, of course, because the Russians had been here one day earlier than in Insterburg. There were a few bedsteads around, and in a carefully locked room pills and ointments, sent by UNRRA. A small room with a very comfortable bed had been assigned to me.

The first three days in the hospital were uneventful. As everywhere else, most of the people who came were women and girls wanting to know if there was any remedy yet for their disease. It is dreadful how callous we have become where they are concerned.

At my colleague's request I drew up a list of everything needed in a normal operating room. He's going to try and get some of it in Warsaw.

Thursday, January 17

As my colleague was expected to be back today, I decided to push off to the west. As soon as it was dark I got my rucksack from the Gray Sisters, stole away to the station and jumped onto the first freight train which came. It was going east, so I would have to look out for a chance to change somewhere into one going the other way.

At the first stop on the open line I walked toward the engine and found a German crew guarded by two jovial Russians, who allowed me to travel with them in the cab. They were taking parts of a factory to Russia and were hoping to be back in Germany in two or three months. I offered my services as a fireman, but they advised against it, because they themselves had papers with Russian and Polish entries, which were frequently checked.

I had to get out at Allenstein. It was so dark on the platform that I ran no risk of being discovered. There were a lot of freight trains standing at and near the station; the empty ones were going west. I approached several German engineers, but none of them wanted to take me along. They were evidently under great pressure. When at last it began to grow light again, there was nothing for me to do but to crawl into an empty car at the rear of a train which moved off soon afterwards.

Friday, January 18

Towards noon we were back in Osterode. The temperature had dropped to about twenty degrees below zero, and I was so frozen that I simply could not travel any longer. I got out and decided

to go straight back to the hospital. It was just possible that nobody had noticed my nocturnal excursion.

Crossing the tracks, I saw to my considerable alarm the commandant of the UB coming towards me. He too seemed startled
to see me. "Doktour, come with!" What does he want? Did he
want to take me to a patient? It would not be the first time. Had
he not been my patient once? Or was he going to arrest me? In
any case I had no choice but to follow him. We walked for a
short while side by side without talking, and entered a house before which a sentry was standing. There I was surrounded by at
least twenty uniformed Russians and Poles. I had walked into
the trap.

Half grinning, half bored, the Russians watched while I was
stripped by two Poles. My beautiful, carefully made up escape
outfit was taken and handed around: a new pair of trousers of an
earlier time, stockings, a pair of shoes—what hadn't I suffered to
bring this ballast all the way! "Ah, Doktour go home!" They
laughed maliciously. Well, it was as clear as daylight that I had
meant to bolt. After the rucksack it was the turn of my pockets,
and all the places where something might have been sewn in.
Two watches came to light and their looks grew grim. I almost
felt ashamed to be still in possession of such things, although
they were mementoes of the dead. Much more dangerous, however, was the small notebook which was put aside for the time
being—my diary. There was nothing in it but short notes on
daily happenings, but that would be enough. The writing was
fortunately very small and in German script, which they might
not be able to read. They left me the fur vest which I wore, and
a loaf of bread. My little Bible would have to be examined. I
asked them why they had arrested me. "You talked political, and
shot with people in Gusenofen." Two reports had been heard
when I was there, they said. The first charge related, of course,
to the services I had held with their permission, the second was

pure bluff. There was nobody in Gusenofen except a few poor, miserable women and children. "Who said that about political talk?" I asked. "German man say." I could not contradict that, because, unfortunately, it was only too possible. Then down with me into the cellar.

A low-ceilinged room, about eighteen feet square, two small windows high up. Thirty men on double-decker bunks, an iron stove in the middle of the room. Except for four or five Poles all the inmates were Germans. One of them drew me down on his bunk and explained the situation to me. They had all been in Russian camps, were released after a few months, came home very ill, found Poles living in their houses, if these were still standing, and had been taken to prison by them under the pretext that they had belonged to the Nazi Party. Until recently, they had had the place to themselves, and had been able to more or less keep clean, but after the Poles had joined them, who were not co-operative, lice had started to spread again. Some of the men were taken out for work by day, usually to sweep the streets. Several had died, not one had been released. There was saltpeter in their food, which badly burned your tongue. He strongly urged me to forget about my belongings and to escape at the first opportunity.

In the afternoon a sentry came for me, and, handing me a coal shovel, ordered me to light the fire in a stove on the second floor. Perhaps they thought I did not know how to do that. I took some live coals from the stove in the guard room, where they were still sprawling on the tables. Keep a stiff upper lip by all means! I felt like a tamer in a lion's cage. On the stairway to the second floor I was alone for a moment. If I could only set the house on fire there would be great confusion, and would give many people a chance to escape! But at that moment the door of a large room opened, and I saw a corpulent Russian officer enthroned on a sofa against the opposite wall. Under the table, at his feet, lay a formidable white mastiff. He did not take any notice of me, evidently I was only meant to light the fire. This accomplished, I was returned to the cellar.

In the evening we were driven out into the yard at the back and given soup in a stable, distributed by a woman doctor who was a prisoner too. After the collapse she had been able to go on practicing in Osterode for a time, then she was taken away by a militia man to attend to his child, and had not been released again. Without the slightest change of expression, as though we were carrying on a harmless conversation, she told me how to get out of the yard. I should try and get into the next stable and from there through the window. While I tried to slip to the back, she tried to divert the attention of the sentry, who had, however, watched and pushed me back with the butt of his rifle.

That night my thoughts wandered in all directions. I did not feel sure whether I ought to escape or not. I had a hunch that they had arrested me because they supposed me to have arranged the religious service in Manchengut in spite of the order forbidding it, or that I had even held it myself, so that in a sense I was here in the cellar as a defender of the Gospel. What should I do? Life was so beautiful, and it was such a pleasure to play a trick on those who gave themselves airs to be the guardians of order. God help me to do the right thing! And lying there on my bunk, I imagined being on my way, up the stairs, across the yard, into the stable, through the window, up the slope, between the houses, along the streets, and in a wide arc around the town to the lake, even though I did not know if it was already frozen.

Night without end. Our Polish fellow-prisoners played practical jokes on one another. A German soldier, escaped from Russia and arrested here three months ago, moaned pitifully. All the others were silent. Now and then somebody got up and shoveled more coals into the stove. Over our heads a roaring noise broke out at short intervals.

Saturday, January 19

Towards seven in the morning the sentry unlocked the door above us, came down the cellar stairs, and opened our door. An old man went up with him to make coffee. I sneaked after him and stopped on the topmost step. The door was not quite closed, and the sentry stood behind it. A long time passed; it was freezing cold, and I began to become stiff. Outside the day dawned. All at once the sentry was called from somewhere, he answered, and moved away a few steps—as if in a dream, my hand pushed the door open, I was out in the yard, reached the stable, crawled through the window, ran up the slope—supposing someone would look out of a window!—reached the block of houses, was on the street, ran west, then to the left, and then more and more east in a wide arc. I wanted to put my pursuers on a wrong track as much as possible, because of the dog, the only one I was afraid of. I picked up a handy piece of iron from a ruined house to defend myself with, ran past the hospital, across the Hohenstein road, through gardens—luckily people were not yet about— and then across the open country. Later I crossed the railroad tracks and took the road to Jablonken, in the direction of Lake Schilling. Nothing but snow and flat country. Later bushy pines, bumpy ground, sandy soil. Single trees, stiff with hoarfrost, were beginning to glow in the rosy flush of dawn. On the ground still blue shadows. I ran and ran until suddenly the shore was steeply falling away into the lake before me. On the other side—the forest, and the sun just rising behind it. I slid down the slope to the lake, knocked a hole into the ice with my iron, and slithered, throwing myself now and then on my belly, over the cracking, crackling ice, and reached the forest. On top of the slope there, among the magnificent trunks of the Taberbrück Forest trees, I sat down and watched the shore from which I had come. Nothing stirred on my tracks.

In a beeline I walked on eastward, across the main stand. Certainly nobody had been there for a year. In the middle of the oldest part a herd of red deer got up, surprised, but did not run away until I was almost in their midst. I felt sure that nobody would follow me here. But then I suddenly heard a big dog baying behind me. All at once I felt very tired, leaned against a tree, and clutched my iron tighter. The baying came nearer, something crashed in the underbrush—good God, a stag at a quick trot and behind it a great shaggy dog. Life flowed back into my veins. I waved my hand, the stag turned aside and trotted away, and the dog turned back and disappeared, his tail between his legs. My heart swelled with gratitude. That morning the whole forest belonged to me.

An hour later I was in Grasnitz. Nobody there could yet have heard of my latest escapade. But for safety's sake I kept out of sight. I found my aunt at home. She had not gone to work because of a sprained muscle and was not at all surprised at my sudden appearance; we had lived through too many unexpected moments together. Up to now nobody had been there to search for me, but it might happen any moment. I stayed in bed while my aunt boiled dumplings for me and kept a lookout for visitors. We discussed what should be done next. In any case, I had to leave again at once. But what of her? Wouldn't the Poles take it out on her? Still, I could not take her with me, with her lame leg, and in such cold weather, nor did we know where to go. So she stayed behind, much more confident than I, waving to me when I left, unnoticed, an hour later—this time with a much smaller bundle.

I thought it safest to walk first to Ponarien, where I had found Preuss three months ago. They would probably not pursue me that far. Taking advantage of small woods, rises in the ground, and other cover I got as far as Brückendorf, where I saw a wagon coming in my direction. I recognized the manager of Langgut by his horses, and had just enough time to slip into an empty house. Dazzled by the midday sun, he drove past without having recognized me.

Beyond Gallinden I took a shortcut through the Tomlack Forest to Reichau and waited there, sitting in the straw of a barn of an abandoned farm until it became dark. It was biting cold. I was quite exhausted, and the anxiety about my aunt dampened my initiative. At dusk I got on my way and reached Ponarien by a detour through the forest. Not a soul to be seen. I knocked on Preuss's door; it was locked. But the coachman's cottage, next door, was open and Frau Klein came out, much afraid. Preuss and his wife and several other families had been turned out in November. Her own husband had been absent for a year. Only Böhnke, the blacksmith, was still here, and she took me to him.

Sunday, January 20

I stayed that night and all next day with the Böhnkes. The housekeeper of the Polish manager, Fräulein Görke, was told of my arrival, and brought me a piece of bacon. Frau Lemke, whose husband was missing, came too and brought two pairs of socks. There were more Poles here than in the fall. Preuss was turned out because they had wanted his property. (We heard later that he and his wife had died on the transport.)

Around ten in the evening I was on my way again. The moon was full and it was much colder. I walked on a country road to Hermenau and then on the highway to Mohrungen. I did not meet anyone. But just outside the town two men turned around a corner and came up to me. It was too late to dodge them so I approached them in the middle of the road. They were regular soldiers, with whom it is always easier to get along. The first one stopped me when I passed, murmured something like "*starosta*," saluted, and let me go on. Perhaps he had taken me for the Polish administrator. After that, the others no longer had any interest in me. Coming into the town I turned right, walked behind the barracks through training grounds with barbed wire fences and frozen trenches, crossed the railroad line, and reached the westbound road again. Judging from the wheeltracks, it was more used than the roads I had walked along earlier, and I should be therefore on my guard.

Soon I reached the forest of Bestendorf and then the village itself. The manor house was still standing. I heard wild shouting and yelling from the village. Around midnight I rested for a moment in a field barn on the left of the road, set fire to some straw to warm my hands, but put it out again at once, not wanting to burn down the barn.

At the crossroads near Maldeuten the problem became acute: should I go to Marienburg and from there farther west, or to the place where my parents and my brother were a year ago? Should I risk having to cross the Weichsel on ice floes, or go home once more to the graves, and then face the consequences? I knew the Russians were in Januschau, but I was irresistibly drawn to that place. Perhaps there were still a few Germans left in the neighborhood. I could not resist the temptation.

The road sign said seven miles to Saalfeld. The old place names were in Russian lettering again. From the distance Saalfeld looked badly damaged. I left it on my right and crossed the railroad line to Liebemühl; there, too, the tracks had been removed. The next village, Weinsdorf, showed considerable damage. I walked through it, suddenly heard footsteps, and took cover behind the church. Two men hurried past, shivering with cold, and disappeared into a house. After another hour of walking, Gerswalde loomed up before me in the moonlit mist. I deliberated whether or not I should go through the village, but decided to turn left, where I came upon Lake Geserich, walked past a long row of wooden fishermen's huts, where nothing stirred, crossed the wide frozen surface of the lake, and came ashore again near the forester's lodge Eichenlaube. A herd of wild pigs broke quite fearlessly through the young oak trees in the moonlight. Nobody seemed to disturb them here. A last look at the lake, then I crossed the road to Schwalgendorf, went through the main stand, and reached again the main road at the border of the province.

West Prussia! Finckenstein Forest! How homelike it felt! The Heide Mill was still standing and seemed to be in operation. The roads leading to it were marked with wide ruts as they had never been before. Then the Januschau Forest. There too were wide ruts in the main driveway like in a big thoroughfare. I wondered what the Russians were doing here. But on the right and left in the main stand, everything was still as it used to be: the view of the lake between the stems of the beech trees, and every curve of the road full of a thousand memories of nights and days in a former existence. One man alone could hardly comprehend it all. But after a march of almost forty miles, I was again in a mental state in which I could imagine that somebody was walking by my side.

Out in the field the road had been widened still more, and the ground on both sides of the avenue looked as if a steam roller had been driven over it. It was dawning when I crossed the field to get to the park. The lodge was burned down. A few minutes, and I would see the graves. And then I was really standing where the dearest people had found their last rest. I looked across the fields in the early morning light, and could not help smiling when I saw that the graves had been dug up and that broken tools were left in them, which were quite inadequate for digging. What did you look for here, you foolish people? I thought. Evidently you tried hard to find something.

I took a few steps to get the view through the park. The dear old house was still standing. A glaring lamp on the porch, lighted windows, doors slamming, cursing, the noise of wheels— that was the Russians.

Slowly it was growing lighter, and I had to find a place to stay. I could still manage to walk the two miles to the manor farm in Brausen, still hoping to find a few Germans. Just before Brausen, where the road crossed the big ditch, a Russian overtook me at the usual high-stepping trot, but did not show any interest in me. Shortly afterwards I met a wagon with four muffled figures sitting in it. The wagon stopped; I stopped too. For a moment we looked searchingly at one another—it was old Tiedtke with three girls from Januschau on their way to work. They told me briefly the most important facts: anybody from Januschau who was still alive was now in Brausen. The trek of last winter had only got as far as somewhere near Stuhm, some twenty-five miles away. My mother and my brother had been shot there by the Russians, and sixteen other people from Januschau had been killed as well.

I asked them with whom I could stay in Brausen and they suggested Lasner, who might be able to put me up. They pointed out the house where he was now living, but warned me to be very cautious because the village was guarded. Soon afterwards, singing loudly, I strode past the sentry who was leaning against the turnpike in a fur cap and slippers, his automatic under his arm. Ten minutes later I was lying safe and sound in Lasner's bed.

JANUSCHAU
January 21 to August 2, 1946

Monday, January 21

A few slices of bread with delicious beet syrup restored my strength, for aside from the pain in my travel-worn feet, I had been very short of breath in the end. To my astonishment I heard that the commandant's thermometer stood at 22° below zero, which I had not realized, in spite of my relatively thin clothing.

I learned that the land and all the surrounding estates were still in the hands of the Russians. All the livestock, all the stores in the granaries, and all movable matters had been accumulated here. The paddocks were piled high with threshing machines, plows, wagons, and other machinery from the whole neighborhood. Only the ruined town of Rosenberg and the evacuated villages had been ceded to the Poles. There were some hundred Germans in Brausen: women, children, and old men, besides a lot of Russians, whose numbers were constantly changing. The commandant was said to be a man with whom it was easy to get on. No work was done in the fields, only the cattle were tended— almost 140 cows, the remainder of the herds lost in the winter, and also a few pigs. They were fed on sugar beet parings supplied by the factory in Rosenberg. The entire village was living on these parings as well. Work in the cowbarn was much coveted because of the leftover skim milk. Nobody had died of starvation here, in the beginning only a few people from cold and diseases. Potatoes were still plentiful for several hundred acres had been planted in the spring. The grain had been harvested, and some of it was still stored in sacks in the granary. People here were evidently less afraid of the Russians than in the other places where I came across them. Some of them had even become rather intimate with those who had been here for some time.

In the evening I was taken to the house across the road where the old forester H. and his wife were living together with two married daughters and their three children. His lodge in the Zolnick Forest had burned down. He was now employed by the Russians as a trapper and woodcutter, and had to accompany them when they went hunting. The daughters worked on the farm, one in the dairy and the other in the commandant's henhouse. Their home, consisting of one large room and a small kitchen which could be divided by a curtain, they now had to themselves. Until a few weeks ago they had been forced to share it with another family and several single persons; but after the Russians had taken a number of people to the west, they had been able to spread out a little more, and were therefore in a position to take me in. The bed behind the curtain in the kitchen was given to me, and with unspeakable content I stretched out my tired legs in it.

Tuesday, January 22

We discussed what was now to become of me. It was too cold to continue my journey, and I could not remain hidden much longer, for the news of my presence had probably got about everywhere. H. thought that he should take me to the commandant and tell him that I was a doctor who belonged here and had come back at last.

The farmyard was closed by a tall wooden gate, with a portrait of Stalin on top of it. Some of the Russians occupied the entirely undamaged farmhouse. The commandant, a fat, elderly man with the rank of lieutenant, was just entering the house from the garden, wearing nothing but a short fur coat and a pair of top boots. I was introduced to him and he agreed, without asking for further information, that I should remain here and attend to the sick. I should live with H. More assured than when we arrived, we took our leave, winding our way through the crowd of Russians camping on the floor in their usual casual fashion.

In the evening I was told about the flight. The fugitives had left Januschau with the trek a year ago, the children and old people in the wagons, all the others on foot. When they had reached the outskirts of Stuhm they sent a bicyclist ahead to Marienburg, to see if there was any hope of getting the trek across the Nogat Bridge. He came back, saying it was doubtful, for innumerable other treks were also heading for the bridge. This confirmed the opinions of my brother and the chief-inspector that the flight would be, in any case, senseless. So they stayed at a small manor farm near Altmark and waited there for the Russians, who came towards evening on January 25. In the ensuing chaos, which needs no description because it was the same everywhere, my brother was severely wounded with a knife. My mother had been able to bind up his wound temporarily when other Russians came, asked who he was, and shot him and my mother together. I was deeply grateful to know that it had been over so quickly, for ever since I had heard that they had not escaped from West Prussia, I had been haunted by the thought of their possible fate.

During the encounter with the Russians another sixteen persons had been shot or burned alive. The women had suffered as they had everywhere else. Any young men left were carried off. In spite of his forester's uniform, H. had, surprisingly, lost only his boots, and afterwards was able to remain in hiding for a week with his family at an out-of-the-way farm. Then, half-starved, they went home through the deep snow and reached Januschau, almost at the end of their tether. They and many others were put up in the school where the women were again treated brutally. Then they were sent to Brausen where gradually most of the former inhabitants gathered again. A German who could speak Polish and understood Russian became the confidential agent of the Russians and, although up to that time a quite harmless person, did his fellow-sufferers a lot of harm, until he died in the summer to the general relief.

Wednesday, January 23

My feet had recovered sufficiently for me to accompany the daughters of the house, Frau S. and Frau L., on an expedition they had planned for some time. They wanted to see the district town of Rosenberg for once from the inside, and to try at the same time to barter a tablecloth, which they had succeeded in burying, with the Poles for some fat. We left the village unobtrusively and reached our destination without incidents.

The town was a pitiful sight, the market square a heap of ruins. We saw a few Poles on the streets, but to all appearance none of the former inhabitants were left. After some hesitation we entered a small store. The heavily made-up saleswoman— "Warzawianka," according to the sign over her door—looked us up and down, a cigarette in the corner of her mouth. We showed her the tablecloth and a lively bargaining began. She spoke broken German. But when we spotted two Russians sitting at the back of the store, we retreated slowly, before an agreement had been reached. In the next store, a bakery next to the post office, we had better luck. The owner, a friendly woman, gave us rolls and money for the tablecloth. They were the first rolls I had seen in a year. The bakeress warned us against the militia. We slunk through the ruins of the town. On our way back I glanced quickly at the empty hospital which had not been destroyed and even had panes in some windows.

Thursday, January 24

Today I held my first consultation in one of the new houses for two families, where Nadja, a Russian hospital nurse had been practicing alone up to now. The front door stood open because it did not fit the door frame. There was a considerable snowdrift in the hallway, and a bench beside it for waiting patients. The door to the consulting room had no handle, because all door handles had been wrenched off and carried away at the beginning. Nadja gave me one for my personal use. Our services were chiefly needed for festering legs. The medicaments we have are some loose pills, the remains of some ointments from German army supplies, and some unidentifiable mixtures in beer bottles with labels written in Russian. Nadja is quiet and easy-going, speaks passable German, and doesn't think much of cleanliness.

Saturday, January 26

The Russians went hunting today, taking their ammunition with them in two potato sacks. They came back in the evening with one red deer and one wild pig; several animals had been wounded. As the beaters took part in the hunting as well, some two thousand cartridges had been fired. Even though hunts of this kind take place twice a week, I was told that there are still many red deer left. (The last time we hunted here, thirty-six cartridges were fired, and our bag consisted of sixteen head of game.)

In the evening H.'s daughter-in-law came through the forest from Schwalgendorf, bringing us some fish. She hadn't seen her in-laws for quite some time. Her father had formerly taken a lease on the Geserich and several other lakes. She had come back from the flight alone, and was cooking for the Russians now living in her house, and also continuing the fishing. Before that she had worked a few months for the Russians in a machine shop somewhere near Marienwerder. Her husband and his brother had fallen in Russia. The presence of this strong and fearless young woman had a reassuring effect on all of us.

Sunday, January 27

My anxiety about my aunt in Grasnitz increased daily. What had happened to her? Had the Poles carried her away, or had nothing further happened? I could find no rest until I had made sure of her fate; I must try and get there once more.

In the afternoon I accompanied, therefore, young Frau H. back to Schwalgendorf. Because of the Russians, we avoided Januschau; I knew that they had a depot of about a thousand horses there. The forest was untouched; the old, cut timber was still lying about everywhere. A year ago we had been hunting here, well aware that it would be for the last time. It seemed almost incredible that I should be walking here again. We went past the lakes, crossed the East-West Prussian border, which is also the boundary of the Januschau estate, and saw the "white man" standing at the roadside. It was a white-washed man of wood whom somebody had once set up at a fork in the road to frighten his guests when they had to drive past it at night. Now there was only half of him left; the Russians had shot away the back of his head.

Half an hour later we were in Schwalgendorf, the big fishing village on the Geserich Lake. A number of Germans are still living there, as usual women, children, and old men. The younger men, if still alive, are either in prison or in the west. Nobody has heard from them. We visited the old fisherman, Kuczmarski.

The people there live mostly on fish filched from the Russian catches. All the men are called up for the fishing.

I stayed for a while and then went down the steps to the shore of the lake and walked over the ice to the village of Weepers, for I had been told of a fisherman there, who was thought to have a map of the countryside. I found him at home, and, after some persuasion, succeeded in getting him to show me his map. As he wouldn't let me take it with me, I studied it very carefully and made a small sketch of the main roads and villages lying in the direction I wanted. The old man shook his head skeptically and warned me against the Poles.

At dusk I passed through Gablauken where some Germans were living with whom I exchanged a few words. By the time it was completely dark I had reached the last outlet of the lake at a spot known as Kragger Corner, which I knew by name although I had never been there before. I now started walking along the canal, thinking it would be a short cut, but it took me too far away from the right direction and I had to turn back and follow the route I had marked on my map. This led me through a village and back to the canal which I followed for some distance through meadowland to Liegen. From there I went straight across the fields to the little town of Liebemühl, which had been so badly damaged that I was sure it was un-inhabited. On the right and left of the road ruins rose stark in the light of the rising moon. Nowhere a sign of life, although it could not have been more than six P.M. Luckily, the bridge across the canal was still standing.

When I crossed the market square, the church clock struck suddenly, clear and sharp, making me jump. When I had come to the end of the town, where the road branched off on the right to Osterode, on the left to Mohrungen, I saw a light to my left and was stopped by a Polish militia man. He asked where I was going, and, with a sneer, clutched my arm when he realized that I was not a Pole. I pulled the hammer out of my belt and he let go. I gave him a push and, before he had regained his balance, I ran for a short way along the road to Osterode, turned left and tried to get to the forest across the fields. Running in the frozen plowland I suddenly wondered what would happen if I stupidly broke my ankle. Another mile or so and I was safely in the forest. The sentry would hardly have risked pursuing me in the darkness.

Cautiously walking along the edge of the forest, I came upon the road to Mohrungen, walked for a while along it, waiting eagerly for the next turning, where a wood path branched off which I did not want to miss. Otherwise it would have meant a great detour for me. I soon recognized the critical spot, but started back when I saw a huge black object apparently blocking the path I had looked for. I stared at it for quite some time before realizing that it was one of the many shell-battered tanks.

The path through the forest showed human footprints which soon turned to the right. Later I noticed only tracks of game. It was now impossible to miss the right direction, for the sky was clear and the North Star showed me the way. I soon found myself surrounded by a herd of wild pigs which peacefully broke up to either side. Later, in a clearing, a herd of red deer let me approach them quite close. Then I was unexpectedly on a road again. I looked around: on my right not far away another road branched off in an eastward direction. Eck-Schilling! I sat down on a stone to rest for a few minutes, deeply grateful to have reached this unmistakable spot in the middle of the forest. After another hour's walk along the road to the east I came again upon a characteristic landmark—an especially sturdy pine, bending over the road, from left to right, into an arch. I took it instinctively for a sign that a village must be quite near. I became wary again, noticed that there were fewer trees, spotted a house to the left, a high fence to the right, and behind it a paddock and

more houses. It could only be Taberbrück, the most coveted
forestry administration in the whole province. It was from here
that Napoleon took the wood called "Bois de Tabres" for Paris.

I now had to turn right, and crawled through the fence,
jumped over a few thinly frozen ditches, passed quite close to
the foresters' lodges which seemed to be inhabited, found the
road to Dungen, and came out of the forest. I gave the village a
wide berth. When I broke through the ice in a big ditch, dogs
started barking. But then I was on familiar ground, crossing the
Grasnitz Forest. Soon I reached my aunt's house and tapped
on her window, in breathless expectation. A figure appeared—
it was she. I stepped out of the darkness.

Nothing much had happened since I left. Once the militia
had come to inquire about me, without giving special reasons.
The villagers believed me to be in prison in Osterode. It was
not yet midnight, so I had plenty of time to sleep.

Monday, January 28

My aunt did not go to work today because of her lame leg.
We spent the day together, talking of the dead and thinking of
all those of whose survival we were not sure. Towards ten at
night I set off again. My old shoes would not do any longer and
I put them in my rucksack. I slipped into a pair of felt boots
which I had repaired a short while back. I also took with me a
New Testament and a small book of watchwords for 1935, which
agreed with the current year as to Sundays and holy days. I
walked to Liebemühl the way I had come, but then turned right
and went along the canal, looking for the railroad bridge which
was far outside the town. Fortunately it was still there. When
I crossed it, holding my breath, the church clock struck again—
twice.

After this a long walk across the open country; there was no risk of losing my way on such a starlit night. When I had arrived at Kragger Corner the soles of my boots were worn out, so I walked on on the ice of the lake, although it was a slight detour. When I reached Weepers it was almost day. I stopped at the house of the old fisherman and asked him to give me the exact direction across the lake. Half an hour later Schwalgendorf loomed before me out of the mist. I could briefly rest at Kuczmarski's, where I had fish for breakfast, and my rucksack was filled with fish to take home with me.

When I came to the Zollnicker Berg and was again in West Prussia, I discovered too late that the Russians were out hunting. They drove past me and one of them aimed at me; there might have been trouble, but H. was with them on the sleigh and saved the situation. I was allowed to go on.

On my way out I had found a dead fox and had hidden it at the edge of the forest. The skin was still in good condition and might bring in a little money if the Poles should like to have it. I slung the animal over my shoulder and was back in Brausen around noon, completely exhausted.

In the afternoon I saw patients. A short, twenty-two-year-old Armenian with the rank of lieutenant, the so-called "medical lieutenant," had arrived to practice medicine, and had been quartered next to the consulting room. He has a smattering of German and admitted to me that he did not know anything about medicine. "Sick people come, Hans, you look, I talk," this is how he has planned our collaboration. He never stops singing and whistling German hits ("Marianka," etc.). He had been in Berlin before coming here, and has a lady friend there, whose attractions he described to me with the most intimate details. Obviously he likes me and wants me to share the kitchen with him, which two Russian women have just vacated.

In the evening we skinned the fox, and in the meantime H.'s

daughters set to work to make the kitchen habitable. They scrubbed the walls and brought the floor to light with the help of a garden hoe. Before we went to bed I read aloud from the Bible.

February 1

The weather has suddenly changed; it is thawing and raining. I took a walk through the forest and found close to Zollnick the blood trail of a stag from yesterday's hunt. It ended in a pool of blood close to the road to Peterkau. Evidently the dead stag had been picked up there by a Polish timber cart. On my way back I passed the spot where, on New Year's Eve 1933, I had bagged a very strong wild boar, and then I crossed the Klavier Bridge where more than twenty years ago I shot my first snipe. The small fir tree under which I found it had meanwhile become an imposing tree.

H. went to Schwalgendorf today to see the new Polish head forester who is afraid to come here because of the Russians, and had sent H.'s daughter-in-law to tell H. to come and see him some day. All the woods in the neighborhood are in his charge —more than 50,000 acres. But he needs competent assistants. He seems to be a passionate hunter, with great understanding and love for the forest and the countryside. He has also taken an interest in the people of Schwalgendorf, and gives them work in the forest so that they can earn a little money. H. is hoping that some time there may be a chance for him to move over there.

February 3

The commandant has allowed me to use a cart to get some wood for my room. I drove to the so-called Milking Place near

the edge of the forest and loaded two cubic meters of alder wood
on it. All the other carts were out for wood, too, because the
steam engine, used for generating electric light, uses up twelve
cubic meters daily. Thousands of cubic meters are still lying in
the forest, everything that had been cut in 1943 and 1944 and
could no longer be carted away, including the 180-year-old stand
of pines just beyond the border, which we always used to show
our guests when they wanted to see first-rate timber. Now the
magnificent trunks are lying in all directions, slowly rotting.
The annual rings are still just visible.

Many women and the twelve- to fourteen-year-old boys are
employed by the Russians as drivers. The impudence of the boys
can hardly be beaten. It sometimes makes you gasp to hear their
remarks in the presence of the Russians, who, after all, understand by this time many German words. But they do not seem
to mind, first of all because they are on principle against any
discipline of children, and secondly, because they themselves are
using swearwords all day long, even if they tell one another
the simplest and most trivial things. "Damn women" has to be
said at least once in every sentence, though they may only want
a light for their cigarette. Even German swearwords, learned
during the war, have crept into their language—if their jargon
can be called a language.

A bath tub has been put up in the dairy, and I have permission to use it. Besides there is an Armenian at the school who
cuts people's hair. It is a special treat, gratefully appreciated by
all of us as a proof of Russian culture.

February 4

Today's temperature is 40 degrees F with strong winds, but
hunting went on just the same. Result: one deer, one fox, one
squirrel. The number of shots fired has been estimated at 2,000.

I went with Frau L. to trade in Rosenberg. We got two pounds of bacon worth 400 zloty for a tablecloth. The H.'s had hidden still other things which were, however, soon discovered. Even here the Russians still go on searching for hidden treasures, using long, pointed iron rods, which the blacksmith has to make for them. We heard that some of our local Russians would soon be transferred to Liegnitz in Silesia—their next headquarters. Michael, my Armenian colleague, invited three other Armenians and me to a schnapps party. The schnapps had been made by the former dairyman—now also responsible for the cattle—out of beet parings, and was very cloudy. You could drink it only if you stuffed your nose with bread—advice a Russian gave me. I had a splitting headache all night, and in the next room Michael was singing, instead of "Marianka," very oriental, warbling songs, which gave me visions of a sunbaked Karst landscape with herds of goats.

February 6

Temperature 33°F. The ground has been thawing out for some days. All the drains are clogged. From one house door to another, and across to the pump, we either walk on planks or jump from one brick to another. The dairyman made me a pair of clogs.

I visited patients in the nearby villages of Faulen and Albrechtau, where Russians, Poles, and Germans are living together. The manure from the stables is carted to the park and piled up several feet high. Plows, reapers, harrows, and threshers are lying around in the paddock. The manor house in Faulen has been burned down. Most of the houses in Albrechtau are still standing; the road to it has been enlarged by traffic to the width of a hundred yards.

My practice is increasing. Many people come to have their teeth extracted, because they have heard that I am in possession of a dentist's forceps. I got a small stove for my room, made by a "specialist"; it gets red-hot in a second and cold just as quickly. I've been sawing and chopping up wood. In the evening I tried to make shoes with binder twine. The day ended with a reading from the Bible.

February 9

The afternoon was free because the Russians have to go to the polls tomorrow. A little Lithuanian painter, who lives above me, has painted forty-five portraits of Stalin for the occasion. We used our free time to make syrup. Owing to the lack of space each of us has to keep strictly to the place assigned to him. The sacks of beet parings had been "semi-officially" obtained from the granary. A small fruit press, saved by the H.'s, wanders around the village from hand to hand; when people knock on our door, we know they have come to ask for "de press."

February 10

Today all the Russians here and from the neighborhood, and the Lithuanians who work for them, went to Bellschwitz to the "elections." Obviously they got a lot of schnapps there.

We separated binder twine for knitting. Frau L., as the expert, sat on a stool high up on top of the linen chest, and divided the twine with upraised arms. Two of us sat at her feet and wound it into balls, which were again divided. All kinds of necessary garments are meant to be crocheted or knitted out of this material. Special praise is due to the firm which invented this binder twine for binding grain in sheaves; they probably never dreamed what a help it would be some day to hundreds and thousands of people.

February 11

Michael had visitors: a first and a second lieutenant, both of them ladies. First lieutenant took precedence and had been described to me before in great detail. Second lieutenant was meanwhile busy with the wash, and tried unsuccessfully to hang it out on a wire in a violent snowstorm.

February 13

Some of the Russians came to have their bloody heads treated. As long as it is nothing serious, enormous head bandages are particularly appreciated.

B., the dairyman, is the only young man among four hundred natives. He had happened not to be with the trek when the Russians came, and had later found his way back here from Pomerania via several detours. He is clever in his dealings with the Russians and has therefore been allowed to take charge of the cattle again. The butter is intended for Liegnitz; but as a wagon is going there only once a month, it has been stored meanwhile in the granary in tin tubs. They have recently started making curds from the skimmed milk in a bath tub, which is kept over a fire to accelerate the process. The slightly burned curds are distributed as a part of the five-day food ration to the workers, to whom I belong.

Sunday, February 17

Clear and stormy weather. With three small milk cans full of syrup, which we wanted to exchange for fish, Frau L. and I went to Schwalgendorf, as usual by-passing Januschau. Without stopping once, we walked the whole way on the double-quick.

As a surprise, Kuczmarski gave us real bread and butter, for he still owns a goat. His daughter, Frau Bucholz, had secretly collected some patients who had asked her to let them come should I ever be in her house again. My dentist's forceps are in great demand. Recently, some Polish families arrived in Schwalgendorf. Loaded with fish, we reached home by moonlight, with a gale blowing.

February 18

A northeaster and driving snow. Tiles fell from the roofs. All the hay wagons which were expected from Peterkau today had been overturned. In the forest a slanting tree swept H. from a cart loaded with timber; he was brought home quite dazed and half frozen. Michael left today for good, and I moved into his room.

February 19

In yesterday's storm some thirty old firs at the edge of the nearby forest were uprooted and fell, all in the same direction, into the main stand. In the forest itself much damage has been done by the wind.

I went again to Rosenberg with Frau L. The bakeress bought the fox for 500 zloty. The price of one pound of sugar is 90 zloty.

At night Nadja called me to come and see the present wife of the commandant who was writhing with pains in her belly. She had taken something that did not agree with her. Nadja seemed to know what was wrong and made her drink two quarts of milk three times running and throw it up again. All that good milk! We could have done with it so well.

February 20

I tried to give some lessons to Alice and Peter L., aged eight and seven, respectively. All beginnings are difficult—for both parties. In the evening a wagon came to take me to Faulen. I sat in the back with Nadja, two Russians sat in the front. We drove away from the front door at full gallop. After ten yards we were stuck on a heap of stones, the wagon split in two, leaving Nadja and me in the back, while the front of the wagon with the Russians disappeared into the darkness. I got out and walked on, but halfway there a second wagon, escorted by men on horseback, overtook me. Reluctantly I climbed up; the coachman drove standing, flogging the horses with the end of the reins, determined not to let the riders get by. The wagon bounded through snowdrifts, but did not come to harm.

In Faulen I found thirty to forty people standing and smoking around the bed of a young Russian who had a deep knife wound under his right collar bone. He shouted at me, asking if he was to die. I said, yes, unless all the others left the room at once. A shower of swearwords from the patient struck home, and they promptly cleared out. He was able to breathe again and soon calmed down, making it possible for me to take the necessary measures. He seems to have had a narrow escape.

February 21

Frau Petschat has made me a new pair of trousers out of two sacks—bright yellow, with patch pockets and gathered around the ankles. It is the latest wear for both men and women. In the evening I went to the farm to get a sack of beet parings. Frau L. had put it up in a place where I could pick it up—from the garden of the farm, through a window of the stable. I came back with my burden, unnoticed, through deep snow, conscious that I had already become a thief. Twenty wagons, driven by women and girls, are driving daily to Riesenburg, returning in the evening with beet parings. Riesenburg is Polish, but the sugar plant is guarded by Russians.

February 23

Eight degrees below and hoarfrost. Later it became warmer and stormy again. The Russians celebrated Red Army Day; all I saw of it was bloody heads. I always ask them, as a joke, "What's wrong with you?" "Head kaput!" is the automatic answer. In the evening a regular blizzard set in. I whittled hooks out of a very hard piece of beechwood to be used for crocheting shoes. In addition to binder twine we need also the rubber of tires and wire for it, both of which are available in plenty, for the bicycles are ruined, and the wires are hanging down from the telephone poles.

March 3

Moderately cold; a strong southeastern wind. I went to Schwalgendorf and saw patients at the house of Frau Buchholz. The Polish head forester dropped in and was very friendly; he speaks German well. After having looked at me for a while he asked if I wasn't very cold, and would I allow him to give me something to put on. I was almost offended by this slight for my costume of which I am very proud. My patients gave us fish again, and also cotton yarn, a great quantity of which has been discovered in Weepers.

March 5

It is thawing and raining. All able-bodied people spent the day in Rosenberg loading potatoes, and did not get back till nine in the evening. An hour later the men were alerted again and I joined them. We drove off in several wagons; it was so dark that we could hardly see where we were going. Russians and Germans from the whole neighborhood were assembled near the station. As we could not see anything, we started burning the wooden handbarrows, standing about everywhere. We were standing among several potato pits along the railroad line on which stood a freight train. Our people began hacking open a pit. In the darkness you were treading on potatoes everywhere. No control was possible; it was left to each of us to decide how to get the potatoes into the train. We carried them over in sacks, always getting entangled in the signal wires. At times nobody did anything at all. When it began to dawn, some two hundred men squatted in the open pits, tired and numb with cold. We were supposed to get some soup soon, but as nothing had happened by noon, I took my leave and went home to my patients. The safest way to walk through Rosenberg in these times is wearing clogs, and shouldering a pitchfork. The Poles call the town Susz.

It is difficult to distinguish between Russian soldiers and Russian civilians. Their clothes are similar and all of them carry guns. Most of our Russians have been prisoners in Germany and are now afraid of Russia.

March 7

Several women came from Schwalgendorf to have their teeth extracted. In the afternoon I went to Rosenberg to bargain for

sugar, bacon, onions, and yeast. With the yeast we make a kind
of beer out of beet syrup in a milk can. When it is three days
old, it is quite good to drink. Three thousand Russian soldiers
are expected in Rosenberg. The Poles are allowed to live there
only temporarily. The Russians are restless and talk of war. There
is a rumor that American and English troops have drawn up
near the Elbe and have armed the Germans as well. Today is
Russian Mothers' Day.

March 10

Today is Sunday, a day the Russians do not keep. I baptized
the youngest grandchild of the Lassners, the last pure German
child in the village. The mother's birthday was celebrated in the
evening and the Russians were also invited. Three of the old
men who had worked here for a year came too. They had made
themselves musical instruments out of boxes and wires. The
melody to their noise was supplied by an asthmatic accordion.
As a finale the Russians danced their national dances like mad-
men.

March 11

Wassili, called Washko, the brigadier, went hunting yesterday and wounded a red deer near Klein-Brausen. He followed
the blood trail across the lake marsh and the Heidemühler Forest
as far as a "river" which he could not cross. The "river" is the
connection between two forest lakes. I went there today and
picked up the trail on the other side of the "flow." Three hundred
yards farther was the dead deer—an oldish hind with calf. I cut
it open and hung the liver on a tree to save it from poaching
dogs, two of which I had seen quite nearby. I could walk only
very slowly in the soft, melting snow and did not reach home

till late in the afternoon. Washko, to whom I reported, was very surprised and ordered the horses to be harnessed at once to drive to the place for the deer. I begged him to distribute the venison in the village. He promised it and came with me in the cart. When we arrived at the spot where the deer was lying it was quite dark, and he asked me somewhat perplexed how I had found the way. "I know every tree here," I said. But this was obviously beyond him. When we got back he told me that I might distribute the venison myself.

March 12

The dairyman helped me to skin the deer. In earlier times we did not make much of an animal like that; this time it will be a treat for a few hundred people who have not seen any meat for months.

There are rumors of war among the Russians. Stalin is said to have made a speech against England. A great many horses are shipped to other places. I heard that in Januschau many horses have been slaughtered for canning.

March 15

Yesterday morning I went to Nipkau to get some medicaments from a Russian pharmacist, especially something for the itch. On the way back I was stopped in Rosenberg by the UB, the Polish Gestapo, and locked in a prison cell. My companion there was a young Pole who had killed somebody in a brawl. He prayed all night. As we had only one mattress, we took turns lying down. In the morning we were let out into the yard and told to take containers from the rubbish pile with us for our food. I found half a preserving jar and had coffee poured into it, which I used to rinse it with. In the afternoon I was brought before the commandant who was not only interested in the medicaments, but also in a tablecloth found in my rucksack. He was in mufti and spoke German well—maybe he was a Russian. After some discussion, and after I had told him that the Russians in Brausen were waiting for me, he gave me, to my surprise, five hundred zloty for the tablecloth and sent me back to Nipkau escorted by a sentry. The sentry conferred for a long time with the pharmacist who had given me the medicaments and then left me there. I asked him to give me a certificate of discharge so that I would not be arrested again, but he could not do it. Instead, I was given something to eat and then told to wait for the next Russian cart going to Brausen. "When will that be?" I asked. "Well, perhaps tomorrow, perhaps in three days. You stay here, eat, sleep. No worry." So I napped until it was dark, and then walked back to Brausen, giving Rosenberg a wide berth. In the evening we sat around at Lassner's, talking about what to do if it should really come to a war, and the Russians should suddenly leave, taking with them everything which is still useful. Should we not try and hide at least a few cows in some remote forest farm?

March 17, Reminiscere Sunday

Fourteen degrees below and a lot of fresh snow. The Russians went hunting again. Result: three deer, one wild pig, two rabbits, a boar and a stag wounded. Unfortunately I couldn't follow up the latter this time, as I am in bed with a temperature.

March 20

Yesterday, in addition to fish, we brought a live rooster from Schwalgendorf. A few chicken have gradually been discovered here and there. We ourselves have no less than five, but we have lost our rooster, which a small Russian boy killed with a Tesching rifle. We brought the new one back with us as a surprise. Schlichting drove us back from Schwalgendorf in his sleigh, to show his gratitude for a tooth extraction. He still has an old horse.

In the evening the Lithuanian painter came to supper. We were celebrating the birthday of my grandfather Oldenburg. We had fish in various forms, hot and cold, served with all the trimmings. Frau S. had learned cooking in a large household, and Frau L. ran a bakery for three years. The lamp was hanging very low over the table so that the beds could not be seen. The Lithuanian shook his head in wonder at the sight of everything our womenfolk had managed to produce in spite of the general poverty. He said that this urge to resist chaos was one of the reasons Germans were such a mystery to the Russians.

March 22

Powerful spring gale. Starlings, pewees, and cranes have arrived. The village pond dashes high waves. On the village road the water is eighteen inches deep, and we have to go a long way around to the pump with our pitchers. The Russians suddenly took it into their heads to store ice in the icehouse which should have been done long before. The women are standing in the cesspool in the farmyard trying to remove with poles the middle piece still floating there. The Russian tailor came in the evening and brought me a pair of gray trousers, to the bottom of which he has sown with a sure eye eighteen inches of black lining material.

March 24

Walking through the small wood full of bird calls, I came upon the tanner. He works on the small and medium-sized oaks with a plane because the bark is needed for tanning. This means that they all get a complete girdle, three feet deep, which will hardly do them any good. I tried to convince him that it would be easier and better to fell a couple of oaks and then to strip them completely of their bark, but he couldn't see my point. They are quite indifferent to what is going to become of things. What can it be—this complete aversion to order, this lack of any relationship to something that has grown? You do not find it in any animal except perhaps in a domestic one, which has been deprived of the basis of its existence, and then it happens only from fear. Time and again I ask myself what are actually the origins of humanity? Is it possible for man to remain a purely natural being after God has spoken to him? Isn't Christ's saying, "Man shall not live by bread alone, but by every word that proceedeth out of the mouth of God," a plain statement and significant for an obligation which we cannot escape?

March 26

Spring is arriving in force. I went to Januschau and restored the graves. Five swans were swimming on the flooded meadow beside the Heidemühler road. In the little pavilion in the park which was built for my mother's fifth birthday, the Russians have established a schnapps still. On my way back I passed by Dead Lake and looked for fish. A few ducks were swimming around on it; there was still some ice in the middle.

In the afternoon we went shopping in Rosenberg after having received some money for another tablecloth. By now we have made some friends among the storekeepers; even "Warsawianka" smiles a little, as much as her puffy and heavily made-up face allows. At the hospital snowdrops are in bloom. I took one of the last remaining windowpanes from there for my room. Within ten minutes three rats were caught in our trap; they are always nibbling at our shoes and shoelaces and are particularly keen on fish, which we have to hang up on wires for that reason.

March 31

I went to Schwalgendorf with Frau L. for the first time in the shoes I made myself. The island in Lake Tromnitz is already peopled with herons and cormorants; the latter are increasing at an alarming rate and have driven some of the herons over to the other island. Their way of strutting around reminds me of the Russians. There was still some ice on the Geserich, which melted during the day; when we left, the sun glittered in innumerable little ripples. When it was almost dark we were attacked by two Russians just outside Brausen. They knocked me over the head and dragged Frau L. away. I lay awake all night, wondering whether it would have happened if I had carried the hammer with me. Frau L. soon came home.

April 1

With my four school children and four-year-old Helga S. I went to Albrechtau to see the church. Almost everything in it has been removed, but the altar is still there and so is the angel above the font who has lost only one foot. The children asked some important questions, and inevitably brought up the central problem: Why did God let the serpent into Paradise? The people in Albrechtau are keeping some sheep and young cattle. A few Russians are living there on good terms with German families.

April 3

Some Russians arrived with trucks to get potatoes for Königsberg, they said. I succeeded in speaking to one of the drivers who

declared he knew the Sisters "with the big caps," and took a
note from me to Sister Raphaela, begging her to advise everybody to try and get through to the country, if possible, and that
they should do their best to come here. Unfortunately, it is not
very likely that she will get my scrawl.

It is the most lovely spring weather with a temperature of 68°F.
H. and I went to Merinos where the sheep of Finckenstein used
to be washed. The village is deserted. The shore of the lake was
speckled blue with more frogs than I had ever seen on it, and
pike were stirring among the reeds.

April 5

The forest is full of anemones, hepaticas, and daphne. I bathed
in the Januschau Lake and watched the fish for a while. A ring
snake swam past me. On my way through the young pines I
unexpectedly came upon a Russian I did not know who was
going hunting. Fortunately, he was as startled as I, and asked
me if I had seen any *"ķossas,"* evidently meaning deer. I tried
to think where he would do the least harm and sent him to
Annhof, the old fishing hut by the lake.

April 7

I went to the lake with some fish traps but could not set them,
because a boat was lying there, and shots were fired quite close
to me. I am afraid for the swans which can hardly be missed
because of their size, especially when sitting on their nests and
hatching their eggs. The abundance of blossoms in the forest
is overwhelming.

Some of our Russians are moving to Bellschwitz today, and
our people are afraid of being taken with them. The Russians
cannot understand it. "But have house there too," they say. For

them there is no such thing as living in a permanent place. When they move out, they take everything with them, even the windows. We sent eight-year-old Alice to see if a certain party of Russians had gone. "No," she reported, "the windows are still in."

Anatolj, on whom I recently operated by candle light, opening an enormous abscess on his leg with a razor blade, came to celebrate with me, bringing some schnapps he had made himself. Fortunately, I saw him coming just in time to escape through the window.

Frau Aust, the old forester's wife from Faulen, is living in Klein-Albrechtau with her older sister in a small room below the Poles. They had once escaped as far as Pomerania, but had been forced to return. Frau Aust's husband died last summer. The two women are knitting stockings and gloves for us out of binder twine.

April 11

A crowd of Russians have come to requisition the potato pits beside the Rosenberg road, our last reserve. I had seen it coming for quite some time, but unfortunately had not taken any precautions. We could easily have opened one of the pits and made a depot somewhere in the field. At night I sneaked to the opened pits to see how many potatoes were left, dug a three feet deep hole in the field and began to fill it with potatoes from the pit. I had just filled the second sack when I was challenged from the road. I took to my heels at once and ran across the fields; the sentry fired three shots in my direction. Once out of reach I took a roundabout way which led me through the Little Wood. What a glorious spring night! The screech owl hooted its weird call. Two badgers chased each other, snarling, on the path; one of them turned a somersault from fright when it brushed against

my trouserleg. I moved stealthily up to my house door through
the tall weeds and crept unseen into my bed.

April 14

Yesterday young Frau H. came from Schwalgendorf to bring
me fish for my birthday, and we had a grand celebration. Today,
Sunday, three of us took her home again. We had left the park
of Januschau behind us and were going across the field toward
Zollnick Forest when a herd of red deer came trotting from the
left. Suddenly, a couple of shots were fired behind us. We turned
round and saw some Russians standing before the door of the
manor house, firing at the deer from a distance of at least eight
hundred yards—or perhaps at us. But their automatics did
not carry too far; the bullets hit the field far behind us.

When we were quite near the forest, a second herd ran swiftly
across the field further left, a magnificent sight. They were using
the same runs as before. From former habit I ran along the edge
of the wood and let one deer after another trot past me into
the forest.

Such a walk through the forest, past the lakes where the life
of the waterbirds becomes more and more animated, is always
a thrilling experience. In the old days a drive to Schwalgendorf
had always been considered a major undertaking. Now we are
walking the same distance without counting the miles. Our life
consists in any case much more of movement, and our feet fulfill
only now their true purpose. The militia from Saalfeld was just
visiting Schwalgendorf, and when we entered the village I was
promptly arrested. But as I am working for the Russians I was
set free. We are gradually learning to play Russians and Poles
against each other. On our way home we avoided Januschau
altogether by walking along the chain of lakes via the Annhof
fishery, and from there along the edge of the forest. At twilight

we crossed the Milking Place—a pasture ground with birches and alders at the edge of the wood, and snipes flew past in such large numbers as I had always wished to see but never had.

April 16

Another day of sunshine and warmth. In the old days we would have worried about the drought and have longed for rain, but as nothing has been sown in the fields we can enjoy the weather with an easy conscience. The Russians have no interest whatsoever in the country, because they are probably leaving it soon, and the few Poles cultivate only enough for their needs.

The birches are showing the first green. Late in the evening I took the Lithuanian painter for a stroll through the Little Wood, under the full moon. At first he was rather shy, but then we sat down on a fallen tree, and he began to tell me about his wife and two small children whom he had to leave behind when the Russians carried him away. He has heard nothing from them for almost two years. I tried to comfort him with the only consolation we have on earth, and urged him not to give himself up so much to despair and schnapps, the effects of which have already left their distinct marks on him.

April 17

Four women from Schwalgendorf visited us on their way to the militia in Rosenberg; two of them are going there to look for their husbands, whom the militia took with them in order to play a trick on the Russians. In the evening two of the women dropped in again on their way home. The other two went on to Charlottenwerder because they had gathered from various hints that their husbands had been taken there.

Late in the evening, after two heavy thunderstorms had come down north and south of us, I was a guest of the Lithuanians. Eleven of them are living in one large room. Out of one large and one small glass, which were passed around, we all drank beet beer and beet schnapps, while student songs were sung to German tunes.

April 18

The Russians really seem to be leaving; new orders are issued every day. H. wants to talk with the Polish head forester and try to find accommodations in Schwalgendorf, where several houses are still standing empty, and I went with him to visit patients, this time a Polish family who had recently arrived. We returned with a great deal of fish. The two old men from Schwalgendorf, one of whom Schwarz, the carpenter, are actually held by the militia in Charlottenwerder. If the Russians do not come and get them out, they intend trying to escape during the Easter holidays.

Our official food rations have become very scanty and are only distributed now to twenty "workers," including myself. But there are still several sacks of musty flour in the granary, and the two girls working at night at the mill have decided to let the people of the village benefit from it. We, too, were to get a sack. I presented myself, therefore, as arranged, at the yardgate at one in the morning and was escorted into the mill; then the Russian who worked the engine, had to switch off the light until I had safely crossed the yard, carrying back a hundred-weight sack on my shoulder.

April 19, Good Friday

I went to see patients in Little and Great Albrechtau. In one of the houses I found two women and six children, both boys

and girls, sitting around a table and knitting. The binder twine
is inexhaustible. In the evening I read the story of the Passion
according to St. Luke.

April 21, Easter Sunday

I held a service in my dispensary which we arranged very
festively. There was some very good singing in spite of the lack
of hymnbooks. Even the Russian tailor who seems to belong to
a sect joined us. I chose as my text the story of the Resurrection
in the Gospel of St. John. As my listeners were nearly all women
it seemed the most suitable.

In the afternoon we hid little Easter eggs the size of peas,
which I had obtained in Rosenberg, in the gravelpit of the
Little Wood. The children were radiantly happy. On our way
back from there we suddenly saw a fountain rising above the
forest, and heard a detonation. The commandant was fishing the
Dead Lake with explosives, and I found later the surface of
the lake covered with small dead fishes. There was another bang
at Annhof. They had towed the boat to the cart and had driven
with it a mile and a quarter across country to the next lake. The
other Russians celebrated the day with schnapps and a great
free-for-all in the village. The women stood in the doorways,
watching with rapt attention.

April 22

With gaping head wounds from yesterday's brawl, three Rus-
sians came to me for treatment. They had wanted to steal the
Lithuanians' schnapps and had broken into their house, but
had been knocked down with a fence post by the biggest of the
Lithuanians and thrown out of a window on the other side.
The whole village had watched them running in at the front

and flying out again at the back. Today the tall Lithuanian is in the lockup.

Noticing a thick cloud of smoke in the direction of the Dead Lake, I went there and found a raging forest fire. From the shore, where the Russians had lit a fire, the dry underbrush was burning in a semi-circle over a stretch of almost three hundred yards. I took off my shirt and succeeded in beating a few breaches with fir branches. Standing on a footpath which the fire was approaching on a diagonal front, I succeeded to my surprise in smothering it altogether. Fortunately it had not yet caught the treetops. The stumps went on smoldering. It is so dry and hot that we must be prepared for more outbreaks of fire, especially since the Russians are building fires everywhere to fry the exploded fish on the spot.

April 25

In the morning I took a bucket with me to the Dead Lake and extinguished stumps. In the afternoon a long walk with H. Another huge cloud of smoke hung over the forest, this time quite far away. They have started to give us "pay." I rank next after the dairyman and the blacksmith and get seventy-seven Polish zloty a month. (The price of one pound of sugar is ninety zloty.) For the others the pay drops gradually to eighteen zloty. Three Russians are busy in their "office" working out the different amounts on calculating machines.

April 28

At last rain during the night; lovely summer weather again all day. I went with Frau S. to Schwalgendorf, via Annhof and Zollnick. The latter was burned down and consists now only of the forester's lodge, standing in the heart of the forest on a small clearing between two lakes. In the yard under the maple tree was a grave with a cross of birchwood and a steel helmet. Frau S. showed me a chest buried in the barn, which the Poles had found and opened. The hunting guns are still buried in the ground beside the empty chest. We took some chives with us from the garden. Later we crossed the border near the Weisse Bruch, which was my favorite stand on our hunting parties, because the lack of underbrush allowed me to see through the whole forest, and there was almost always some game in sight. On stalking expeditions, too, I often got in a shot there.

In the middle of the forest we found a mowing machine and a dead man lying near it. In the four-year-old pine plantation in the state forest we both stopped at the same moment with a shout of delight, "Morels!" Morels already! And what beauties! We soon had filled our rucksacks, but left them lying there, so that the people in Schwalgendorf would not become envious. From the garden of the deserted forester's lodge in Alt-Schwalge we took the first rhubarb, and from a crow's nest in easy climbing reach, two eggs for H.'s birthday. Two young tree plantations have been burned down in Schwalgendorf and an out-of-the-way farmhouse as well. The Pole who had lived there had only intended to burn off the old grass in his meadow. On the way home we passed the lakes again; a swan was lying dead on its nest near the shore. The reeds are getting taller; rollers and hoopooes have arrived. We have been going barefoot for weeks.

Stimulated by our constantly going barefoot, I have read the Gospel story of the washing of the feet from quite a new angle than in previous years. For when you come home barefoot in the evening, the need to wash your feet or to have them washed, is actually very great, and you begin to understand why our Saviour used just this particular means of making vivid some aspect of the most important relationship between Christians. What is involved here is, after all, our becoming clean, our maintaining fellowship with Christ and with one another. I believe we Protestants make things too hard for ourselves on this point. Like Peter we think that forgiveness of sin always involves cleansing of the whole man. But Jesus said to Peter: "He that is washed needeth not save to wash his feet." And "Now ye are clean through the word which I have spoken to you." Did not Jesus speak to us, too? But it seems to me that we do not properly lay claim to this our fundamental cleanliness, and we therefore bear about the weights on our conscience for an unnecessary long time. If we kept the image of the washing of the feet before our eyes, we should probably soon learn to regard our sins—accumulating daily, almost unavoidable—as undesirable as we do street dirt on our bare feet. And then we would make use, in a quite different way than before, of the possibility of having them taken away by our Divine Companion along the road.

April 30

Yesterday and today—the birthdays of the H.s', both husband and wife. We had a birthday cake. There is almost no work to do now. The pigs are gone and only the cattle are left. The cows have been lowing in the stalls for days, because they can smell the fresh grass; but the Russians were afraid to let them out into the paddock. We have at last persuaded them to do so, and the animals have been capering around there all morning, almost crazy with joy. In the evening Frau S. and I worked in the burial ground and planted flowers on the graves. At sundown we walked home, shouldering our rakes and spades.

Looking after the graves of my loved ones is one of the happiest tasks I am allowed to carry out these days. How great is God's kindness to grant me this happiness and to let me love life in spite of all we have endured. My youngest brother was the first to go. When he was eighteen, he was killed at Maubeuge,

ten days after the beginning of the French campaign. After having taken part in twelve reconnaissance patrols, some of which
he led himself, he lost his life in an encounter with French
tanks, when he was shot in the head. His death was a shattering
blow for me. I had not seen him for almost a year. The last time
we had met was here in Januschau, a few months after he had
graduated from school, and was serving in the labor battalion.
We all dimly felt the war coming. We went hunting in order to
be together. Before I left at four the next morning, I went into
his room as he had asked me to do. He was awake. For a moment we looked at each other hesitantly, but before the anxious
question about the future could come up his indestructible sense
of fun flashed out and saved the happiness of the moment. His
image is always present to me, but not as a stable motionless picture, but always astir, coming and going, giving and receiving.
I see him coming downstairs and greeting people who are waiting for him—a little slower than usual, a little more embarrassed
than necessary, a slight wrinkle of annoyance on his forehead
because of all the eyes directed upon him—but powerless to prevent a wave of his own joy of life communicating itself to those
waiting for him. With him, a new element had come into the
life of us children. Even before he was born my mother had been
different than usual; she somehow seemed to be treading on air,
and the child always made this impression of lightness on people.
In his presence the world grew wider, the sky more lofty; objects
of dispute lost their importance, and violent impulses were
checked by a feeling of shame. His personality lent a quite new
and much clearer aspect to the rather muddled self-understand-
ing of our brotherly relationship. We looked upon him as
being truly one of us, and yet we treated him in a rather cautious manner, because we felt that he did not belong to us;
he would go his own way and we wouldn't be able to stop him.
I shall always remember how someone who had watched him

closely, said to my mother: "You will have to let that one travel
early—a great deal, I mean." He was five years old. Very early all
the children in the neighborhood gathered around him without
having been called by him, and grown-up people liked him to
tease them in a playful way, for it was so pleasant; I have never
known anybody to be jealous of him for any reason. "I walk
across bridges though I'm able to fly,"—these words from a poem
always recur to me when I think of him.

When he fell he was buried by a brother ten years older than
him, who was serving in the same regiment, with the help of
eight comrades, by the roadside, wrapped in a tarpaulin. And
when the French campaign was ended, his brother did what was
forbidden: he dug him up and brought him secretly to Januschau, thinking it would be his mother's wish. The grave has
been here ever since.

At his side lies the next youngest brother, who died six weeks
later. At the age of eighteen he had had a heavy fall from his
horse on the race course of Karlshorst, and had never really recovered from it. The death of his dearly loved brother dealt
him the last blow. He hardly spoke at all during those last few
weeks, and then a sudden brain hemorrhage put an end to his
life. When I think of him, I am always gripped by a deep sense
of guilt. From birth, he was smaller than his brothers and developed at first more slowly; but by sheer force of will, he made
up for the lost time, became a splendid horseman, learned more
easily than his brothers, showed a more stable character, and
resembled the younger in the sense that he was completely un-
selfish and was always standing up for the underdog. But he
lacked the compensating element—an inner sense of assurance.
Too much had been demanded of him all his life, even a year
after his skull had been fractured. We let him go and join the
army when he was no more than a shadow of his former self.
We were blind at that time. He carried on with the remains of

his strength until he finally collapsed. Now it all comes back to me, and I can guess at what he suffered.

A few steps away there is a stone bearing the name of the brother nearest to me in age, with whom I was in a constant state of feud during my whole childhood. He was harsh, passionate, very touchy, and it was not until he had become a soldier that he was able to master his temperamental personality and to show his human qualities to the best advantage. After the French campaign in which our youngest brother had fallen by his side, he served in Russia, first before Moscow and then in command of a reconnoitering division before Leningrad. It was when he was transferred there, in November 1942, that we saw him for the last time. He had spent three days in Berlin, had informed himself of the situation, realizing something of the abyss above which our leadership was playing its reckless game, and was prepared to face the inevitable consequences. "I know it is wrong for me to go back to the front now, to my division," he said to me. "Once you are out there with your men, you think that everything is all right as long as you do your duty. Yet everything is lost by now, and you are only driving your men to their ruin. I should be doing something quite different. But three days are simply not enough to make up one's mind, so I must choose the easier way once more." In the night of January 14th to the 15th he appeared to me in a dream as a gigantic figure. Before the news reached us by telephone, I knew that he had fallen. He had waited with his division on the shore of Lake Ladoga for the attack of the Russians who were advancing across the ice in successive waves, and at first had succeeded in holding them up. Then he had rushed to drag a wounded soldier out of the danger zone and had been mortally wounded. Somebody told me that only the day before he had said to his men that you could not die a better death than in saving a comrade.

My oldest and last surviving brother and my mother should be buried here too, but although they were killed not far from this place, their bodies can never be brought here, because I was told that many weeks after their death they were buried in a mass grave somewhere. My brother, who was too old to share in our childish rivalries, and had often criticized our sometimes foolish behavior, was nevertheless devoted to us and felt responsible for us. He had spent the whole of the war in Poland, the Danube Provinces and southern Russia, and had only come home now and then for several months to look after his Januschau estate. He had obtained leave for this a few days before the collapse of East Prussia, and we had talked to each other over the telephone. It is an immense relief for me to know that he and my mother were together at the time of their deaths.

I find it difficult to talk of my mother. She is still so near, that is, she will be forever near, even if I should have many more years to live. She was the decisive influence on our lives, much more than my father. Although we took a passionate interest in his strictly defined occupation of horse breeding, we naturally felt him to belong to an older generation. We never felt this with our mother. We could not help conforming our lives to hers, and this led sometimes to emotional conflicts. But I do not know what sort of a man I would have become without my mother. She was the measure of all things for us, and we were always anxious to live in harmony with her. Not that we always shared her every single opinion or did what she expected us to—on the contrary, it sometimes heightened our zest for life to swim against the current of her ideas, though only within her reach, so that in case of an emergency we could be hauled on board again by her. She was a woman of action, standing in the center of events, indeed, the stream of events flowed right through her. Her spontaneous actions sometimes gave us a painful shock, but they always resulted in the straightening out of a false situation, the exposure of a hidden untruth. She could act wrongly, and still be perfectly right. Right and wrong as alternatives meant, in any case, far less to her than great and small. She could wound, but she healed even more easily, and when it came to difficult decisions, she could help you out of an awkward situation with the assurance of a sleepwalker. After my youngest brother had fallen she went through a serious crisis. It began with that kind of "floating" which we had noticed before his birth. His friends and comrades came to see her, and their orphaned state upheld her. But they fell too, one after another. Then she stopped eating. Although the ties of affection with the rest of us remained as strong as before, she seemed at times so remote, when she believed nobody observed her, that I felt her decline could no longer be arrested. But the fresh demands on her, her contacts with persecuted Jews in Berlin, where my parents were then living, the increasing disquieting news from the front, the air raids—all this combined to rouse her spirits again. When my brother was killed in Russia she was staying with me in Insterburg and I had to break the news to her in the morning. Hard as it was, I am grateful now that I was allowed to do it. When I took her to the station that evening she said: "Don't imagine that I have ever wished to die. I know that I am the most fortunate of mothers."

May 1

The first of May really does credit to its name. In recent years we have nearly always had snow at this time. This year the trees have been in leaf for a long while, the oaks are getting green, lilies of the valley are out, cockchafers are buzzing and the cuckoo is calling. In honor of the day we went on a big outing; we even took four-year-old Helga with us, sometimes on foot, sometimes carried piggyback. She slept peacefully all the way home, buttoned up in an overcoat hung on a pole which two of us carried

on our shoulders. Our objective was the Uroviec, a beautiful lake
near Schwalgendorf which we had only passed until now. It is
said to be 240 feet deep, and the water is the clearest imaginable.
When we had got there, we first filled our rucksacks with morels,
and then bathed in radiant sunshine in the lake below the Alt-
Schwalge forester's lodge, where a small landing stage runs out
into the water. There Frau H., who had come to the birthday
party, left us again, and we made a wide detour through the
forest and took some more rhubarb from the garden at Annhof,
coming home late in the evening.

May 4

We started making a garden for ourselves, digging up the
ground directly behind the house and rooting out a thick tangle
of burdocks, nettles, thistles, and horseradish. Then we spread
pressed beet parings, in the process of fermenting, over the whole
as manure. The garden measures twenty-one feet by twenty-one
feet. We got poles and wire netting for a fence from the forest.
People laugh at us, because the Russians will tear everything up,
they say, and because we won't be here long enough to see things
growing. But we do not let them discourage us; we enjoy the
work and somebody will certainly benefit from it later. In the
evening we put some plants in. In a kind of plant nursery in
Faulen Frau H. has picked up ten small tomato plants, which
we put in along the wall. We also hope to get seeds in Rosenberg.

Two German soldiers came to see me today; they are working
for the Russians in Januschau, but I hadn't seen them before.
One of them brought his wife who has the usual disease, con-
tracted from the Russians. The commandant in Schönberg kept
her a prisoner for a long time, and there is still danger that he
may send for her again. It must be frightful in Schönberg, the

commandant is a sadist. It is a blessing that we have nothing to do with him.

Our fat commandant left here today; the cattle are to go too very soon.

May 8

During the day it was warm and cloudy, but in the evening it became clear and very cold. We are afraid for the countless blossoms on fruit trees and bushes in this unusual spring. Two young women and I went to Schwalgendorf to get potatoes in a baby buggy. There are none left here, and we want some to plant. On our way back, partly along sandy paths, partly through the main stand, we had a lot of trouble with our load. One of us always had to walk ahead a hundred yards, while the other two pulled and pushed the buggy whose axles were no longer parallel to each other. It tipped over more than once and we had to collect the contents over again. On the last part of the journey the wheels had become so completely locked that we had to pull the buggy across the fields like a sledge, and it was almost midnight when we arrived home.

May 9

Today the Russians are celebrating the anniversary of our capitulation. Many of them can no longer stand the smell of schnapps, and stuff bread into their noses. What they value most in drinking is the aftereffect, not the taste. I visited patients in Rasenfeld. There are some typhus cases among the Germans. Afterwards we went to Merinos and got rhubarb, our chief food at present, boiled in syrup.

Schwalgendorf has had mail from the Reich! Two women

came to tell us about it. People are affected by it in very different ways, for not all the news is pleasant. Many husbands who were thought to be lost have shown up again, but not all of them seem inclined to get in contact again with their wives and families, having formed new liaisons elsewhere. Some of the letters are real scandalmongery which threatens to disrupt the harmony gradually established in the heterogeneous community of the village.

May 12

This morning there was slight frost again; it is the week of the "Ice Saints." We've covered our tomato plants with paper bags. It grew warmer during the day. A German soldier who works for the Russians in Rasenfeld, came with a serious injury to his hand. The Russian who brought him drove us to Nipkau where we could give him an anti-tetanus injection. Going back we drove most of the time at a gallop with the result that the backboard of the closed wagon fell out and was left lying on the road, because the driver did not consider it worth his while to stop for such a trifle.

In the evening I went fishing in the lake at Januschau, opposite the bathing place, where the osprey has built its aerie in a fir tree. The lake, about a mile and a quarter long, entirely surrounded by woods and connected with the neighboring lakes by "flows," is one of the strongest attractions for me because peace and quiet has returned, and life is in no way different from what it used to be. The only thing I really miss among the calls of the larger and smaller ducks, the divers, the moor hawk, and the osprey, is the occasional barking of dogs from the Annhof fishery across the water, which always broke out as soon as anyone approached. Even a pair of swans is still here, although as a result of the disturbances in the spring they have not succeeded in hatching their young. On my way home I walked for miles through fields choked with weeds, out of which clouds of midges and other vermin rose into the air.

May 14

Sun and wind; in the evening very warm and a storm. A most unusual year. I went to Gross-Albrechtau to baptize two children of Russian origin. The attitude of the mothers to these children, of which only a minority are the result of rape, differs very much, and it is difficult to foresee what their future will be like. Some of them seem to be loved in a quite simple and natural way; others are only accepted because they are there, many are looked upon as a mere nuisance. But for the moment the existence of these children presents no problem here. Later on, if people should ever return to more orderly conditions, difficulties will probably arise now and then. At the present time, owing to the excessive supply of men, many women are so much under the spell of their own demons that it is not likely that they will listen to reason.

On my way back I looked up old Frau Aust who is working in the gardens of several Poles and is paid in food for herself and her invalid sister.

When I came home toward evening I found, to my intense surprise, a letter waiting for me, which had come from the west and had been forwarded by my aunt. It was from my sister, dated January 21, so one of my own letters must have got through after all. My sister tells me a great deal about people who are still alive and well, among them near relatives of my aunt. Almost stunned, I left the house again and roamed the countryside. I could only gradually take in the fact that there are still people waiting for me. With this letter a new period has begun. Lost in thought, I went as far as Grünhof, a small village on the other side of the forest, which is still uninhabited. In one of its weed-grown gardens a single iris flashed like a blue flame. It seemed to me a symbol of my former existence which is ready to flower once more.

May 15

I took a letter to Rosenberg. In the post office, which I entered rather cautiously, a friendly Polish woman asked me—in spite of my peculiar costume—if I was a "studierter." She offered me the books in her house. Very grateful, less for the books than for her friendly attitude, I nodded and let her show me, in the distance, her house on the Riesenburg Street. Frau S., too, has recently made some contacts in Rosenberg, and goes there daily to work for a family with two children.

Three days ago all our cattle were driven to Rosenberg to be shipped away by rail. Today the whole herd has come back again for some unknown reason. Late in the evening the new commandant consulted me about a very painful pleurisy. He is considerably thinner than his predecessor, and seems to have an aversion to schnapps. He has shot to pieces some of the distilleries in the village, but some are still left.

May 17

The neighboring manor of Falkenau is completely abandoned and partially destroyed. I went there to forage in the gardens, where I found a forest of rhubarb which no one had discovered. When I walked through the empty stables, an indistinct shape slipped before me out of the door and disappeared around the corner. I was just able to see that it was a human being, and I ran a short way after it, but did not find any trace. In a corner, sheltered from the wind, I came across six glorious yellow tulips.

The cattle went to Rosenberg today for the second time. A

hundred head were put on a train to be slaughtered in Liegnitz—
all of them excellent milch cows. The remaining forty came back.

May 19, Cantate Sunday

I, too, feel like singing. I have decided to visit my aunt, because
we have to talk over all the exciting news from the west which
the letter has brought us. I pulled a baby buggy behind me as
far as Schwalgendorf, which I intended to fill with potatoes and
pick up on my way back. After giving some medical advice to a
few families there, I went on eastward with a full rucksack.
Young Frau H. rowed me across the lake to Weepers. Beyond
Gablauken I overtook four German women carrying containers
of water. They were going to the graves of their husbands and
sons who had been taken away a year ago and were later found
dead not far from the village. They had buried them and set up
a small cross made of two boards which had since been shot to
pieces. I sat down beside it, while the women tended the grave,
and then we sang, and I read a psalm.

Afterwards I followed the canal through the meadows, exchanged a few words with some German women living in Liegen, and then ran across country through some paddocks past
Liebemühl, and crossed the canal by the railroad bridge. I nodded,
in passing, to two Polish anglers standing there who stared
after me rather bewildered.

Soon I was in the Taberbrück Forest again. The beech foliage
had suffered in places from the frost. This time I walked on a
long straight lane with many hunting stands, called "pulpits,"
which ended at a lattice gate, similar to a barn door. Snipes flew
up in greater numbers than I had ever seen; it was probably the
second flight which is usually disregarded. I waited by the gate
till it was dark. I heard bugle calls from Taberbrück, obviously
blown by an expert. How familiar they sounded! It seemed silly

to have to again by-pass the next villages. But I was soon in the Grasnitz woods where the ground was dotted with glow worms. I heard the snuffling of many wild pigs near the burial ground. Then I was standing before the house door. It was locked on the outside, and I started back at the sight of a piece of stamped paper which was stuck on it.

Cautiously I tapped on the window of the next house and stepped back into the darkness. Frau Langanke opened the door, let me in and called down Gross and Fräulein Jokuteit from their attic rooms. They burst into tears. A few days earlier my aunt had been taken away at night by at least twelve armed men, presumably to Allenstein. No reason had been given. We spent the whole night together, discussing the incident and the possibilities of finding out more. They fed me the best they had, and refused to accept what I had brought with me. The chicken, Lorchen, had not taken any food after my aunt left, and had suddenly dropped dead.

During the whole day I remained hidden and set out again about nine o'clock in the loveliest summer weather. The snipes were again on the wing. Three times I came upon red deer. The night hawks churred incessantly and followed me with the peculiar trilling and clapping of their mating flight. There was always a spice of danger in walking under the "pulpits," but the risk of any one of them being occupied was never as small as at the present time.

After I had crossed the bridge at Liebemühl a fox barked at me. I took cover in a roadside ditch when a group of men were coming toward me at dawn. The dew had shrunk my homemade shoes so tightly that I had to take them off and walk barefoot. I reached Weepers about five in the morning, where Frau P., the former innkeeper's wife, made me some coffee and took care of my passage across the lake. Nobody has a boat on this side, so we walked along the shore and over the dam which is built in the water as far as the next island. From there she shouted across the water between her cupped hands until a dog barked on the second island, and a woman appeared at once on its shore. We waved to her; she unmoored a boat, came over and took me to Schwalgendorf.

May 24

Again there are rumors that the Russians have left Januschau and that the manor house is empty. I went there and approached it, quite unconcerned, from the park side, first stopping in surprise at the side of a fiery bush, twice a man's height,—our *azalea pontic,* over and over covered with blossoms in four different shades of red. Trying to see the front of the house, I popped into a bunch of at least twenty Russians. Quickly I turned to the nearest and asked him zealously if there were any sick people around. They directed me to the village where one of the two German soldiers was actually sick in bed. I was glad to have got out of it so easily. All around the manor house are rubbish heaps as everywhere else. The big stone balls had been thrown down from their pedestals; in front of the porch on the garden side is a Russian grave enclosed by a fence on which washing was drying. In the park decaying horses were lying around. Out of a rubbish pile stuck one of the two remarkable antlers which had been lying on the table in the hall for decades. I took it with me as a memento. Afterward I also inspected a small forest farm, called Gräberberg, with a house standing in a small clearing. Nobody seemed to have been there for months. Paper and broken dishes were lying knee-deep in all the rooms, but nothing was of any use. In the garden stood a forest of rhubarb, some of which found its way into my rucksack.

May 26, Rogation Sunday

I held a service in my two rooms. Many came—Washko had sent them home from work for this purpose. Although I hardly ever exchange a word with him, I have the feeling that we understand each other to a certain extent. Our people like him. In the afternoon I again saw patients in Schwalgendorf. On the way back we found that the forester's lodge Alt-Schwalge, empty before, is occupied again. The new forester called me in to see his sick wife, and later gave me a pound of bacon in return for the consultation. We then took a dip in the Uroviec. The Russians are said to have recently fished four tons of carp there at one single draft.

June 7

Some unusual incidents happened today in Schwalgendorf. When we arrived, the place was occupied by Polish partisans; forty of them had come in two trucks and had locked up the local Russians, in their undershorts, in their own cellars. Other Russians who had apparently arranged to meet there and had arrived during the day, were disarmed in the village street *coram publico,* stripped and put into the cellars too. Their horses were unharnessed and ridden around. I myself was employed by the partisans in a medical capacity, and afterwards invited to the meal which Frau H. had just cooked for the Russians. Nobody was allowed to leave the village during the day. Late in the evening the partisans buzzed off again. We stayed the night in Schwalgendorf and left at four the next morning, loaded with potatoes, fish, and honey, which the other Polish forester had given us. He was particularly nice to us, and his wife as well. He used to work in the Corridor Zone, and his wife was a teacher in Lodz.

There are a few colonies of bees again. Old Jepp, the miller, has managed to pull through seven swarms but still keeps them secret. Last winter the Russians opened all the hives they found, and took out the honey; now they find some only occasionally in hollow trees along the roads, and have engaged people to search for such trees and cut them. Most of these trees then fall across the road and are not removed, from sheer indolence, so that all the traffic has to go through the ditches into the fields, and the roads have become more than fifty yards wide in places. But this is not important because the fields are not cultivated anyway.

We came home about eight o'clock in the morning. The partisans had been here at night, had stopped at the farm and fired on the steam engine which was in operation. A Russian who happened to have a handgrenade in his pocket, flung it over the garden fence. The tire of a truck was hit and punctured, whereupon the partisans left the truck with their booty standing and took to their heels. The Russians went on shooting for another hour.

June 9, Whitsunday

I held a service in the dispensary and read the story of Pentecost. Shooting was going on all the time. Two trucks full of Russians arrived to wait for the partisans. In the evening some thirty strange Russians went into the houses. There seems no hope that the women will ever be left in peace.

Most of the Germans in Schwalgendorf now call themselves "Masuren." This is a new invention and probably intended to emphasize their membership of the Polish race and to deny their German extraction. I cannot very well dissuade them from becoming "Masuren," since it is less important at the moment to represent the German way of life than to remain alive. A few of them still have things hidden away, which they want gradually to sell to the Poles or exchange for food. I am sometimes called for advice on these transactions and have to act as a go-between, because the people are too easily robbed, once it is known that they have any possessions left. Frau Tiedtke still has some of her husband's suits buried. Her house was burned down, and she is living with a crippled sister and an epileptic one. The epileptic one has fits whenever she sees any Russians. She once jumped out of their burning house from the balcony.

Our Russians are very excited about the partisans and shoot at anything moving. They fired on the old H.s when the latter were gathering herbs in the big ditch.

June 14

We spent the morning digging, and planted potatoes in the afternoon. Suddenly alarm signals: a truck with heavily armed men with steel helmets drove through the village. The Russians were lying hidden in the weeds and did not make a move. An hour later the same truck returned and again they let it pass in silence.

Two Poles who used to work in Zollnick visited H. and brought schnapps with them. They want to settle in the neighborhood and behaved in a very friendly fashion, although H. had once given one of them a sound thrashing. After I had given the children lessons, I retired to the Little Wood, met two black storks in the drive, and picked blueberries. Our Russians talk of war, but they often do it. The partisans have been in Fincken-stein and slaughtered some pigs.

June 16

Today all the Russian soldiers suddenly left; only the com-mandant and two civilians are staying. Nobody knows what this means. We picked wild strawberries, chopped wood and made shoes. On my way to some typhus patients I met some Poles on bicycles who were looking for an empty house to live in. They were leading a cow by a rope, and asked if I knew where there was a "billy cow."

Faulen has been handed over to the Poles, and we hear that Januschau and Schönberg will soon be evacuated. We can see the Poles plowing and planting potatoes everywhere.

We have set a hen on eighteen eggs under my writing table, the only place where it can hatch fairly undisturbed. A Russian came from a great distance to have a tooth extracted and paid me a hundred zloty for the job.

June 23

After the Sunday service we picked several pails full of blueberries and wild strawberries at Annhof and Zollnick. We had no competitors for nobody dares to go so far into the forest, especially the Poles and the Russians, who are afraid of the partisans.

The grave in the yard at Zollnick has been opened again, and the empty chest in the barn has gone, together with the rifles buried alongside. The pump in the yard which was still giving water has been dismounted.

All types of agricultural machines which had been hauled away five days ago on trucks and tractors were brought back today and dumped in the field behind the school. The Poles are not meant to have them.

July 2

The heat has been brooding over our village for days. I was called to work with some Russians in Albrechtau, where another threshing machine has been found hidden in a barn belonging to the Poles. With great difficulty it was hauled as far as here, and left standing in the middle of the village street. Eight other threshing machines were already lying in the paddock. Aside from this work, we are spending all our days in the fields. The three- and four-year-old clover is cut and brought in. It stands as thick and tall as reeds and winds itself around our legs like wire. Who is to be fed with it is a mystery. At any rate it will keep us busy for a long time for the whole region is full of it. It is extraordinary how the rabbits have increased in the clover; both boys and girls are very clever at catching the young.

I'm not well. My mouth is completely dried out and I have to carry a can of water around with me and to take a sip every ten minutes. Marushka, the dreaded commanderess—a Pole, they say—always used to come to the field, riding on a fat white horse, to be at once greeted by the women and girls with a torrent of swearwords. Now she has to work with us as a punishment for having attacked a supposed rival out of jealousy and beaten her with a big piece of firewood. In the breaks between work we have picked raspberries from the bushes along the fields. The linden trees are in bloom.

Ten days ago we had bad luck. In the morning, just as we were trying to slip away, barefoot, to Schwalgendorf with four pitchers of syrup, Frau L. and I ran into the commandant and were locked up in the school cellar. After spending a night there, Frau L. was released. The guard brought me good food every day from the Russian kitchen, and I was also handed all sorts of berries through the bars of my window. My dispensary has been cleared out, and they have apparently found some very dangerous poison, probably in one of the beer bottles with Russian labels which had belonged to my predecessor Nadja. Everybody was very excited, and I was to be punished. A woman of our village had also told the Russians that I was a spy and in cahoots with the partisans. Things looked rather critical, and on top of everything I had come down with a chill and a high temperature; all my mosquito and flea bites began to fester, and I got cramps in my calves. On the third day I was let out and taken to the commanderess. She shouted at me and took my temperature herself, because she did not believe that I was actually sick. I answered her in much the same tone, which is always the best tactic. To my great surprise I was then allowed to move into the attic room above my former quarters. I am living there now. I believe Waschko has put in a good word for me.

July 7

We need not work today because of the rain. The women mend sacks as usual. More than a hundred small Russian cars came through the village. We retreated again into the Little Wood to pick berries. Although we are not really allowed to leave the village, we know that our movements cannot be checked in the tall weeds. Burdocks and thistles have grown so high that we can walk among them almost upright without being seen. New stills have been set up among them too.

July 13

After days of sunshine and gales it is raining again. I have been sitting all day in the smithy sharpening blades for the reaping machine. Yesterday I worked with three Lithuanians in the granary, where the flour is slowly rotting in the sacks. A truck drove up, made a too sharp turn and knocked down the small projecting part of the manor house kitchen. The barn is full of ruined cars and various pieces of furniture piled up in a jumble. The other day the commandant was grabbed by the tall Lithuanian whom he was about to arrest, and kicked so violently to the ground that he remained lying on the doorstep. The Lithuanian was locked up, but is meanwhile at large again. In the afternoon we shoveled rotten beet parings from the granary into the yard.

The Russians are in a state of excitement again because of changes in official plans. Cattle are to be sent here again from Silesia. The pigs which have grown extremely fat on the beet parings are not allowed to be slaughtered but are given some sort of laxative to make them thin again. Now and then a horse disappears, probably sold secretly by the Russians themselves; one was found recently, after a wide search, at a Pole's house about eighteen miles away. The Pole had bought it from a Russian who turns up here only occasionally. Nobody knows where he lives. The commandant has outlawed him; anybody who sees him is to shoot him down.

August 2

For two weeks I had a high temperature and a splitting headache, and sometimes was almost delirious. Now I am terribly weak and laid up in bed in H.'s kitchen this last week, because nursing me in my broiling hot attic had become too difficult. The mice ran back and forth along the beam over my head, and when I called out nobody could hear me. All this started on a Sunday. We were working in the hayfield near Gross-Albrechtau in a scorching heat and had a short break at noon in the church. I had been feeling ill all morning and saw the fat Marushka, lording it over again on her white horse, as through a veil. In the afternoon Russian soldiers drove up in a truck to take the Lithuanians from the field, probably to Russia. One of them escaped and disappeared in the forest; the tall one had decamped some days earlier. We did not get home until after sundown, and next morning I could not get up. Now I am slowly beginning to recover.

The partisans have been in Januschau taking all the horses and also the boots and guns of the six Russians still left there. One of the Russians came running past us here, on his way to Nipkau for reinforcements. He was arrested in Rosenberg by the UB and locked in the cellar for a night. We never know here who is actually against whom. Although the Polish police are mortal enemies of the partisans, they never miss an opportunity of playing a trick on the Russians.

In our little garden behind the house everything is growing luxuriously in the tropical heat: cucumbers, tomatoes, and onions. The Rosenberg Poles have sent me a message that I must come over to them as soon as possible, because their doctor has been imprisoned. They have turned the former health office into a hospital. Frau S. has put my name down there as a patient in any case.

· 8 ·

ROSENBERG
August 6, 1946 to May, 1947

I have been in Rosenberg these two last days. The Polish doctor received me very kindly, and so did the German woman who is working here as a nurse. The house is quite close to the shore of the lake. Frau S. came to take me there, and we left the village and reached the highway unnoticed. There we parted company. My escort went through the town where she is now well known. I chose the road through the fields around the lake. But some workmen were on the road and saw us walking in different directions. One of them bicycled into the town to alert the militia. As a result, Frau S. reached the hospital hours later than I did, having been thoroughly searched and questioned.

I have a room of my own on the first floor with a view over the lake, and a lovely bed with white sheets. For the present I rank as a patient, and only hope that the Russians will not come and take me back at once. We get good food from American cans.

There are thirty beds in the hospital, nearly all of them occupied. I am allowed to make the rounds with the doctor. About the diagnoses I am slightly skeptical. Half of the patients are supposed to have typhus and the others pneumonia, but most of them look remarkably well. The typhus cases, both men and women, can be recognized by their shaven heads. This measure seems to me not only very draconic but also quite unnecessary, since it is done only in cases of spotted fever, of which there can be no question here. No temperature charts are kept. There are enormous quantities of drugs available, but the choice is minimal; they have all been sent by America and are labeled only in English and French, so that their use has been up to now rather problematic. Among them are 180,000 sleeping pills, besides bottles of concentrated hydrochloric and sulphuric acid. But the most coveted and therefore most closely guarded item is a container with ten quarts of pure unmethylated alcohol. To the regret of the Polish nurses, Nurse Erna has the key.

Here, too, prevails the most loathsome of all diseases which has haunted us at every turn. Fortunately we now have drugs in plently at our disposal. At present, about forty treatments are under way, all of them with the same hypodermic syringe. Nurse Erna who never had any medical or even nursing training, but got stranded here by accident, has already become astonishingly competent in giving intravenous injections. Ten to fifteen patients come to her every day, healthy young men, and women too. Many new cases have lately swelled the number. You dare not imagine what the future consequences will be.

Rosenberg, which the Poles call Susz, used to be a peaceful small town of about six thousand inhabitants, the center of a district in which the large landed estates predominated. Now the town is lying in ruins, the country all around is desolate, and most of the beautiful manor houses have been reduced to rubble and ashes. Around the ruined inner town the Poles have moved into the houses left standing, but only very few seem to be definitely settled. The majority are in a state of constant unrest, and the train, which is running once or twice over this section of the line, is packed with adventurers who come and go, because they have not yet found any place to stay, or to look for more favorable opportunities. They come from every part of Poland and represent the most diverse types, eastern and west-

ern, who have hardly anything in common as regards their character and mentality. There is obviously a fundamental dividing
line between east and west running straight through Poland.
The only thing they have in common is that they all have lost
their roots, otherwise they would probably not come here of their
own free will, to a country which is lying waste, and with which
they have no connection, except perhaps for the few who worked
here on the land during the war and are now trying to build up
a new existence for themselves on the deserted farms. The others
first came here a year and a half ago, immediately behind the
Russian army. They are relatively well off because they could
secure a lot of things which had been overlooked in the houses at
the first looting. They are more or less adequately dressed and
already represent a certain, if loose, social stratum.

Every newcomer tries to set up a business or to take upon himself an office. We already have a mayor, a priest, a doctor, a lady
dentist, a lawyer, a forestry official, a postmaster, a stationmaster,
a chimneysweep, a barber, a shoemaker, a tailor, etc., although
none of them seems to be very good in his field. Moreover, trades-
men of all kinds, from baker, butcher and innkeeper to a simple
matchseller. They all make a living, and their activities are
limited only by the general poverty, and also by the presence of
the militia and the UB which discharge their dreaded offices according to rather primitive and temperamental points of view.

Only very few Germans are still living in the town; they can
be counted on the fingers of both hands: two old men and a
couple of women and children who sweep the streets, remove the
rubble and do domestic work in Polish families. Any other Germans left in this district live on the estates, chiefly under Russian
supervision and in closed groups. Left to their own resources,
they would hardly find the means to live and would be at everybody's mercy.

The small hospital in which I am working gives me a chance

to observe all this from a relatively comprehensive viewpoint. On the whole I am treated with great courtesy, having been fortunate to make a favorable impression in the very first days by some successful minor surgery.

My first patient was an eighty-year-old peasant with an enormous carbuncle on his neck, who was brought to us in a wagon by his anxious relatives. Doubting very much whether the old man could still be saved, I pointed out the seriousness of the situation and made preparations for the operation. The two Polish nurses, who assured me they had often seen surgery of this kind, wanted to assist me, but rushed out of the room, horrified, after I had made the first of four long incisions. They thought I was going to cut off the patient's head. The old man felt the relief at once, recovered, and has promised to send me a goose as soon as his neck is completely healed. He lives with his eighty-year-old wife on the farm of his sons, on the other side of the lake. I go over there every third day to change his dressing. The second dramatic case was an arrested birth. The midwife called me in desperation, and after the requisite examination we went into the kitchen and boiled the forceps, which is available fortunately, in a saucepan. The child came fairly quickly into the world, the midwife continually crossing herself because she was sure that the child was still too high up for me to reach with the forceps. After the successful outcome of these and some other rather tricky cases, I am beginning to feel safe to a certain extent. Moreover, I am told that signatures to a letter to the militia have been collected, asking that they should give me as much liberty to move as possible. In any case, if things should become critical, I have a strong rope in readiness in my room, by which I can let myself down from the window, for I do not intend to let them put me under lock and key once more.

Thanks to the daily injections, with which I assist Nurse Erna, I have come to know quite a number of young policemen, and it looks to me as if they would not bother me so long as nothing special happens. All the same, things became critical one Sunday morning, when two elderly men in uniform whom I had not seen before, entered the hospital and asked for me. Contrary to their usual behavior on the arrival of men, the two nurses retreated into the farthest corner. We stood for some time facing one another in silence. They looked me up and down. To my question as to whether they were ill they first made no reply; then one of them pointed to his teeth, while the other walked slowly up and down behind my back. I stared at the immaculate set of teeth of the man in front of me, thinking: "Wouldn't that suit you fine, you chap behind me! If you only move a finger, I'll be on the stairs with one bound, out of the window and lost in the woods, before you can count ten." But the inspection of my reverse side had apparently given no occasion for an intervention, and the two visitors left the house without saying good-bye. The two nurses came out of their hiding place at once, congratulating me on this unexpected outcome of the encounter. Those two were the most dangerous men in the whole district, they told me, the Commandants of the UB and the militia.

My first drive to see a patient took me almost the whole day. A peasant came to fetch me with a horse about the size of a normal goat, and we proceeded, along sandy roads, at a snail's pace, much more slowly than I would have walked the nine miles to Heinrichau. The very sick man was lifted onto the wagon—it would have been much simpler, if the peasant had brought him to us in the first place—and we drove back a different road, through Neudeck and Langenau, the two Hindenburg estates. The Reich president's manor house burned down, and the one in Langenau as well, and the village Neudeck also badly damaged. The fields, of course, choked in weeds, as usual.

I am often called to sick people in the town itself and in the neighborhood, which gives me an insight into their lives. In many cases the people are not legally married; the young couples have met each other more or less by chance and will probably stay together only for a short time. All the same, the birth rate is surprisingly high, and Cecylia, the midwife, is glad to have found help in me, even for uncomplicated cases, because she cannot cope with all of them alone. I often stay for hours, sometimes whole nights, with a family until the arrival of the child, which is usually welcomed with joy in spite of everything. Sleeping at intervals on some chair or other or on the floor, and offered now and then a schnapps, I get to hear many things which these people would normally not relate. The war had knocked them about in a pitiful way, and it was hard to tell from which side, west or east, they had suffered more harm and injustice. I often feel deeply ashamed when they respond to a kind word with a readiness to restrain their justifiable feelings of revenge, looking upon all that was done to them in Hitler's name as an aberration alien to the German character. And it is just those who have lost and suffered most with whom one can talk most easily about these matters. But it does not surprise me, for it is the same all over the world, especially where people know something about forgiveness.

Except for a few who are sitting at the receiving end of American generosity and know how to feather their nest, they are all very poor, and will have no chance for a long time to have more than the barest necessities of life. There is too much confusion and arbitrary procedure, too little mutual trust; clothing and food are too expensive, and schnapps relatively too cheap. There is hardly a man who does not resort to it immoderately to cheer himself up. Although I too like the taste of Czysta Vodka, compared to the horrid beet schnapps, but drinking it in the morning on an empty stomach is a bit of a strain, and hinders me considerably in the exercise of my medical duties. On the other hand, it is often the only way to avoid hurting people's feelings. The women like to drink vodka as much as the men, and many of them are clearly showing the effects of it.

Thanks to American relief the food in the hospital is excellent. Besides, patients occasionally bring us secretly something to eat. Some of them even pay in cash up to 100 zloty for a tooth extraction, and between 500 and 700 zloty for a delivery—unimaginable sums in our circumstances. You can buy a pound of sugar for 80 zloty, potatoes for 600 to 700 zloty a hundredweight, and two pounds of bacon for 800 to 900 zloty. The price of rye is 1500 zloty, of wheat 2,000 zloty a hundredweight. Nothing else interests us at present, for food is scarce everywhere, and as I personally get everything I need at the hospital, I can pass on to our people everything I earn in addition. They even come from far away to visit me, and I am very glad that my Polish fellow workers make no difficulties in this respect. If it is necessary, we are even allowed to take them into the hospital without having to pay for it, and to treat them exactly as the Polish patients. They even give tacit consent if we hospitalize someone who is not really sick but only needs protection and care.

Fortunately the American drugs include many useful narcotics which have become very popular, though at first I had to overcome strong resistance to their use. Now all at once all patients want to have something injected into their veins when I make an incision or pull a tooth, and every day two or three people are lying about in the dining room, sleeping away the effects of their narcosis.

There is usually a certain amount of trouble with the young men of the militia and the UB, well nourished fellows who are used to alcohol and therefore not easy to narcotize. The scenes I go through with them should be filmed and transmitted to posterity; they can hardly be described in words. As a first move I invite them to take the handgrenades out of their trouser pockets, to which they usually do not react, merely looking at me with contempt as though this was none of my business. In the end I take them out myself and deposit them in a safe place. Then the person concerned is strapped to a field-operating table and given the injection, which, however, in most cases only lasts until I start with the extraction. Then it may happen that the patient gets up with an effort, bending the table, crashes to the floor with it, gets up again and dances around the room with the table on his back, while I hang on to one of his molars with the forceps, only concerned to prevent him from crashing into one of the two windows or into the glass cabinet. With Nurse Erna's help I usually succeed in obtaining the desired result, while the other two nurses regularly make off in a funk.

Aside from the forceps for pulling teeth and the one for obstetrics, my surgical equipment is very primitive. Major incisions are made with razor blades; the only existing scalpel I keep in my bed so that it will not be used for sharpening pencils, cutting string and even rougher purposes. A red pencil which I had procured with great difficulty for the temperature charts, could not be found for a long time, till the color of the housemaid's lips set me on the right track, and I discovered it on the windowsill in the kitchen. The curettages, so often necessary in the cases of women brought to us unconscious from loss of blood, I perform with a sharp spoon, because we do not have a curette, nor any chance to get one. No major operation can be performed here anyhow; all such cases have to be sent to Marienwerder, now called Kwidzyn. The ambulance, donated by America, had been intended for this purpose, but is mostly used for business trips to Danzig, Allenstein, or Warsaw, so that, as a rule, we have to look around for other means of transportation. This takes a long time because the UB, which has the only other car, a small Volkswagen, at its disposal, usually has other uses for it. So it ends in our having to be satisfied with a horsedrawn vehicle of some sort, which naturally takes hours to get there.

It is not rare that we get people with shot wounds, and also not surprising, considering the enormous number of automatics which people carry here with them. The militia once brought me a case in the middle of the night. I woke up to find at least twelve men, covered with dust, bursting into my room with bull's eye lanterns. On the operating table, downstairs, lay one of their comrades with a bullet in the region of the groin. As the missile might be lodged in the abdomen, which would necessitate a major operation, I advised them to get the man to Marienwerder with all possible speed. Whereupon they all vanished as quickly as they had come, ostensibly to look for a car, and left me alone with the injured man. Not till six hours later did a few of them reappear to take the patient away, after having drowned their fright in a bar. According to their story, they had come upon partisans, had fired at random and hit one of their own men.

The language problem here is no longer very difficult for me. Most of the Poles know a little German, especially when they are sick, and I myself have picked up, meanwhile, the most necessary words, so that I can talk with them fairly fluently about matters of food and illness, even though I have to disregard the extremely difficult grammar. My Polish is very much like their German, which they speak, using only nominatives, infinitives and no articles: "Doktour, come to wife, child come"—a kind of Esperanto, familiar to every German who has had to do with Poles. You have, of course, to be versed in Polish swearwords if you want to have it your way. I had practiced them for quite some time and had used them in some cases. My greatest success in this respect was on a ward with four young men who had all been admitted for observation because of venereal disease. The little Polish nurse Jadja could not manage them and called me for help. "Herr Doktor, please come, the men are so fresh!" "Well, what can I do? They won't listen to me." "Oh, just curse them—that's what the cheeky fellows need!" I ran upstairs, flung the door open, shouted all my swearwords one after another, and then continued in German: "You boys, just wait until I know enough Polish, then I'll teach you something!" Speechless at first, they roared with laughter, and from then on were quite easy to manage.

Even my knowledge of English and French has been useful here. The postmaster and various other people have come to have letters from France and America translated and answered for them, and besides, all the medicaments we possess are labeled in those languages.

Russian patients are not much liked in this hospital. Jadja usually announces them in the following way: "Herr Doktor, there is a Russian here, and what a one! If you don't come quickly, he'll smash everything up!" It is usually not as bad as that. But they feel themselves, of course, to be the masters who can take whatever they want. There was the case of a Russian woman who was unable to give birth to a dead child, when I was called to help with the forceps. It was a precarious business, because three Russians were standing in front of the door and were only prevented with difficulty from coming in. Of course there was a major laceration which had to be stitched, but the whole affair turned out well for me; a week later the three Russians returned and took the woman away, neither paying any attention to us nor giving any token of gratitude to the hospital.

When I was walking on the streets, people at first treated me with great reserve. Nobody greeted me and I sometimes felt rather lonely. Now the atmosphere has become more relaxed, especially after the barber drew me into his shop when I passed and cut my hair for nothing, all in view of the people waiting there. It is really a very pleasant feeling to be publicly regarded as a human being again.

Of the two churches here, the Catholic one has been restored and mass is now said regularly. The priest has a difficult office, because in the absence of any working judicial authority, he is consulted by the population to settle their disputes. Particularly drastic cases are announced in the sermon which is frequently attended by even the less religious-minded people.

Summer is almost gone, and I have not had time to resume my old walks and visit again the accustomed places and people. But the people come to me and inform me about the happenings in their areas. The wife of the new forester in Schwalgendorf came to us for her delivery. Her husband has been in prison in Allenstein for some time. The head forester came to us as a patient. Frau Tiedtke sent me things for barter; she wants me to try and get a goat for her. On September 13 the H.s will be moving to Schwalgendorf where the head forester has work for him. Frau L. will become the latter's housekeeper. The Russians are going to hand over Brausen to the Poles, and are anyway leaving the district very soon. They are taking everything with them that can still be used; even the houses are quickly looted once more. There is now only one Russian in Januschau, temporarily on guard; otherwise the village is empty. In Schönberg the Russians turned all the Germans out into the street, within two hours.

On September 30 H. came on his bicycle to take me to his sick daughter. I took the bicycle to get there quicker and found Frau L. already better, was shown their new house, and made some calls. I spent the evening with the head forester who had shot a very strong, older stag. We inspected the antlers in the cellar where the head was being boiled down. For supper we had stag's liver, and he gave me a piece of it to take it with me.

On October 13, a Sunday, Nurse Erna went with me for a walk through the forest of Januschau. We have had some sharp night frosts, but under the crystal-clear sky the land still vibrates in its autumnal glory, and the golden beech foliage was reflected in the deep blue water of the lakes. We passed the Januschau manor house, where a single, glowing-red trail of wild vine had climbed the bare white wall up to the roof. Through the front door, which still made the old familiar noise, we stepped into the hall and had a look at the garden room—one huge jumble. From the straw which covered the floor a man got up—the Russian guard. He looked at us inquiringly, uncertain what he should do, and was obviously relieved when we decided not to inspect any more of the house. In the forest the timber, cut long ago, was still lying about. We heard a few shots in the distance. When we approached Zollnick, three men with bicycles suddenly took cover in the underbrush ahead of us. I was inclined to retreat, but my companion insisted that we should go on. When we reached the spot, the head forester and two forestry officials came out of the bushes, and we hailed one another with relief. They had thought we were Russians, who had been lately disturbing the forest again.

The season of the yellow boletus was over—there had never been so many as this year. In the Zollnick clearing the cranberries were riping. Cormorants, herons, ospreys, hoopooes, blue rollers and most of the waterfowl had left. But where the beech grove slopes down to the lake a pair of swans were swimming in slow circles round each other on the still water.

It was such a joy to show all this to another human being, to talk about the past and how everything looked here then—about my grandfather Oldenburg whose name will always be connected with this part of the country, as long as the concepts Prussia and Germany still exist; about his humanity, which endeared him so quickly to everybody, and to which countless anecdotes bear witness; about the moral support which his mere existence meant for everyone who was in danger of losing his home in the changing times, and did not know how to measure up to his responsibility before God for his family, his tenants, his homeland and his country; and about my close relation with him, of which I am extremely proud, and which has been the reason why he is always present to me when it comes to questions of human behavior.

I told my companion of all the exciting events in which we had been allowed to take part from early childhood, not least among them the visits of the old Field Marshal Hindenburg. How the whole village participated, lining the road on his arrival and flattening noses against the dining room windows in the evening.

Ever since September I have been getting letters from the west, from different kinds of people, one almost every day. How the post can do this is a mystery. The letters take four weeks, apparently via Warsaw, but as far as I can see they are not censored. My replies, too, reach their destination almost regularly. In the hospital, I am extremely envied for these letters, Jadja hands them to me half admiringly, half reproachfully, "Doctor, another letter already!" She takes it for granted that they are all written by women. The address has, of course, to be written entirely in Polish. I have had two letters from my father written in French. One day the post office sent for me, because a very suspicious-looking letter had come for me. The address was written in huge letters diagonally across the envelope. I recognized the handwriting from a distance, and could not help laughing at the fuss the Poles were making about it. To me it did mean, however, something special, for it was from Count Brünneck, one of the best-known and most highly respected men of our province. The Russians have made his manor house at Bellschwitz their headquarters, and are rolling their cigarettes in the pages of his famous collection of books.

These letters have brought the west still more palpably near, and my longing to see the people again, to whom I am so deeply attached, becomes stronger every day. Moreover, I keep thinking that I might be able to do something there for the people in Königsberg. On the other hand I also feel my obligations here, and would not like to give up my post without some definite guidance. I must find out, too, what is going to become of my aunt. Through an intermediary, I got a letter from her from Osterode, where she is a prisoner, and I have been able to send her some money through the same channel.

In the middle of October the frost became more severe and toward the end of the month it began to snow. This early onset of winter has made conditions in the hospital more and more difficult. The heating still functions, but nobody sees to getting in coke, although it would be easy to do so. The only warm place is the kitchen, which we usually avoid, because it is the focus of gossip and slander. Violent squabbles are going on there, occasionally leading to blows, and mainly caused by jealousy or superstition.

One morning horror reigned; two white lines of human footprints could be seen on the coal-black, soot-covered ceiling, one set large, one set small. The evening before I had been the last there, and had tried very hard to make friends with the two-year-old daughter of the janitor. She always ran away from me, screaming, whereas her five-year-old brother was not shy at all, and always wanted to ride on my shoulders. It suddenly occurred to me to lift him up by his legs and let him walk, head downward, along the ceiling with his bare feet. The effect, which surprised me too, made the children shout with joy. The little girl immediately jumped up to me, and I had to trace a ghostly trail with her feet too. I should have liked to put mine next to theirs, but even so it was sufficient to create a wild excitement among the others.

Superstition in its most primitive forms is running riot here. Cards are laid three times a day, and faces are cheerful or depressed according to what comes out. It does not matter in the least whether what is prophesied lies within the range of temporal and spatial possibilities. The prospect of having two children plus a husband before the year is out is enough to be in high spirits for the whole morning.

Light and water supplies are also getting lower and lower. The wires are still there, and the electric lights still burn at times, but one bulb after another disappears and cannot be replaced. I am anxiously guarding a big 500-watt bulb, which we screw in and out when we need it in the operating or delivery room. I managed to "repair" another bulb, which did not burn any longer; that is to say, I turned it in a way that the ends of the wires were again connected. As a result I now find the most impossible objects put on my desk for repair.

Up to now water could be pumped; but one pipe after another freezes, and only two pumps are now workable for the whole town, one of them at the railroad station. Water for washing dishes is drawn by us from the lake, less than twenty steps away, where we have cut a hole in the ice.

Among the German female patients who come to us, are some with whom we are very much on our guard, because they are obviously acting as spies for the Russians. One of them, of whose pure German extraction I became very doubtful in the course of our conversation, claimed to be a distant relative of my grandfather. When I had given her proof that this was hardly possible, she switched to another subject. Letters had come from the west lately, she said, intimating that G.S. would soon be back in East Prussia. Certainly this could only mean "German soldiers," and what did I think of it? I advised her, quite naively, to be more careful about repeating such things; she should not get upset by such foolish letters; if she should ever be in trouble I would try to help her. Whereupon she disappeared rather suddenly, and I realized only later that our conversation had been planned as a provocation.

Meanwhile, I have again christened a few Russian children and held little celebrations on these occasions. That the mothers wish to have their children baptized seems to me sufficient reason to do it, although I am reasonably sure that the actual motive is sometimes a very obvious one. They find it interesting that I come to see them, and have no other way of attracting me, as long as they are not sick. But once I refused to baptize a child right away, saying that I would like to have a preliminary talk with the mother, whom I had known in the past, and whose sort of life with the Russians seemed to me no longer admissible, even allowing for all the unleashed demons. The talk took place and I am now waiting for the woman to call again.

On November 24 Jadja came to me very excited and announced: "Doctor, there is a woman who looks like you." I jumped to my feet—my aunt was standing behind her. She had escaped from Osterode, traveled on a transport train as far as Deutsch Eylau, and came from there on foot. We have made preparations for her: she was first admitted as a patient, and then will live with a Polish family as domestic help. The whole house shared my delight, and everything was done to make her stay in the hospital a pleasant one, after all the hardships she had been through. We spent three happy days together. A very timely present was a live duck which a Polish patient had put in my wardrode while I was out, and it was the *pièce de résistance* of a festival to which Frau S. was also invited. But it was a farewell party at the same time, for my aunt did not want to stay here, but to try and get through to the west where her family is waiting for her. A Polish woman friend got her a ticket to Stettin, and with this ticket she started off on November 27—without papers a rather risky undertaking. After a week of worry we had a letter from her from Stettin. She had used the bribe money which she had taken with her, to smuggle herself into a camp for emigrants, and was staying there until the next transport left. As this might not be for some time, she had taken a job in the camp kitchen, and was very sorry that she had left her clogs with us. She had to stand in ankle-deep mud all day.

Just at that time I was taken by the militia on some drives in their cars. The first was at night, in the American "Sanitarka," to Deutsch Eylau, now Ilawa, to see a man of the UB who had been wounded by a shot. The beautiful town is unutterably ruined and recognizable only by its lake. Fortunately I did not have to put up with the menacing atmosphere of the UB for long; the matter was soon settled, and we could take the man with us. The tempo on our way back was terrifying, thanks to the alcohol which had been consumed; we only braked once, very abruptly, to pick up a rabbit which had been run over.

The next was a drive in the militia's Volkswagen, in a westerly direction to Bischofswerder. A man had come from there, seeking a doctor for a friend who was in great pain. The man had been on the road three days without finding one. This was sufficient excuse for the militia to tear through the countryside with me as if we were out to rescue a drowning man. The northwester, blowing into our faces, was so strong that every time we passed a village we were almost flung against the walls of the houses. Four miles from our destination we struck a curbstone and tore off the right front tire and the mudguard. This was, however, not so important for on our right the road was slightly higher and we could do without the right tire. It merely meant that we now got a constant spray of sand into our faces. There had not been a windshield anyway. I pulled my overcoat over my head and watched the right curb of the road through a button-hole.

For a short time everything was all right, but then we crashed into one of the wrecks lying in the road ditch—actually I had jumped out a few yards farther back. The drive had come to an end. We had another half hour to walk to the house of the sick man. As we opened the door, he took a deep breath, leaned back and declared that now everything was all right. Afraid of a sharp pain in his left side, he had not dared breathe normally for the last three days, and had only waited for the doctor to come. I stayed with him until the car was repaired, and then we drove home again at the same breakneck speed.

On December 10 they came for me again in a snowstorm, without telling me at first what was the matter. In Riesenburg, now Prabuty, two trains had collided, practically the only ones running on this line. Several cars had been telescoped, and the injured had already been transferred into a hospital train which would take them to Marienburg. Thirty-five people had been hurt in the accident, some were dead, others had crushed legs. I was also taken to Marienburg, where we arrived at the hospital with our casualties toward eight in the evening. Forewarned, I was prepared not to speak a word of German; but I was spontaneously greeted in German by my colleague and his assistants who gave me a warm welcome. We attended to the wounded in the operating room until morning; then I was given a room, and after a few hours sleep, a breakfast with real coffee. Encouraged by all this kindness, I took a short walk through the city. Unlike the modern part, the old town with its characteristic arcades is completely destroyed. The castle, recognizable now only by its outlines, towers into the sky like the carcass of a gigantic goose. Not a soul to be seen anywhere. I was the only person present who grieved for the past.

Shortly before Christmas I again went to Deutsch Eylau by car. Two patients had to be picked up in Raudnitz. I got out in Deutsch Eylau and visited Frau F., the former owner of the beauty parlor, who is going to make a warm jacket for me. In return I am going to make her a pair of shoes and to pay her something as well. She lives in one of the small wooden dwellings built on wooden piles above the surface of the lake. All the remaining Germans are living there together in a kind of ghetto. The town proper has been destroyed; the Poles live in the outskirts. Now that I have received a shirt from UNRRA and a patient has made me a pair of leather shoes, my clothes have gradually become rather normal-looking. We have also obtained a lot of dress material for Christmas presents.

I have done a great deal of bartering for the people in Schwalgendorf. For a sun lamp which she brought me secretly, Frau Tiedtke got another goat. As I could not test the lamp in the hospital because of the failure of the electric current, I gave it, in good faith, though rather unwisely, to a patient, a professional electrician. For three days I heard nothing from him; then the fact that the lamp was functioning could no longer be denied, for the man was going around town with a fiery-red face.

I managed to acquire in the market, without attracting attention, a young pig weighing fifty pounds, which the man who sold it to me, agreed to bring to a prearranged place. It was taken over by Frau L., who had come by night with a pushcart. Five hours return march through the forest, and she had it safely at home as a surprise for her parents.

I met the lady dentist who works here, when I had to attend to her one-year-old child. She speaks German fluently and treats me very kindly. Her drilling apparatus, worked by foot, is in great demand by the Russians, but she does not allow herself to be easily bullied. If an extraction is needed she sometimes sends the people to me. Her husband is working in Bromberg. There are two different ways of getting there, either through Thorn, which is quite a detour, or through Marienwerder, which, on the other hand, demands some courage, for the new railroad bridge, built over the Weichsel by German prisoners of war under Russian supervision, is said to be very rickety and creaking in its joints already.

We spent Christmas peacefully in every regard. I was invited to supper by the lady dentist and her husband, afterwards attended Midnight Mass, and was then called for a delivery in town. On Christmas Day I set off with a heavy rucksack, sat for a while with old Frau Aust and her older sister, who are the only Germans still living in Albrechtau, stayed a few hours in Brausen, paid a short visit to the graves in Januschau and reached Schwalgendorf before dark. There I called on several persons, spent the night with the H.s and was driven back next morning to Rosenberg by one of the Polish foresters in his one-horse carriage.

For some days it has been bitterly cold, but without snow. To my great astonishment I could clearly see Venus at noon in the leaden-gray winter sky. Nowadays I see so many things that I had not noticed before, and I have come to attach great significance to apparently simple and obvious matters. My inner ear has been sharpened too and I am more disposed to follow spontaneous impulses. I have never found it as easy to make up my mind as in these days. I suddenly feel that I should go to Schwalgendorf at once, and when I arrive there a few hours later, I'm sure to be greeted with the words: "Ah, there you are already! We were just wondering how to get you here."

The first thing I did in the New Year was to drop a brick. Not wanting to seem to be a spoilsport, I accepted the challenge of the assembled staff to lift up one of the six flowerpots, standing upside down in a row on the window sill. Under the one I lifted appeared a card with the picture of a small grave. They were all aghast, and declared that it did not count; that I had lifted the pot too quickly, and should try once more. Again the grave appeared. "You see?" I said. To me, it was like a rap on my fingers. Nobody dared to say anything more. But it was quite a good cure for us all. Since then the laying of cards is somewhat out of fashion.

In these days I was called several times to the dying, once to Schwalgendorf where I stayed overnight, and then to Gollnau to the father of nine children. Another man, however, of whom I had thought was long since under the ground, turned up suddenly, quite cheerful, and thanked me for my visit.

In Brausen the Russians are making preparations for their definite departure. I went there to say goodbye to Washko and thank him for having intervened for me in a ticklish situation. He looked at me half suspiciously, half astonished, and called me in. We sat down at a table with two other Russians; tobacco was offered and we smoked in silence—it was an ordeal. At last I got up, saying goodbye; they responded briefly and I was outside, taking three deep breaths. We had not understood each other. My thanks had been out of place and therefore embarrassing. He had not done it for the reason I had thought. What a pity! He will only remember me as an oddity.

In the first half of January it was twenty below zero. For three days we had no coal, and had to send most of the patients home. Those who remained got all the blankets, in spite of which their cheeks and noses froze. Six of us slept on the floor in the room of our fireman and medical orderly, near the small iron stove. During the day I was always outdoors and did not feel the cold so much. There was hardly any village within a radius of five miles which I did not visit in those days, many of them for the first time. From many of these walks I came back only at night, twice from Charlottenwerder along the railroad tracks, once from Gross-Albrechtau where another Russian child was due. Great-grandmother, grandmother, and the sixteen-year-old expectant mother were all assembled in the room. The dim lamplight barely enabled us to discover that, among the Russians in question, the friendly little Mongol was without a doubt the father of the child. "Just look, and from slit-eye to boot," said the grandmother, holding the baby for the mother to see.

On January 16 it suddenly started thawing. My Polish colleague came with the ambulance to take me for a drive to Stradem near Deutsch Eylau, to examine one of his patients. On the way I told him of my first drive with the Poles and its premature end in a ditch. It was exactly a year ago to the day. He had first listened only with half an ear, then he suddenly asked: "Where did you say it happened?" I described the place, whereupon he stopped the car and told me about the accident, which he had observed more closely than we had. He had been sitting in the car which stopped beside us on the road when we clambered out of the ditch. He had expected to find us all reduced to pulp.

On January 20 we brought Frau Aust and her invalid sister here from Albrechtau, because the fresh cold wave had been too much for them. Frau Aust was put up with the bakeress as a nurse to the children, and her sister was hospitalized. Unfortunately, this arrangement was of short duration, for the sister died, and Frau Aust herself had to come to us as a patient. She had fainted from the cold in her room which had no heat.

The people in the town have come to the conclusion that I am now qualified for social life, which is very well-meant but at the same time likely to misrepresent my real situation. I was twice invited to a party where, believe it or not, they were playing bridge. When the third invitation came, I was fortunately saved by an operation. On the fourth occasion I had to explain my refusal more plainly, even at the risk of not being understood. But my outlawed state and my fool's license suit me better than being apparently admitted into a swanky milieu. Not long ago I was almost on the point of extricating myself from this development by flight, interpreting the calls to the west in the letters of my friends as a command. I approached some Russians who were leaving for Liegnitz, but then again became so irresolute that I was glad when Nurse Erna discovered my plan and convinced me that I should stay here.

In these days I got the first direct news from Königsberg in a letter from Else Peto, which had reached an address in the west and was forwarded to me from there. What I read was not surprising to me but moved me deeply. Erika had died on December 22, 1945; in her last weeks she had been praying for me.

At the beginning of February the ground was covered with deep snow. A covey of twenty partridges appeared near the hospital. We were drawing our water now only from the lake, because the last pump had frozen. The ice was more than thirty inches thick, and each pail we drew up was full of tiny fish. The commissioners were taken aback when I offered them one to wash their hands in.

It was still extremely cold; but the white blanket of snow and the gradually higher sun stimulated our spirit of enterprise. We drove to Schwalgendorf on two occasions with the sleigh and a borrowed horse, very slowly, and mostly walking alongside to spare the horse, but we all enjoyed it immensely. We planned our route so that it was possible to drive almost all the way, twelve miles, through the forest.

February 19 was the coldest of the many cold days—forty below. The snow was so deep that the trains could not run, and the cold continued until well into March. I was in bed for a week with the flu, part of the time without heat, reading *Quo Vadis,* trying to acquaint myself with a Polish author. In primitive times like these one does read quite differently and much more intensively than usual. Anyway, this book which I had read as a teenager and had always regarded as a kind of popular thriller now moved me deeply. And I was even more impressed by Bergengruen's *Grand Tyrant,* and actually shed tears of joy reading the last two chapters.

By the middle of March I was on my legs again, and well

enough to undertake a brisk walk to Schwalgendorf. Frau L. came to accompany me there, and we tramped in single file, through snow and wind, along the track she had made in coming, changing positions from time to time. I arrived perspiring profusely and weak in the knees. Frau Aust who had been there for some weeks—we had brought her over in the sleigh—had erysipelas and a high temperature. I thought of all the people in Königsberg who had died of it; but thank God she seemed to be getting better again. While I was there it began to thaw. I stayed one day in Schwalgendorf, rested, made a lot of calls, pulled some teeth, and spent an evening in pleasant conversation. Next day I went back past the Heide Mill. A white-tailed osprey flew over the still frozen Geserich Lake. The miller took me in his sleigh as far as Albrechtau.

I often go to Finckenstein where a number of Germans are still working under Polish administrators. In the old days it took your breath away when you entered the castle yard through the wrought-iron gate. Now the burned-down castle no longer gives the slightest idea of the atmosphere which it had radiated for two centuries. The only reminder of culture was the dachshund belonging to the keeper of the granary, the first real dog among the thousands of mongrels I had seen for the last two years. Its owner, who used to live on the Polish side, on Lake Karrasch, got it from Schönberg. He told me that a carpet, embroidered with many coats of arms, had been found in Januschau, and was now lying on the bed of one of his colleagues, not far from there. It was the so-called wedding carpet of my family, and, of course, I started speculating how to get it back without attracting attention.

Spring is arriving again in full force. The night of March 23-24 was full of the whistling and whirring of innumerable wings; in the morning the starlings were singing on the rooftops, ducks and pigeons were sailing high above the lake, and on the opposite shore you could see the peewees tumbling during their mating flight. The ice was melting rapidly. In the midday sun the first butterflies ventured out, and the temperature jumped about twenty degrees.

Two days later I took a walk in the forest. Cranes were calling, the herons were standing in their nests on the island. On the shore of the lake where the ice had melted ducks and divers were fluttering in the water. What a blessing to be allowed to witness the awakening of nature once more.

March 30 was Palm Sunday. I asked Frau S. to go with me by train to Heinrode and walk from there to the place where my mother and my brother had come to their deaths more than two years ago. She had been present at that time and could show me everything exactly. In Altmark we called on the Catholic priest with whom they had spent the night before, with the trek, before the Russians arrived. We stayed there for dinner and then went on a very muddy road to the little village of Kontken, close to the railroad line, where the trek came to an end. Children were playing at the wall of the house where the dead were finally left lying. At some distance from there, in the garden lots, stood a simple wooden cross without an inscription. A man, living nearby, came up and told us that he had arrived here three weeks later, as the first of the Poles, and had buried the dead. Except for the one in the garden lots, they were all lying beside the house wall where the children were now playing.

While we were walking back to the railroad station, skeins of wild geese flew very low over the flat land. We sat down in the ditch, waiting for the train, and read the Palm Sunday Gospel of Christ's entry into Jerusalem.

We went to Schwalgendorf again at Easter. Frau S. has given up her job in Rosenberg and is going to remain with her parents and help them. On Easter Monday I was called from one house to another, both by Germans and Poles, and had to eat something everywhere, the last in the house of the forestry secretary and her mother, who always addressed me as "Professor."

Since the Russians left, conditions have daily become worse for the Germans in Faulen and many other places. They can actually survive only by begging and stealing. The wife of Schmolla, the shepherd, is particularly bad off; she has managed to bring up five small children, and now goes around clothed in nothing but a tattered blanket into which she has cut holes for her arms. She is no longer quite right in her head, and several times has been on the point of jumping into the pond. Until now, however, I have been able to save her from the worst. For months past people have been led to believe that the next transport to Germany would be starting soon, and that they all would be taken on it. Now they are squatting, fifteen to twenty in one room, with their belongings in bundles, waiting for the start. For the people in Brausen, too, life becomes more miserable every day.

Two women are living all by themselves in Januschau. They seem slightly better off, and have evidently found our buried silver, as I gathered from a Polish storekeeper to whom they had recently sold three silver goblets fitting into one another. He showed them to me and is willing to sell them to me for five hundred zloty, the price which he paid for them—a ridiculous sum. He has many other objects in his store which once belonged to us. But it is not worth while telling him that for he has always been very nice to me, especially after I painlessly extracted several of his teeth. To me the women wisely offered only a lot of hymn-books, and our family Bible, which they have found. I accepted them gratefully and deposited them in Schwalgendorf.

It is astonishing how the poultry has increased in such a short time. They constitute the main food for the peasants; they also like to bring me eggs as payment for medical treatment. They are relatively cheaper than everything else. Fifteen to twenty eggs for pulling teeth or for any other treatment is nothing unusual, and with them I make many needy people happy. There are also a lot of chickens in the town; the dressmaker, for instance, is surrounded in her room by six sitting hens. People keep their livestock, even the larger kind, as close as possible, because they have become so used to having it stolen, or to be themselves turned out of their houses, having to leave behind everything they haven't close at hand.

On April 10 a young Polish woman I know came to the hospital and whispered to me that the UB in Deutsch Eylau wanted to speak to me as soon as possible; it would be best for me to take the next train. I asked her what this meant, and if I hadn't better make myself scarce right away. She assured me that it would not be necessary, that it had nothing to do with me. So with very mixed feelings I headed for the lion's den. Whatever the reason may be, calls of this kind can be made only with great reluctance. The mere setup is frightening, and the noises you hear suggest something horrible behind each door. This impression remains, even if you are suddenly addressed in German, in a relatively friendly fashion—this might also be a trick. But this time it really had nothing to do with me, only with conditions in the hospital. The information I supplied was very meager, because I had no reason to expose anybody. They wanted to know in particular what had happened to the alcohol sent from America. I did not keep it a secret that we took a sip once in a while, which amused them immensely. Then, hardly believing my ears, I received something like thanks for my hitherto unpaid services, and found myself safe and sound on the street again.

After several cold days it became warm again in the middle of April. On the nineteenth we began going barefoot in the forest, and I took a dip in the Uroviec. The first swallow had arrived. When I came out of the water I saw two stags getting up from the wallow on the opposite shore of the lake. A few days later the student of forestry from Schwalgendorf came with two bicycles to take me to a patient. As I wanted to show him more of this lovely region, we rode back through the forest. His chain broke, and we had to push our bicycles. He became rather frightened when it slowly grew dark and we got deeper and deeper into the forest. But then we came to the Tromnitz Lake and I showed him the cormorants which he had heard about. It was pitch dark when we finally came out of the forest and were, to his great relief, right in front of the forestry office.

On Sunday, April 27, I went to Januschau to look for peewee's eggs. The woods were full of anemones, hepaticas and daphne in bloom. Near the carp pond, in the large forest glade, which had been so important for us in our hunting days, I came upon four stags. With a bunch of flowers for the graves, I crossed the waste fields on the footpath which we had trodden out on our walks last year to Schwalgendorf. Near the Crown Prince's ditch I found a nest with four peewee's eggs but left them there, because we did not really need them. The peewee thanked me with jubilant cries, and I responded with an indescribable cry of joy. How a shout that nobody hears can liberate the soul. I have lately learned a number of tunes and hymns from the hymnal which I had not known before, and sing them at the top of my voice on my walks.

I often go to Finckenstein and the villages around, mostly on foot and sometimes in hopeless vehicles. Something always happens on these drives; either we run into a tree or a ditch, or the horse refuses to go on, a wheel comes off, the pole breaks— if there is one—or the harness comes apart. Besides, even without a breakdown, it takes much longer than on foot; but I do not want to offend the good people, who are so proud that they are able to drive.

On April 29 I ran over to Schwalgendorf for Frau Aust. I

had been told that a small transport would leave next morning for Germany via Stettin, and she was anxious to see her son, who has a forester's lodge in the west. A peasant in Schwalgendorf lent us his horse, and we were back in Rosenberg just in time to shove Frau Aust into a group of women assembled at the station. But, unfortunately, we had no luck. The women were chased away; no transport was leaving, and they were not allowed to travel on the ordinary train. I have now lodged Frau Aust in Brausen, so as to have her nearer in any case.

On May 4 I was called to Brausen for a delivery. It was freezing hard at sunrise. Just as I was about to leave, the news came that cars would be coming about ten o'clock to take all the people to the camp in Deutsch Eylau. From there they would be transported to Germany; I decided to wait for this. The cars actually came, and everything had to be done at full speed. Each person was allowed to take only one small package. Frau Aust was smuggled in, although she was not on the official list.

Once they had safely started I went back to Rosenberg, and heard to my great relief, that the Germans in Faulen were being taken too. They really had nothing left to live on. In the afternoon I was lying on my bed, wondering if I should make myself another pair of shoes, when suddenly three militia men came into my room, saying: "Doktour, want to go home?" "Yes, very much," I said; "when?" "Come now!" "How much can I take with me?" "Forty pounds." "I haven't got that much."

I quickly put my things into the rucksack and said farewell to my rather bewildered feminine staff. Then I was taken along to the guardhouse, where people kept coming to say goodbye. They will not be left without a doctor, because a few weeks ago a very nice colleague arrived to take the place of Dr. B. who has joined the Navy, and he already knew the ropes. This is probably the only reason they are letting me go.

I had to spend the night in the guardhouse. The commander

took me over to his apartment for supper, and also wanted me to sleep there in spite of the narrow space. But his new colleague did not like the idea, and I was sent back to the guardhouse, where I found an almost naked Russian who, meanwhile, had been arrested for disorderly conduct, and was now interrogated and thoroughly punched and kicked about.

In the morning I was escorted to the railroad station, along with a German soldier who had been working here as a blacksmith, and accompanied by people who waved to us in a friendly manner. We went to Deutsch Eylau, and were taken to the camp, where the people who had been transported the day before, were already assembled.

We waited three days for the transport; our railroad car was to be coupled to a train coming from Allenstein. We were not really supposed to leave the camp, but the militia kept calling me to see their families. This was an occasion for me to be able to exchange all my Polish money, which I would have had to hand over otherwise, for foodstuff. The militia men were very skeptical about our destination, and besides thought it very unlikely that as a doctor I would be allowed to leave Poland. I should be prepared, they said, to be taken out of the train on the way and employed at some other place.

To our surprise we got soup twice a day in the camp, and the farewell-rifling was not too drastic either. Fortunately the district magistrate whom I had met before was present. He at least prevented our clothes being ripped up, though a few things which had been sewn in had to be given up. I would have liked to save my three silver goblets and asked the district magistrate about them. State property should be given up, he replied; but as my name was engraved on the goblets, the case seemed doubtful. He thought it over and finally made a sign to the leader of the rifling procedure, and the whole thing was called off.

Before we were finally escorted to the station, a curious scene took place. We were ordered to line up more or less in closed ranks, some four hundred persons, and then the district magistrate asked me to say a few words to the crowd on his behalf. With some consternation I asked him what approximately he would have said. He would like to emphasize, he answered, that the manner in which we, as Germans, were treated here, was not mere chicanery, but according to orders. The Germans had done the same to the Poles. We must all therefore suffer for it, even though as individuals we might not have shared in the guilt. So I stepped forward and said more or less the following: "Dear fellow countrymen, listen all of you! The district magistrate here is very sorry that we have to leave our homeland in this condition. But he cannot help it, because our people did the same to the Poles, and that is unfortunately true. But we want to thank him for the good soup we were given in the camp, and we beg him to see to it that the next transport is treated as well. And now let us hope that we really do get to Germany."

That same evening we were slowly moving in a freight train across the country, thirty people to a car, via Thorn, Bromberg and Posen. The fields everywhere were as deserted as ours, but the towns looked much better. We were allowed to open the doors during the journey and hang our legs out.

After two days we arrived in Kohlfurt; there we joined other transports and were detained for two days, dusted with a powder against lice and checked once more. The two German doctors working there let me spend the night in their quarters. They would have liked to go with us if it had been possible. But in spite of the nearness of the frontier it was as difficult to escape here as it had been for us. Wading by night through the heavily guarded Neisse was the only chance left to them.

And then we went on, as in a dream, slowly, slowly across a small river, and at the next stop we were permitted to get out without being pulled in again. We were in Germany.

We reached Wehrkirch towards evening, and were welcomed by a large poster with a portrait of Thälmann. The sick were taken from the train and treated kindly. At night our train rolled on to Hoyerswerda, where we arrived in the morning and were conducted into the Elsterhorst Camp, our last checking-off station. It consisted of a rectangular enclosure, fenced in with a lot of barbed wire, and divided in two by a road with barracks on either side. A few hundred yards away a similar enclosure, surrounded by pines, had been fenced in for the sick, and many doctors and nurses were working there. They admitted me into their circle, gave me a room and allowed me to assist at their examinations. They also assigned me a ward.

At the sight of my patients I felt myself carried back to the Königsberg days. They were almost without exception dystrophics, so-called victims of starvation, barely alive, skeletons with mask-like faces and swollen legs. What had I done to deserve to go around among them in perfect health of body and mind? They came from a section of our camp, which was isolated by an extra barbed wire fence, a section in which the so-called "roughs" were housed—younger men who had been carried off to Russia from the Danube provinces because of their German nationality, and were now deported to Germany. They are said to have become like brutes and were therefore shut off most severely from the outside world. Not far away was their graveyard, a small rectangle in the white sand with small crosses made from twigs. You had to be very careful when speaking to them, for you felt instinctively that you should do only what is absolutely necessary. Above all, no questions, no stirring up any emotions. One small flicker of the soul—and the spark of life might be extinguished.

We were still in the camp on Whitsunday, but then our ways parted; that is, we evaded the imminent typhus quarantine by flight. After I had helped Frau Aust to slip out under the barbed wire into the arms of her nephew waiting outside, noth-

ing could hold me back any longer. I flung my rucksack over the
fence, clambered after it and took the next train to Berlin.

And then the reunion! In the first days and weeks I went
around almost drunk with joy. So few people really knew the
truth of all the sufferings and experiences we had gone through
in the east, and what a lot there was to tell! But one day it happened that a person to whom I was describing things took a
piece of bread out of her pocket while I was talking, broke it and
handed me half of it—a customary gesture in those days of food
shortage. Then I knew that it was time to take the first steps
along the road offering me a new existence. And I was faced with
the question: What will this new life be like? Will it be a casual
one, a life which need not be lived at all? Or will I, along with
those who have gone through the same experience, be allowed,
by the grace of God, to bear witness by our lives to all we have
seen and heard?

DATE DUE

PRINTED IN U.S.A.

GAYLORD